THE GODDESS NATURA
IN MEDIEVAL LITERATURE

The Goddess Natura
in Medieval Literature

GEORGE D. ECONOMOU

HARVARD UNIVERSITY PRESS
Cambridge, Massachusetts, 1972

TO MY PARENTS

Εἰ Θέλημα Θεοῦ ἐστι τοῦ εὐδοκοῦντος πάντα,
εἰ ἔχω τοῦ πατρὸς εὐχὴν καὶ τῆς καλῆς μητρός μου . . .

If it is the will of God who approves all things
if I have my father's blessing and my good mother's . . .

Digenis Akritas

PREFACE

The personification of nature has for long been recognized as a commonplace of medieval literature. More recently, medievalists have noted that one main line of tradition involves a single figure, the goddess Natura, who developed out of a background of classical philosophy and Christian theology and was elaborated through the work of Latin and vernacular poets from the middle of the twelfth century through the sixteenth century. Some of the greatest poets of the Middle Ages are directly involved with this tradition.

Just as Boethius' *Consolation of Philosophy* provides the information necessary for understanding most instances of the concept of fortune in medieval texts, the tradition of the goddess Natura helps to explain most instances of nature. An extraordinarily rich complex of concepts and literary motifs come together in the characterization of the goddess. For example, in the thirteenth canto of the *Paradiso* a question of Dante's about the wisdom and perfection of Solomon prompts a lesson from Saint Thomas Aquinas on the creation of all things, eternal and temporal. By describing the descent of the divine creative light from its source in the Trinity through the angelic hierarchies to the heavens, and thence to matter, Aquinas explains the principle of creation that directly made Adam and Christ (who are therefore more perfect than Solomon) and indirectly made all earthly creatures, those brief contingencies generated with or without seed. On the lowest, earthly level of creation, "the wax of things" is imperfect, for nature always transmits the seal to it defectively, "working like an artist who has the skill of his art and a hand that trembles" (76–78). These lines contain a number of ideas that are important in the tradition of the goddess Natura. Implicit in the passage are the concepts of nature as a secondary creative force in the cosmos, the *vicaria Dei*, and as a definite poetic personality who stamps matter with the seal of the idea. Dante also appropriates the traditional threefold division of creativity— God's, nature's, and man's in imitation of nature—although he alters it for the occasion with characteristic brilliance. He suppresses the last category because it is not pertinent, but retains the concept of human art striving to imitate nature (traditionally in vain during the Middle Ages) within his characterization of nature itself. Nature thus becomes the artist who knows the perfect form—being close to the source of divine light—but who always falls short in execution—being the creative principle of the physical universe and a fallen world.

The aim of this study is to investigate the sources and development of the tradition of Natura for its own sake and to provide a solid basis for further study of the figure and the literary forms with which it is associated. Whatever success I may have had is owed largely to the many people who have generously given me their assistance. To Professor W. T. H. Jackson of Columbia University I owe a profound debt of gratitude. It was he who first urged me to study Natura and who provided guidance, encouragement, and information through every stage of the work's previous incarnation as a doctoral dissertation. Since then he has given me valuable advice whenever it has been sought.

Special thanks are due to Professors William Nelson and Howard H. Schless, also of Columbia, who raised objections that saved me from embarrassment and made suggestions that led to improvements. Professors Marjorie Nicolson and Paul O. Kristeller read the first chapter and made useful recommendations. My good friends Joan Ferrante of Columbia and Tom T. Tashiro of The City College of New York read more than one draft of the book and gave me excellent advice. To them I express my gratitude once again, as I do to my parents, my sister, and my wife Rochelle for their support and encouragement.

I wish to thank Long Island University for generous grants, both financial and in released time, which helped make possible the writing, typing, and publication of this book. Grateful acknowledgment is made to *The Chaucer Review*, in which parts of this work earlier appeared in considerably different form. I am indebted to the Harvard University Press for permission to quote from several volumes in the Loeb Classical Library series, and to the Houghton Mifflin Company for permission to quote from *The Works of Geoffrey Chaucer*.

CONTENTS

THE GODDESS NATURA
IN MEDIEVAL LITERATURE

I THE PHILOSOPHICAL BACKGROUND

The development of the goddess Natura in the allegorical poetry of the Middle Ages not only represents a significant chapter in the history of the influence of the classical heritage on the thought and letters of medieval culture, but also indicates the genius of that culture to give, in the words of M.-D. Chenu, "new birth, new existence in all the changed conditions of times, places, and persons," to the materials of antiquity that it had inherited. A history of Natura, therefore, involves the history of ideas and literary forms or, to put it more accurately, the history of the mutations of certain ideas and forms as they were appropriated and used by thinkers and writers of successive generations and periods. The road which begins with the Ionian one, that principle or nature "from which things come," and ends with the personified *vicaria Dei* (vicar or deputy of God) in the poems of Alan of Lille, Jean de Meun, and Chaucer, is indeed a road of many turns and junctures, passing through many landscapes and climates, from the grand designs of Plato, Aristotle, and Plotinus, to the equally magnificent vision of the universe of the school of Chartres.[1]

The medieval poems with which this study is primarily concerned—the *De mundi universitate* of Bernard Silvestris, the *Anticlaudianus* and *De planctu naturae* of Alan of Lille, the *Roman de la Rose* of Jean de Meun, and Chaucer's *Parlement of Foules*—have in common a general concept of the goddess Natura as the *mater generationis*, the intermediary, subordinate, or vicar of God in the universe. This concept has for some time been recognized as a development of medieval Platonism, particularly that which is associated with the intellectual activity of Chartres during the renaissance of the twelfth century.[2] Yet each of these works is the product of a man's imagination as well as of a cultural atmosphere, which in turn is indebted to the philosophy and poetry of the past. Natura's history is in fact in the mainstream of intellectual and artistic tradition flowing from ancient Greece and Rome to medieval Europe. Equally important with the philosophical tradition is the poetic, in which Natura appears as a true allegorical personification, a tradition stretching from Claudian in the fourth century to Chaucer in the fourteenth and beyond.[3] Any attempt to trace the evolution of the figure thus requires a painstaking and patient investigation of its sources in antiquity.

Perhaps no single term in the history of Western thought has enjoyed as many meanings and interpretations as have the Greek *physis* and the Latin *natura*. Indeed, Cicero's statement, "Naturam ipsam definire difficile est," expresses the sentiments of many philosophers and historians who have wrestled with the problems of differentiation and definition of this multivalenced word. Almost every author who has attempted definition, in ancient, medieval, and modern times, has had to admit that *nature* has meant many things to many men. In his *Metaphysics*, Aristotle lists seven meanings. In his commentary on the *Timaeus*, Proclus surveys the several meanings used by earlier philosophers before discussing Plato's. In his presentation of the philosophical systems of Epicurus, Zeno, and the Academics in the *De natura deorum*, Cicero is careful to include their definitions of nature. Boethius defines nature in four ways in his *Contra Evtychen*. In the *Didascalicon*, Hugh of Saint Victor reports that men in former times used the word in three special senses, and John of Salisbury finds it necessary to discuss the various meanings of nature in his *Metalogicon*.[4] As this sampling of classical and medieval writers might suggest, modern students of those periods have found it necessary to classify the meanings of nature with even greater comprehensiveness. Pauly-Wissowa devotes thirty-five columns to "Physis." Arthur O. Lovejoy and George Boas list no less than sixty-six meanings of nature. Ernst Robert Curtius presents fourteen functions of Natura in Latin allegorical poetry. And R. G. Collingwood has brilliantly traced and interpreted the views of nature from ancient to modern times.[5]

The concepts of nature that were developed and explored by the Chartrian philosophers and poets, particularly Alan of Lille, who did more than any other author to establish and fix the characterization of the goddess Natura, represent an aggregate of ideas. The term nature could stand for the general order of all creation as a single, harmonious whole, whose study might lead to an understanding of the model on which this created world is formed. It could stand for the Platonic intermediary between the intelligible and material worlds; or for the divinely ordained power that presides over the continuity and preservation of whatever lives in the sublunary world; or for a creative principle directly subordinated to the mind and will of God.[6] These are the meanings of nature to be sought out in the philosophical texts of antiquity. The personification of nature in these texts should not be equated with the allegorical figure in a sustained narrative poem, however, for such an allegorical figure is always a character, whereas personification in expository writing may be no more than the means of making an abstraction concrete and thus accessible to the reader.[7]

ARISTOTLE'S SURVEY OF PHYSIS

In the philosophical lexicon of the *Metaphysics*, Aristotle discusses seven meanings of physis or nature.[8] The first "historian" of the term, he surveys the earliest meanings of the word in Greek philosophy before stating his own definition. His first definition of nature as "the genesis of growing things" (1014b.16–18) refers to the etymological sense of "origin" or "birth," a sense that is found nowhere in Greek literature.[9] Also unrecorded elsewhere is Aristotle's second meaning: "that immanent part of a growing thing, from which its growth first proceeds" (1014b.18–19). The third meaning—"the source from which the primary movement in each natural object is present in it in virtue of its own essence" (1014b.19–20), such as fire rising by nature—corresponds to the normal, untechnical Greek usage.

The fourth definition is the one emphasized by the pre-Socratics.

"Nature" means the primary material of which any natural object consists or out of which it is made, which is relatively unshaped and cannot be changed from its own potency, as e.g. bronze is said to be the nature of a statue and of bronze utensils, and wood the nature of wooden things; and so in all other cases; for when a product is made out of these materials, the first matter is preserved throughout. For it is in this way that people call the elements of natural objects, also their nature, some naming fire, others earth, others air, others water, others something else of the sort, and some naming more than one of these, and others all of them (1014b.25–35).

This includes obvious references to Thales (water), Anaximenes (air), Anaximander (*apeiron* in which were contained in latent or potential form the four antagonistic elements or their properties), Xenophanes (earth), Heraclitus (fire), and Empedocles (all). Though nature meant the primal matter of the existent for the pre-Socratics, they also understood it in the sense of meaning "the real constitution or character of things," including the ways things behave. The most important aspect of their meaning is the relation between these two senses. This attempt to explain the behavior of things by reference to the substance of which they were composed was soon supplanted by the Pythagorean attempt to explain the behavior of things by reference to their form, regarding the structure of things as something that could be explained mathematically.[10]

Aristotle's fifth and sixth definitions represent the philosophical and ordinary usage in the fifth century. Nature as the essence or form of natural objects aptly illustrates the shift from the Ionian concept: "Hence as regards the things that are or come to be by nature, though that *from which* they naturally come to be or are is already present, we say they have not their nature yet, unless they have their form or shape" (1015a.5). This definition is circular, for it leaves "natural objects" undefined. In the sixth definition, Aristotle posits a more general meaning: "By an extension of meaning from this sense of 'nature' every essence in general has come to be called a 'nature,' because the nature of a thing is one kind of essence" (1015a.10). The circle is removed in this definition, but the term is now too broad to be meaningful. So Aristotle eliminates the circle by defining natural things specifically as having a source of movement in themselves:

From what has been said, then, it is plain that nature in the primary and strict sense is the essence of things which have in themselves, as such, a source of movement; for the matter is called the nature because it is qualified to receive this, and processes of becoming and growing are called nature because they are movements proceeding from this. And nature in this sense is the source of the movement of natural objects, being present in them, either potentially or in complete reality (1015a.15).

Aristotle regards this definition as the true meaning of nature. Coupled with his distinction between the two kinds of movement in the universe—the translunary, which he called heaven, and the sublunary, which he called nature—this definition ultimately stands behind some of the most prominent features of the medieval Natura.[11]

In arriving at his definition, Aristotle was not thoroughly repudiating Plato and the pre-Socratics, for one idea that they all held in common was that the world of nature was characterized by movement—by process, growth, and change.[12] But the investigation of how Plato and Aristotle classify movements and speculate about the source of movement in a cosmological context reveals the profound and often irreconcilable differences in their visions of reality. Such an exploration is an indispensable background to the personified Natura of medieval allegory, for as mater generationis, or in the words of Alan, as "mundanae regionis regina," she is the goddess who presides over movement in that part of the universe which is most subject to movement and change, the sublunary world.[13]

PLATO AND ARISTOTLE

Since movement is the essential characteristic of nature for Plato and Aristotle, both wished to establish which form of movement among the many movements in the world is to be accorded primacy. Both asserted that locomotion, an eternal self-caused movement, is the prime movement in the world, and in proving the possibility of such movement, both were concerned with a question of physics. But when they identified this movement with the first movement in the universe and showed that it caused all cosmic changes,

they were concerned with a question of cosmology.[14]
Here arises a fundamental and profound difference between
the two, namely, that Plato makes his world-soul the first
mover, while Aristotle, not recognizing the Platonic world-
soul (a self-moved mover), puts "at the point of origin for
all cosmic or physical movements ... two entities, the
Prime Mover who is himself unmoved and the *primum
mobile* which is set in motion by him."[15]

Aristotle argues for the necessary perfection of the first
principle, upon which "depend the heavens and the world
of nature" (*Meta.* 1072b.15). He also advances the notion
that this principle, which he calls God because it is the
entity which ultimately accounts for the eternal movement
in the world, is outside the world of movement, that God
does not know the world, that drastically unlike Plato, he
did not will to create it nor provide plans for its history or life.
Yet the primum mobile, the first heaven in which the fixed
stars are set, is actuated by its love for God, the unmoved
mover, the final cause, and it moves eternally in a perfect
circle striving to be as like God as it is possible for a body to
be, and in its turning it produces all other movement.[16]

Aristotle explains all movement or change as the passing
from potential to actual existence (*Physics* III.i–iii). Just as
the primum mobile loves and desires God and strives to
imitate his activity, his self-knowledge, all other things,
which are imperfect (only God is perfect and pure actuality),
strive in their own way for their own perfection. This is in
part a question of the relationship of God to His thoughts,
the ideas or forms, and involves a serious difference with
Plato's concept of that relationship, as explained by Collingwood:

God in the *Timaeus* certainly thinks the forms; therefore, according to Aristotle, God and the forms are not two but one. The forms
are the way in which God thinks, their dialectical structure is the

articulation of His thought: and conversely God is the activity whose diverse aspects we are describing whenever we identify this or that form. This identification of God with the forms removes all objections brought by Aristotle against the Platonic theory of forms; for those objections are directed not against the conception of form as such—Aristotle himself constantly uses the conception—nor yet against the conception of transcendent forms existing apart from all matter—that, too, is a doctrine of his own no less than of Plato's—but against the conception of these forms as purely and simply objective, divorced from the activity of a thinking mind. Plato in the *Timaeus* represents God, in virtue of His creative act of will, as the efficient cause of nature, and the forms, in virtue of their static perfection, as its final cause; Aristotle, identifying God with the forms, conceives one single unmoved mover with a self-contained activity of its own, namely self-knowledge . . . thinking the forms which are the categories of its own thought, and, since that activity is the highest and best possible . . . inspiring the whole of nature with desire for it and a nisus towards reproducing it, everything in its degree and to the best of its power.[17]

That the world loves God, not the reverse, is central for Aristotle, the word for love being *eros*, "the longing of what is essentially imperfect for its own perfection."[18]

Aristotle's division of the universe into the heavens and the world of nature has further ramifications that were to influence one of the goddess Natura's most important characteristics: her rulership in the sublunary world. First, beyond the sphere of the moon, Aristotle introduces his fifth element, ether, which accounts for all heavenly movements, including those of the planets, all of whose movements are circular.[19] Ether, though *sui generis*, immune to becoming or passing away, and subject to less change than fire, air, water, and earth, nevertheless has its own natural movement and place in the cosmos, and in this respect it does not differ from the sublunary four elements, which arrange themselves according to the order of their particular natures. From the view that the translunary world (heaven) is subject to less change than the sublunary world (the circle of the moon bounded by the terrestrial sphere), it follows that the heavens are of a higher nature than the sublunary world. For while the sublunary world is involved in change of substance, quality, and quantity, the heavens undergo only change of place. The sublunary world is thus a world of generation, of becoming, of mutability, and death, and though it strives, it can never attain the near perfection of the eternal and unvarying rotation of the primum mobile, the sphere of the fixed stars, and the uninterrupted motions of the planets: "So also the same place is occupied by the most honoured of perceptible things, the stars and the sun and the moon; and for this reason only the heavenly bodies always keep the same order and arrangement, and are never changed or altered; while the transient things on earth admit many alterations and conditions (*De mundo* 400a)."[20]

This distinction clarifies Aristotle's frequent personification of nature. When he speaks of that world, he means the world of the four elements which extends as far as the circle of the moon. One must not, however, make the mistake of thinking he scoffed at that relatively inferior place, for though its order is of a lesser nature than the heavens', it is order nevertheless, and he frequently graced that order by personifying its principle as Nature.

The striving for perfection on the part of the things of this sublunary world is a teleological matter. That is, all things in moving from the potential to the actual are seeking to fulfill their forms, form being not only the object of desire of the material thing that wishes to embody the form in its own matter, but also the motive of the tendency toward such realization. Thus, nature is identified with form, with *telos*.[21] This is of considerable significance, for Aristotle often personifies nature in relation to teleology: "'Nature like a good householder throws away nothing of which anything useful can be made.' 'Nature does nothing in vain, nothing superfluous.' 'Nature behaves as if it foresaw the future.' To a large extent this is merely a statement of a *de facto* teleology. The world, Aristotle is maintaining, is well-ordered; i.e. everything in it is disposed so as to assure its progress toward its best possible state."[22] Furthermore, Aristotle uses the word as a collective term for the harmonious working of all natural bodies, a sense in which it is not a transcendent principle. Nature is the principle of order in the world, as the *Physics* perfectly illustrates: "Well, but nothing natural or accordant with nature is without order; for nature is the universal determinant of order" (VIII.i.252a). Being such a principle, nature is divine, for she is in a direct line from God, the creator and preserver, who, though far from earth, reaches all things, his power experienced mostly by the body nearest him, less by the next, and so on down to the terrestrial sphere.[23] This principle of order is expressed by Aristotle in a way that clearly foreshadows the medieval concept of the goddess Natura as God's vicegerent: "But God and nature create nothing that does not fulfill a purpose" (*De Caelo* I.iv.271a).

To turn from the nature of Aristotle to that of Plato is to turn, in effect, from a nontranscendent principle of order and continuity in the sublunary world to a principle that lies somewhere between the ideal and the sensible worlds.[24] In other words, at issue is Plato's two-world doctrine, which, as Ingemar Düring points out, was "a bold step in a new direction," one that Aristotle not only could not accept, but which ultimately brought him around to the pre-Platonic tradition.[25] Plato repudiated previous philosophies when he asserted that this world, the world of becoming, change, and motion, is a world of belief, a delusion, and not, as the Ionians had taught, a reality. Reality for Plato is in the transcendent, immaterial, and therefore intelligible world of forms. What links this ideal and eternal world with our own is the world-soul, which, though in an intermediate position between the ideal and sensible worlds, was nevertheless created by the Demiurge "in origin and excellence prior to and older than the body, to be the ruler and mistress, of whom the body was to be the subject" (*Tim.* 34c).

One of the difficulties with Plato is that he does not explicitly define nature, a fact which led C. S. Lewis to claim that the development of Natura in the Middle Ages "in quantity and still more in vitality, is quite out of proportion to the hints supplied in antiquity," and that the student of Natura "will find nothing (where he might hope to find it) in Plato's *Timaeus*."[26] Against such discouragement, however, stands the fact of Plato's enormous influence on subsequent thinkers and writers—Plotinus, Chalcidius, Macrobius, Boethius, the Hermetics, to name a few who are of primary importance to this history. Roughly the first half of the *Timaeus* (up to 53b) was available to medieval readers in Chalcidius' translation, not to mention the passages from numerous other dialogues that are quoted in the commentary. Surely those who studied Chalcidius, men like William of Conches, did not neglect the text to study only the commentary.[27] There is no reason to believe the *Timaeus* was not carefully and thoroughly read in the Middle Ages, which should be motive enough for its consideration.

That Plato situated the origin of movement in the worldsoul was an innovation removing him from the Ionian tradition and later alienating Aristotle. He did, however, follow a line of Ionian thought in conceiving of the material world as a living thing, an animal made by God. "But let us suppose the world to be the very image of that whole of which all other tribes are portions. For the original of the universe contains in itself all intelligible beings, just as this world comprehends us and all other visible creatures. For the deity, intending to make this world like the fairest and most perfect of intelligible beings, framed one visible animal comprehending within itself all other animals of a kindred nature" (*Tim.* 30d). God's desire to fill the world with his creativity is clear here. But the duality is typically Platonic inasmuch as one is not permitted to regard this world without reference to its perfect model. The transcendent, immaterial forms, which underly God's creative act and constitute the eternal, changeless model after which God fashioned the temporal, changing world of nature, are unlike the world of nature, which is alive with movement, "in a process of creation and created" (*Tim.* 28c). Such forms are alive only in the sense that they are dynamically related to each other, but not alive with movement, because they would then be in time and space, which movement implies. The bridge between these two worlds, according to Plato, is the world-soul. God, desiring that all things should be good and as like him as possible, brought the visible world out of disorder into order, and knowing that that which is without intelligence cannot be better than that which has intelligence, and that intelligence cannot be present in anything devoid of soul, "he put intelligence in soul, and soul in body, that he might be the creator of a work which was by nature fairest and best. On this wise, using the language of probability, we may say that the world came into being—a living creature truly endowed with soul and intelligence by the providence of God" (*Tim.* 30b–c).

It is significant that the world-soul is intermediate between the material and immaterial worlds, being the immaterial locus of the world, a characteristic that would elicit from the Neoplatonists, whether philosophers or encyclopedists, a good deal of attention. Though it was to be the Neoplatonists who would place nature as an intermediary partly in the world-soul and partly in the material world in their more elaborate declensions of existence, the starting place was the *Timaeus*, where the world-soul is the "ruler and mistress of the body" (34c).[28] Although Plato's view that the existence of the world-soul is eminently natural, being the originator of all motions in the universe, is nowhere explicitly stated in the *Timaeus*, its future influence was assured by its presence in many of the Neoplatonic texts known to the Middle Ages.[29]

Unlike Aristotle, Plato does not personify nature. He classifies the "three natures" as "that which is in process of generation," "that in which generation takes place," and "that of which the thing generated is a resemblance naturally produced" (*Tim.* 50d). These kinds of being or natures are the uncreated and indestructible forms; the corporeal world, created, in motion, subject to becoming or vanishing, and apprehended by opinion and sense; and the eternal space, the nurse of generation, the indestructible home of all created things. Closest to what Aristotle calls nature, his sublunary world, is Plato's corporeal world, created by the stellar gods at the behest of the Demiurge.

In Plato's mythological account of the creation of the corporeal world, the Demiurge's apparent motive for relegating this task to the gods and the children of the gods is that his proper activity prevents him from creating mortal creatures. He instructs the gods and the lesser gods to complete the job of creation by putting the souls—which he has provided by sowing the remains of the world-soul "diluted to the second and third degree" in the earth, the moon, and "the other instruments of time," the planets (*Tim.* 41d, 42d) —into bodies. Next, he explains to the gods the laws to which the creatures must be subject, namely, the doctrine of metempsychosis. This he does "that he might be guiltless of future evil in any of them" (*Tim.* 42d). This concession, along with the emphasis on the mutability of the bodies in which the souls are to be placed, should clarify the profound difference between the ways in which Plato and Aristotle regarded the material world.[30] Whereas Aristotle saw the sublunary world, though subject to mutability, as fundamentally good, without any evil principle, and chiefly characterized by a striving for perfection, Plato saw the same world of mutability as something to be overcome, to be transcended, where evil is a given necessity. The only principle of nature in Plato to rival or supplement that of Aristotle, is to be found in his concept of the world-soul as refined and elaborated in the Neoplatonic synthesis.[31]

PLOTINUS

The major sources of the philosophy that the Middle Ages regarded as Platonism came from the Latin West in what has been described as "the most tangled lines of descent." Though the history of this descent cannot be settled here, the authors who were its most familiar and widespread purveyors were Chalcidius, Macrobius, and Boethius, in whose works men of the Middle Ages "encountered Plato's thought in different contexts."[32] These Platonisms, or Neoplatonisms, were considerably influenced by Aristotelian thought, and though they held certain ideas in common, they differed in character. Macrobius, for example, probably had no first-hand knowledge of either Aristotelian or Platonic texts but relied rather "on a mass of indirect tradition."[33] Boethius, in contrast, knew both in the original and offered as one of four meanings of nature a virtually literal translation of Aristotle's, "natura est motus principium per se non per accidens."[34]

Despite the superior currency of this Latin tradition and of the Hellenistic concept of the world order as opposed to the speculative symbolism of Plotinus (204–270), Plotinus and those who came under his immediate influence exerted a definite influence on individuals of importance to medieval thought. Augustine read Plotinus in the translations of Victorinus; Proclus, himself profoundly indebted to Plotinus, influenced Boethius and Dionysius the Areopagite, whose works were translated for the West by John Scotus Erigena. Even the works of Macrobius and Chalcidius cannot be seen in proper perspective unless preceded by a brief assessment of the Plotinian contribution.

The concept that the Platonic world-soul acts as a bridge between the ideal and sensible worlds is found preserved in the more logically complete system of Plotinus, wherein the third hypostasis of the divine principle brings the material world into being. The One is utterly transcendent and self-sufficient and yet is the source of all things. The first emanation from the One is nous, which is the divine mind or intellectual principle. In nous multiplicity occurs, for in it exist all the ideas, or exemplars, of all things, both of classes and of individuals, held there indivisibly. Nous is beyond time, possessing the eternity that time imitates, and contains all in its identity. From nous, in turn, emanates the world-soul, which is immaterial but immediately anticipates the material world. In order for the world-soul to impart life to matter, however, Plotinus posits two world-souls: one to contemplate nous and thus receive reflections of the ideas; the other to pass them on, thereby generating in matter by direct contact the beings of the phenomenal world.[35] This second world-soul Plotinus calls nature: "that what we know as Nature is a Soul, offspring of a yet earlier Soul of more powerful life" (*Enneads* III.8.4).[36] Thus, in its creative contact with the material world, nature gives to that world participation in the ideal by transmitting to it images of the ideal received by its higher activity, soul, from nous. Nature, then, in the words of W. R. Inge, becomes "the activity of matter, that which added to Matter, gives it its substantiality and without which Matter is a mere abstraction or non-entity."[37] In giving bodies their reason-principles (their participation in the ideal), nature produces in them an object of vision, involved in "the ultimate purpose of all the acts of the mind and, even further downward, of all sensation, since sensation is also an effort towards knowledge." Thus, the desire of bodies to reproduce their kind is the stirring of reason-principles within them: "the procreative act is the expression of a contemplation, a travail towards the creation of many forms, many objects of contemplation, so that the universe may be filled full with Reason-Principles and that contemplation may be, as nearly as possible, endless . . . So Love, too, is vision with the pursuit of Ideal-Form" (*Enneads* III.8.7). Nature thereby endows bodies with the desire and ability to perpetuate themselves.

MACROBIUS AND CHALCIDIUS

The three Neoplatonic hypostases—along with the concepts of world-soul as creative principle in the material world, of the sublunary world as the realm of generation, decay, and death, as opposed to the divine and immortal translunary world, and of the procreation and continuity of sublunary creatures being governed by nature—were transmitted to the Middle Ages by the commentaries of Macrobius (354–430) on Cicero's *Somnium Scipionis* and of Chalcidius (fl. 325) on the *Timaeus*.

In his commentary on the *Somnium Scipionis*, Macrobius explains how mind, Plotinus' nous, fills the world with its light.

Accordingly, since Mind emanates from the Supreme God and Soul from Mind, indeed, forms and suffuses all below with life, and since this is the one splendor lighting up everything and visible in all, like a countenance reflected in many mirrors arranged in a row, and since all follow on in continuous succession, degenerating step by step in their downward course, the close observer will find that from the Supreme God even to the bottommost dregs of the universe there is one tie, binding at every link and never broken. This is the golden chain of Homer which, he tells us, God ordered to hang down from the sky to earth.[38]

This passage, one of the foremost sources of the Great Chain of Being, briefly describes the Neoplatonic theory of emanation.[39] As for the third hypostasis, the world-soul, Macrobius explains that it creates and fashions bodies ("anima ergo creans sibi condensque corpora") "out of the pure and clearest fount of Mind from whose abundance it had drunk deep at birth, endowed those divine or ethereal bodies, meaning the celestial sphere and the stars which it was first creating, with mind."[40] But the world-soul penetrates below the celestial bodies to the terrestrial sphere, where with difficulty it endows man with the divine mind, for he alone of all creatures is able to sustain a small part of it: "Soul, degenerating as it came into the lower regions and to the earth, discovered that the frailty of the mortal realm made it incapable of sustaining the pure divinity of Mind . . . Man alone was endowed with reason, the power of mind, the seat of which is in the head."[41]

The movement of the incorporeal world-soul brings all of nature into being ("nam ideo ab anima natura incipit") from the motion of the *aplanes*, the celestial sphere of the fixed stars, which it inspires with its eternal motion, to the seven planets that move in countermotion to the celestial sphere, down to the dregs of the universe, the sublunary terrestrial sphere.[42] All things, then, that come into being as a result of the direct contact of the world-soul can be considered in general as nature; but their division into the divine, immortal translunary and the mortal, everchanging sublunary brings one closer to the essential meaning of nature.

Discussing the powers of the number five, Macrobius again gives a capsulate description of the three divine hypostases and of the created world, the celestial and the terrestrial, for they number five and embrace all that is or seems to be ("omnia quaeque sunt quaeque uidentur esse"). There is the highest God ("deus summus"), out of whom

springs the mind ("mens"), in which are contained the
patterns of things ("in qua rerum species continentur");
there is the world-soul, the fount of all souls ("mundi
anima quae animarum omnium fons est"); and finally
there are the heavens ("caelestia") and the terrestrial
world ("terrena natura").[43] This distinction between the
heavens and the terrestrial world is of special significance,
for besides the more traditional opposition of immutability
and mutability, Macrobius includes the Aristotelian division between ether and the four elements, a division Plotinus
and Chalcidius do not make: "Now all things that lie between the topmost border and the moon are holy, im-
perishable, and divine because they always have in them the
same aether and are never subject to the vacillations of
change. Below the moon, air and the realm of change
(natura permutationis) begin together, and the moon,
being the boundary of aether and air, is also the demarca-
tion between the divine and the mortal."[44] Thus, it is clear
that while all the created universe can be considered nature,
there is a sharp distinction between the immortal heavens
moving in the divine ether and the realm of change under
the moon comprising the four elements. The world-soul, as
it turns away from the mind, begins by making celestial
and divine bodies, then degenerates into making bodies that
are subject to change and death.

Yet, as Macrobius later points out, the universe is immortal, and even that which in Cicero's words is mortal in
part ("mundum quadam parte mortalem"), the sublunary
world of the four elements, undergoes only a change of
appearance: "Within the living universe nothing perishes,
but of those things that seem to perish only the appearance
is changed, and that which has ceased to be as it formerly
was returns to its original state and to its component parts
... That which flows off bodies withdraws from them, but
the flow of elements never withdraws from the elements

themselves; and so in this universe no part is mortal according to sound reasoning."[45]

So the copies or images of the ideas as they are embodied in the world are subject to birth and death, but the stuff of which they are made remains.[46] Such is the nature of all sublunary bodies, even that of man, though this change occurs in man only after the soul, which is the true man, departs from his dead body, for soul rules the body as God the universe, being self-moved. This analogy is one of the bases for the concept of microcosm-macrocosm, "the reason why philosophers called the universe a huge man and man a miniature universe (ideo physici mundum magnum hominem et hominem breuem mundum esse dixerunt)."[47]

Besides transmitting these ideas which were to become of major importance in the development of the medieval goddess Natura, Macrobius also personifies nature in some instances. There are two such cases in which the personification is coupled with ideas that shaped Natura's character and the literary attitudes toward her. The first involves nature the craftsman or artist (*artifex*) as participating in the biology of human reproduction: "Once the seed has been deposited in the mint (monetam) where man is coined, nature (artifex natura) begins to work her skill upon it so that on the seventh day she causes a sack to form around the embryo, as thin in texture as the membrane that lies under the shell of an egg enclosing the white."[48]

The image of the mint in which man is coined is one that Alan of Lille borrowed from Macrobius and set in the context of the long speech in which Natura explains her cosmic role in the *De planctu naturae*. God, Natura says, "appointed me as his deputy, the coiner for stamping the classes of things (Me igitur tanquam sui vicariam, rerum generibus sigillandis monetariam destinavit)."[49] The second instance is a reiteration of the idea that nature prefers her secrets to be kept from the ignorant and vulgar:

But in treating of the other gods and the Soul, as I have said, philosophers make use of fabulous narratives; not without a purpose, however, nor merely to entertain, but because they realize that a frank, open exposition of herself is distasteful to Nature, who, just as she has withheld an understanding of herself from the uncouth senses of men by enveloping herself in variegated garments, has also desired to have her secrets handled by more prudent individuals through fabulous narratives.[50]

This notion anticipates the use of allegory and fabulous narrative in some of the treatments of Natura in the Middle Ages.

Personifications of nature in Chalcidius have a wider and deeper significance than those in Macrobius, for they are more integrated with the cosmological material in his commentary. Though C. S. Lewis' argument is correct that personifications of nature in Chalcidius and others "show only a momentary (metaphorical, not allegorical) personification of *Natura*—such personification as any important abstract noun is likely to undergo," it does not help to clarify the central issue.[51] Chalcidius was not writing allegory, nor did his medieval students read his commentary as allegory. The question of his influence on the allegorical poets and their milieu is not concerned so much with the kind of personification (there will be sufficient instances of literary or allegorical personification in the Latin poets) as with the meaning of the term. The fact that the personifications of the term in Chalcidius, Macrobius, and others are metaphorical rather than allegorical does not make those personifications irrelevant. On the contrary, it is reasonable to assume that they would have meant something to poets whose works were concerned with cosmological themes.

The most significant personification of nature occurs in Chalcidius' discussion of the "three natures" of the *Timaeus* —ideas, the corporeal word, and the receptacle of the corporeal world. In his explanation of these three *primae substantiae*, Chalcidius personifies nature as that which brings forth the corporeal image of the idea; that is, nature is made the intermediary between the idea and matter.

. . . and he [Plato] enlightens the mind by representing the matter in such a way that three kinds are seen.—He now takes "kinds" in a figurative sense using it to denote first substances, for neither matter nor the example are kinds. "They are," he says, "first that which comes into existence and originates"— *viz.*, the generated *species* which originates in matter and dissolves in it (quae in silua subsistit et ibidem dissoluitur)—"secondly that in which it originates"—this "in which" is matter itself, for fleeting *species* acquire their being in this—"and, thirdly, that to which originating things owe their likeness," *viz.*, the idea which is the exemplar of all things produced by nature (idea scilicet, quae exemplum est rerum omnium quas natura progenuit), namely those things which are enclosed by matter as in a womb and which are said to be the images of the exemplars. Next he clarifies the problem by a manifest example, for he compares that which receives the *species* to a "mother," matter of course—for matter receives the *species* offered by nature (uidelicet siluae—haec enim recipit a natura proditas species); that from which the image is derived to a "father," namely the idea, for the species mentioned owe their likeness to the idea; and that which originates from these two to a "child," *viz.*, the generated species—for this stands between the really existing nature which is constant and always the same, i.e., the idea, the eternal intellect of the eternal God, and that nature which indeed is but not always the same, *viz.*, matter; for matter by itself is not among the things that are, because it is eternal. Therefore, that which stands between these two natures is not really existing. Since it is the image of what really exists, it seems to exist to some extent, but since it is not permanent and undergoes change, it does not exist in reality, as the exemplars do; for these indeed enjoy true and unchangeable existence. Hence there are the three following realities: that which always is, that which always is not, and that which is not always.[52]

The two personifications of nature—"all things produced by nature" and that which "receives the species offered by nature"—in this context are striking, for they clearly exemplify the concept of nature as a link between the ideal and corporeal worlds. Nature produces the images of the ideas in matter; or matter, to put it another way, receives from nature the species that she offers. To extend Chalcidius' analogy of matter ("silua") as the mother, the idea or intellectual act of God as the father, and the generated species as the child, nature acts as a kind of midwife in the process of creation. Her activity, as implied in this passage though not directly stated, is that of intermediary—one could almost say, of vicaria Dei—for the similarity between her role in this passage and that of Macrobius' nature and Alan's is quite clear.

As it was not uncommon in Neoplatonism to consider nature as the moment of contact between the world-soul and matter, what Chalcidius has done in the passage quoted above is not to allow nature to usurp the offices of world-soul, but rather to show a distinction of the utmost importance. In an earlier section, Chalcidius explained that providence, the mind of God, is the active agent and matter is the receptive one in the creation, in the cosmogony. Providence expresses creative activity through matter, and the way in which the provident spirit pervades the world is comparable to the way in which nature and world-soul pervade and animate bodies:

For the world has not its origin in a mechanical mixture of these two, but the world came into being through both planning of a provident spirit and factors of necessity. In this way Providence was the active agent, whereas matter underwent its action and let itself be adorned willingly. The divine spirit moulds it in such a manner that it is entirely pervaded by it, not as forms are conferred in sculpture, where only the surface is operated upon, but rather in the manner in which nature ("natura") and the soul ("anima") pervade and animate solid bodies.[53]

It is possible that *natura* and *anima* are doublets here and that they are identified with each other in the vivification of the universe. But such a reading does not take into account one very important fact: that when Chalcidius discusses the way in which "the world-soul vivifies the world's body (anima mundi corpus mundi uiuificet)," he is explaining the creation of the heavenly bodies and their movements as time, the moving image of eternity.[54] But when, as in the passage above, he discusses creation out of matter, he uses the term nature to describe the marvelous process of the creation of the world of mutability, the everchanging world under the moon. This distinction, however, must not be construed as meaning that nature replaces world-soul, or that Chalcidius posits a double world-soul. That Chalcidius regarded the world-soul as the animating principle in the universe is manifest throughout his commentary. He quotes from the *Phaedrus* the long passage in which Plato asserts that the immortal and bodiless soul is the first principle of motion in the universe.[55] He echoes Plato's statement that soul is the mistress of the body.[56] And finally, in the section "de ortu animae" (XXVI–LV), he explains the construction of the world-soul. In its elements and in the way that they are mixed together, all things in the world are provided for.[57] When he speaks of "nature," therefore, it is reasonable to assume that he intends the term to represent the vivifying power of the world-soul operating in the lowest regions of the universe and acting upon matter, "which is the beginning and source of bodies (quae . . . exordium et fons est corporum)."[58]

To complete the picture given by Chalcidius of the activity of nature in the sublunary world, one must turn to an earlier section in which he repeats the Aristotelian classification of the three kinds of creativity or work: "For all things which exist are either the work of God, or the work of nature, or the work of a human artist in imitation of nature."[59] This classification—which was the basis for Dante's organization of the third round of the seventh circle of Hell (*Inf.* xiv–xvii), where the pilgrim encountered those who had been violent against God, nature, and art—demonstrates once again the intermediary role of nature between the divine and the earthly, a pattern that was to receive the serious attention of the thinkers of Chartres. The work of nature, as Chalcidius continues, includes all things that are born, grow, and die in the world, the fruits and grains of the earth, the offspring that are conceived by the genitals of animals, and work appointed by God and provided for in the divine mind.

ASCLEPIUS

The Hermetic *Asclepius*, attributed in the Middle Ages to Apuleius, is of special importance because it restates in its own way some of the ideas found in the Neoplatonic tradition. Dating from 250 at the latest and heavily influenced by Plato, the *Asclepius* contains passages that must have been carefully remarked by Chartrian writers who were interested in nature, for the work and others later in the Hermetic tradition were well known to them.[60]

Once again, nature acts as the bridge between the soul ("anima") and matter ("mundus" here rather than "silua"), uniting all things into one whole: "Soul and corporeal substance (mundus) together are embraced by nature, and are by nature's working kept in movement, the manifold qualities of all things that take shape are made to differ among themselves, in such sort that there come into existence individual things of infinitely numerous forms, by reason of the differences of their qualities, and yet all individuals are united to the whole; so that we see that the whole is one, and of the one are all things." A few lines later a more detailed description of nature's working upon matter reminds one of the Chalcidian description: "Matter has been made ready by God beforehand to be the recipient of individual forms of every shape; and nature, fashioning matter in individual forms by means of the four elements, brings into being, up to the height of heaven (ad caelum), all things that will be pleasing in God's sight."[61] God works through nature, Trismegistus teaches his disciple Asclepius, and through her is the maker of all living things. It is interesting to note the "height of heaven," which can be read as meaning all the heavens or up to that point at which the heavens begin, that is, up to the moon. If the latter is correct, this is another instance of the sublunary world being the realm of nature.

Finally, the concept of continuity, the way in which nature's working keeps things in movement, is explained as occurring through the reproductive process, which provides for the immortality of the species although the individual dies: "In the case of the gods, both the kind and the individuals are immortal. All other kinds, though they perish in their individuals, are kept in being by their reproductive fertility. Thus the individuals are mortal, but the kind is everlasting; so that men are mortal, but mankind is immortal."[62] This is the reason that God has endowed all beings with sexuality, so that through procreative power they may sustain all that he has created.[63]

The shaping of the medieval goddess Natura was thus a complex cultural process, with some of her most salient characteristics originating in the philosophical and encyclopedic sources of antiquity. Nature was earlier defined as the general order of all creation, as the point of contact between the world-soul and matter, as the ruler of the sublunary world, as the power presiding over the continuity and preservation of all that live in the lower world, and as a creative principle directly subordinated to the mind and will of God. The immediate relevance of these concepts to the medieval characterization of Natura can be demonstrated by referring to one of the better known passages of medieval poetry that deals with her. In the opening lines of his tale, Chaucer's Physician reinforces his description of Virginia as a young girl of extraordinary beauty and virtue by introducing a speech by the goddess Nature in which she makes a kind of boast about the quality of some of her work, in this case, the noble virgin:

> For Nature hath with sovereyn diligence
> Yformed hire in so greet excellence,
> As though she wolde seyn, "Lo! I, Nature,
> Thus kan I forme and peynte a creature,
> Whan that me list; who kan me countrefete?
> Pigmalion noght, though he ay forge and bete,
> Or grave, or peynte, for I dar wel seyn,
> Apelles, Zanzis, sholde werche in veyn
> Outher to grave, or peynte, or forge, or bete,
> If they presumed me to countrefete.
> For He that is the formere principal
> Hath maked me his vicaire general,
> To forme and peynten erthely creaturis
> Right as me list, and ech thyng in my cure is
> Under the moone, that may wane and waxe;
> And for my werk right no thyng wol I axe;
> My lord and I been ful of oon accord.
> I made hire to the worship of my lord;
> So do I alle myne othere creatures,
> What colour that they han, or what figures."[64]

Besides stating her activities as artifex and queen of the sublunary realm in which she works as the vicaria Dei, this speech of Nature's reveals the threefold division of creativity. Nature, who creates in the sublunary world by divine appointment of the principal creator of the universe, challenges the most famous of human artists to match her work. They cannot match it, of course, and were they to try, their vain attempt would be a presumption. The hierarchy of creativity remains intact and beyond question, although, as students of cultural history and literature know, many issues about the relation between nature and art were soon to be raised.[65] Most likely, Chaucer's immediate sources were Alan of Lille and Jean de Meun, but the fact that almost everything Nature says of herself in this passage can be intelligibly related to the materials of antiquity is a testimony to the viability and continuity of the tradition.

II BOETHIUS AND THE POETIC BACKGROUND

There is no more fitting comment on the scope and nature of Boethius' influence on medieval literature and thought than to trace some of the most prominent characteristics of Natura to his great work, *The Consolation of Philosophy*. Even the form of the work, which is in the Menippean tradition and commonly identified as *prosimetrum* because of its alternating sections of prose and verse, indicates the authority and respect accorded its author by medieval writers, for many were to adopt it as the vehicle of their efforts, particularly when their subject was basically philosophical. For every medieval intellectual he was a bridge to the thought of the ancient world, the "last 'ancient' author" of a Rome that was soon to lose its historic role as the *communis patria*.[1]

THE PHILOSOPHICAL NATURE IN *THE CONSOLATION OF PHILOSOPHY*

The significance, both ethical and cosmological, which Boethius assigns to the word *natura* makes an important contribution to the philosophical continuity of the term.

In the *Consolation* there is an eloquent and considerably clarified statement of much that was said of nature in the philosophical works and commentaries of antiquity. The key question of the *Consolation* is raised in the first book, which brings into sharp focus the major theme that Philosophia will develop in her arguments throughout the work. Boethius—destitute, imprisoned, and calumniated—laments his fallen condition and seeks from his visitor an explanation of the marked difference between the ways in which God governs the affairs of men and the affairs of the rest of His creation (I, m. v, 25–29). Philosophia's reply, generally stated, is based on the same principle that the Natura of the medieval poets would set forth. The irregularities and vicissitudes of man's life are owing to his failure to follow nature and her greatest gift to him, reason. Philosophia reveals man's error by pointing out that he has chosen those things that fortune controls in his quest for happiness (II, pr. v, 38–46). Having concentrated his efforts on acquiring the mundane goods of fortune, he has ignored, or rather, dulled his sense of what nature requires him to do with what she herself has given him.[2] In addition, because fortune is unstable and capricious, he has lost whatever little good he might have had through his pursuit of her mutable, fleeting prizes.

What Philosophia is driving at in her opposition of nature and fortune is that man is a creature crowned with reason and the ability to know himself, a blessed possession that neither fortune nor any other power in the world can take away from him (II, pr. iv, 79–84). Reason, the *summum bonum* of human nature, is the key to his blessedness, to his fulfillment in the Aristotelian sense of *telos* or end. Man alone is capable of depriving himself of blessedness by refusing to live according to the self-knowledge that is its result. Through such error, man can become worse than a beast, for ignorance of self is nature in animals but vice in

man (II, pr. v, 85–89). Thus, the groundwork is laid for
Philosophia to demonstrate to Boethius that fortune is
really in no way responsible for his plight, since he possesses
the unique ability and responsibility among God's creatures
to choose between a life under fortune or a life according to
his distinctive nature. If he makes the right choice, the
motive for asking the question to which the depressed
Boethius sought an answer all but disappears. Then he will
know what it is to be a man and will be in tune with the
universe, as Philosophia sings to him in the closing words of
the second book which Dante found so inspiring:

> O felix hominum genus,
> si uestros animos amor
> quo caelum regitur regat.
> (II, m. viii, 28–30)

(O happy human race, if your souls were ruled by the love that
rules heaven.)

This fundamental contrast between nature and fortune is
dramatically epitomized by the juxtaposition of the heavenly
spheres with fortune's wheel, which she turns that she might
turn things upside down (II, pr. ii, 29–34), for in the contrasted images of wheel and sphere is summarized the choice
mankind must make between immediate and eternal concerns.[3]

Thus far the meaning of the term nature has been limited
to the sense of man's recognition of his nature, with Philosophia demonstrating what it means to realize or fail to
realize the distinctive quality that gives man his nature.[4]
This sense of the term is the same as the third definition of
nature in Boethius' *Contra Evtychen:* "natura est motus
principium per se non per accidens" (I.41–42), since it involves the proper and inherent movement of the body in
question. But there is also a larger sense of the word, since
nature can be affirmed of the totality of things (*Con. Ev.*

I.4–10). In this sense, the term embraces both corporeals and incorporeals, natural bodies and divine ideas. Natural bodies, considered collectively, are "an aggregate, ordained by providence, of participations in divine Ideas."[5] It is thus possible, for Boethius, to speak of the nature of all created things.

The place and role of nature in this sense in the order of the universe is a significant part of Philosophia's explanation of providence and fate in the fourth book. In Boethius, as in the commentaries of Chalcidius, fate is subordinate to providence.[6] Philosophia begins her lesson on this subject with the statement that the generation and progress of all things of mutable nature take their causes, order, and forms from the stability of the divine mind (IV, pr. vi, 22–25). The disposition of these causes, forms, and order in the purity of God's understanding is called providence, where all things, diverse and infinite, are embraced, and where the unfolding of temporal order is unified in the mind of God. But the disposition of this order in time is called fate, the ordering that is inherent in all changeable things, and by means of which providence binds all things together in their proper order ("Ordo namque fatalis ex prouidentiae simplicitate procedit," IV, pr. vi, 43–44). Through analogy with a workman who conceives a form in his mind and then sets himself to making in time what he has seen and what is present to his mind, she explains that so also God by his providence disposes of whatever is to be done with simplicity and stability, and by fate effects in many ways and in time those same things that providence has arranged. Thus, fate is the instrument of providence. It may be aided in its works by divine spirits who serve providence, by the soul, by the service of all nature ("seu tota inseruiente natura"), by the motions of the stars, and by angelic or diabolical powers. No matter what the powers or agents that serve fate, they and fate are subject to providence (IV, pr. vi, 60–63).

However, there are some things that are under providence but above the course of fate. These, Philosophia explains in one of her vivid analogies, are like the innermost of a series of concentric spheres; that is, they revolve about the same axis or center. That which is nearest the center most nearly approaches the simple motion of the center and is itself, as it were, the center about which the outer spheres revolve. The outermost of these spheres will turn in a greater circuit and take a longer course in proportion to its distance from the center. But if the outer sphere is joined to the center, it will be drawn into the motion of that center and will no longer stray. In like manner, that which departs farthest from the first mind is all the more bound by the ties of fate, while that which draws nearer the center is all the more free of fate. And that which clings without action to the supernal mind is completely beyond the necessity of fate. In this manner, reasoning may be compared to under-standing, that which becomes to that which is, time to eternity, the circumference of a circle to the center; such is the difference between the moving course of fate and the stable simplicity of providence. The course of fate moves heaven and the stars, tempers the elements, renews all rising and falling things, constrains the actions and fortunes of men in an unbreakable chain of causes, since this course itself proceeds from the principles of immovable providence. Thus, order is brought to the otherwise changeable and confused.

It is quite clear in this analysis that the function of nature, as the ruling principle of an aggregate of mutable bodies, is part of God's mode of operating the world which is called fate. It is significant that Philosophia does not stress nature's subordination to fate; what she stresses is the subordination of fate, and of those various powers that are collected under the common name of fate, to God's providence, which is itself a function of the divine mind. The emphasis is on the

fact that nature, like all the agencies of fate, depends on
providence for its power and direction. This becomes
especially clear when regarding nature as the presiding power
over the principles of procreation and continuity in the world
of change, that power which, under providence, "renews
all things through reproduction of similar offspring and seeds
(eadem nascentia occidentiaque omnia per similes fetuum
seminumque renouat progressus)" (IV, pr. vi, 84–86).

Like Macrobius and Chalcidius, Boethius describes nature
as a kind of artifex presiding over procreation, as in the
clause, "Cum te matris utero natura produxit" (II, pr. ii,
9). More significant is the section in which Philosophia
teaches that the generation and continuance of mortal
things proceed from the principles of nature and not from
the soul's will. For providence has given to all creatures the
desire for continuance (III, pr. xi, 89–102). This sexual
urge, though it may at times be curbed by the will, is always
present in nature ("natura semper appetit"), for it is the
natural seeking of mortal things for permanent stability
which providence has given living creatures. This dependence of nature, either as a collective principle or as the
singular nature of an individual, on God's providence is
really the source of her strength, and in an ethical sense,
nature is a guide for right behavior, because the individual
who follows nature cannot but follow God ("Nihil est
igitur quod naturam seruans deo contraire conetur," III,
pr. xii, 56–57). For the harmony of the universe, the unified
pattern of various and contrary parts compacted by God, is
held together by God, and the course of nature, which carries
that harmony into time and motion, could not continue on
its certain course were it not for the mind and will of God
("Non tam uero certus naturae ordo procederet," III, pr.
xii, 15–26). By establishing this relationship to providence,
Boethius' explanation foreshadows the future role of Natura
as the vicaria Dei.

PSEUDO-JOHN SCOTUS ERIGENA
AND WILLIAM OF CONCHES

The commentaries on *The Consolation of Philosophy* by pseudo-John Scotus Erigena and William of Conches, one of the major figures in the development of the natural philosophy of the school of Chartres, provide a useful indication of the Boethian contribution to and influence on the shaping of the figure of Natura.[7] Both men observe the Aristotelian classification of the three kinds of creativity already noted in Chalcidius, and both associate nature with procreation. In discussing Boethius' poetic summary of the *Timaeus*, pseudo-John Scotus repeats the formula of "opus Dei, opus naturae aut artificis imitantis naturam," and after explaining that the work of God involves nous—or the divine mind, the word of the Father—and the world-soul, and "that which was once chaos, namely the confusion of elements that is called matter ("hyle")," he goes on to explain the work of nature: "The work of nature is twofold: either when something reproduces out of the falling of seeds, such as a man from a man and trees from trees, or self-reproduces, such as certain trees which reproduce themselves without the falling of seed. The work of an artist imitating nature is such as a statue of someone."[8]

The context of his comments on the work of nature in the created world, however, is the Platonic two-world doctrine:

Whoever have spoken of the world's constitution, whether Catholic or pagan, i.e., those who were gentiles, have asserted that there are two worlds: the one called the archetype of the other one called the sensible, i.e., the exemplary world. In fact, they call the archetypal world the original pattern and model of this sensible world which existed in the divine mind before the sensible world came into being . . . And the idea of this entire world existed in the mind of God, according to the pattern of which idea this sensible world was made.[9]

Though the procreative function of nature is explicitly stated, pseudo-John Scotus' comprehensive view of the two worlds tends to give it little emphasis.

The commentary of William of Conches, however, reveals the Chartrian emphasis on Natura's procreative power and on her stewardship to God, as in his gloss on "Non tam uero certus naturae ordo" (III, pr. xii, 20). "This he [Boethius] proves, namely, that God governs the world through the order of nature, and it is the order of nature by which like are born from like, such as men from men, asses from asses."[10]

Again and again, William's commentaries show the Chartrian interest in and fascination with the world of nature. Simply by virtue of the number of times it is repeated, this classification of three kinds of creativity—God's, nature's, man's—lends dignity and significance to the works of nature and those of man, the microcosm.

William directs attention to another activity of nature: "But whatever exists, is conjoined out of diversities, whether it is conjoined by men, or by the working of nature, or by the working of the Creator; by man, such as the parts of a painting; by nature, such as the limbs and organs (membra) of a man."[11]

The closing phrase suggests the activity of natura artifex and looks forward to the role played in the creation of man by Natura in Bernard Silvestris' *De mundi universitate* and in Alan's *Anticlaudianus*. But the Chartrian view of nature's place and role in the universe, following the formidable authority of Boethius, can perhaps best be summed up by this passage from William: "The work of nature is that by which like are born from like, men from men, asses from asses. But one might say: is this not the work of the Creator by which man is born from man? To which I answer: I subtract nothing from God; God made all things that exist in the world except for evil, but other [or some] things He makes by the working of nature, which is the instrument of divine working, and these are called works of nature that are made by nature in subservience to God."[12]

This defense of his position on the work of nature, based on the concept of nature as a servant of God and in no way diminishing His glory, points forward to the goddess Natura as vicaria Dei and at the same time echoes a problem with which Christians of an earlier time had to deal. For in the multitude of ways that the pagan concepts of nature— philosophical, religious, and literary—filtered into the Christian consciousness, there was indeed a danger that the glory and omnipotence of God might be threatened.

This same passage from William expresses the insistence that God made everything in the world except for evil, an important idea in medieval thought which is also crucial to the development of Natura. William, in his commentary on the *Timaeus*, and pseudo-John Scotus, in his gloss on the *Consolation*, both identify the source of evil as the will rather than nature, and both point out that even the devil's nature is good; it is his will that is evil. To quote pseudo-John Scotus on the question: "But if anyone wish to oppose God he gains nothing. He [Boethius] rightly says *following nature*, because insofar as one follows nature he acts rightly and is ruled by God; insofar, however, as he deviates from God he acts wrongly and against nature. For the devil's nature is good and even his power just: but his will is evil. But God makes good use of his evil; and therefore insofar as one willfully attempts evil to that extent he resists God."[13]

That the will and acts of man be evil in their resistance to nature and God, despite his natural goodness, underlies Alan's *De planctu naturae*, for in that work the basis of the goddess Natura's complaint is that man has deviated from her laws. Thus, Boethius' statement that the desire for continuance in the world may be curbed by the will but is always desired by nature becomes not only the justification of Natura's innocence but also the reason for her dissatisfaction when the will perverts nature's demands. For Alan, the moral responsibility rests with a human race whose will has been corrupted by the Fall, and therefore Natura and her priest Genius complain against and excommunicate individuals whose renegade wills have brought them to acts violating both their laws and God's. William's commentary again sheds light on the problem, for he defines Genius in a way that makes him morally neutral, just as the Boethian procreative force is always present and used for good or ill according to the will. William defines Genius as natural concupiscence, who desires whatever he believes is good, whether it is or not ("Genius est naturalis concupiscentia . . . quum quisque judicat bonum, sive ita sit, sive non, concupiscit"), a definition that underscores the fact that the responsibility for sexual conduct lies with the individual.[14] Alan of Lille and Jean de Meun would make radically different uses of this definition in their characterizations of Genius.

THE POETIC NATURA IN
THE CONSOLATION OF PHILOSOPHY

The *Consolation* is much more than a philosophical document; it is a great work of literature. Its wisdom prompted Dante to give its author a place in the sphere of the sun (*Par.* x.124). Its style was regarded as a model of excellence, and its form, though not original with Boethius, was widely imitated. Translated into the medieval vernaculars more often than any other Latin work, it is the only work of literature that enjoys the distinction of having been translated by two of the Middle Ages' greatest poets, Jean de Meun and Chaucer, both of whom figure significantly in the history of Natura.

In the background of the medieval goddess there is another tradition, a mythological and religious one, which

does not lend itself to analysis as readily as do the philosophical and encyclopedic traditions. It is the anthropological
and psychological complex known as the Great Mother
that existed in the European consciousness.[15] This aspect of
nature was invariably expressed poetically.

One of the most striking features of these poetic expressions
of nature is personification, which is of quite another kind
from that encountered in philosophical works and commentaries. The major distinction that must be kept uppermost is that rhetorical or grammatical personification
merely aids in making an abstraction intellectually more
accessible, while poetic personification concentrates on the
representation of a figure having some character. It would
be difficult, perhaps foolhardy, to try to make a case for the
precedence of a poetic nature over the philosophical in the
development of the medieval figure, for in writers known to
have contributed to the medieval concept of the goddess
this aspect cannot be easily separated from philosophical
values. Rather, it is a question of emphasis and nuance.
Also, poetic personification may often be merely the concrete representation of an abstract or mystical phenomenon
or power which is the object of address or epithetical description.

In the second meter of the third book of the *Consolation*,
the expression of nature differs considerably from, though
without contradicting or confusing, other appearances of
the word in the text.

> Quantas rerum flectat habenas
> Natura potens, quibus immensum
> legibus orbem prouida seruet
> stringatque ligans inresoluto
> singula nexu, placet arguto
> fidibus lentis promere cantu.

(It liketh me to schewe by subtil soong, with slakke and delytable
sown of strenges, how that Nature, myghty, enclyneth and

flytteth the governementz of thynges, and by whiche lawes sche, purveiable, kepith the grete world; and how sche, byndynge, restreyneth alle thynges by a boond that may nat be un-bownde.)[16]

This opening statement of intention to celebrate in poetry the inexorable laws with which Natura directs the spacious world is followed by four illustrations of the power of her ways. The lion, though captive and tame, once he has tasted blood, will break his bonds and return to his life of deadly rage and fury. The bird that sings in the forest may be caught and tendered the most delicate of foods, but should she glimpse the woods that were once her home, she spurns the food and sings of flying the coop. The bough bent downwards by a strong hand will raise itself skyward again once the pressure is removed. And Phoebus, though he sinks in the western waves, always turns his course back to his rising in the east. The meter concludes with a state-ment of the order of Natura's world: all things obey a certain course and rejoice in their return to their proper place; nor is there any order unless each thing join its beginning to its end and make in itself the firm, immutable circle that characterizes the world.

There is nothing in this meter that is inimical to the philosophical concepts of nature. Yet her apparently supreme power, through the omission of any mention of her sub-ordination to God's mind, could be misleading in this hymn were it not for the surrounding philosophical context in which the poem is enclosed. Boethius' use of the poetic tradition in a separate poem, which enables him to describe her power and range in more absolute terms and in a kind of language that differs from his other expositions of nature —the epithet "Natura potens" and the image of the goddess driving the universe as a charioteer would his team ("flectat habenas")—nevertheless demands that the reader refer to other passages in the text that more exactly define her place in the cosmos. As a writer, Boethius keeps the poetic and philosophical separate, knowing that his readers will enjoy the poetic interruption of Philosophia's lectures without losing the intellectual thread of her argument.

THE ORPHIC HYMN TO PHYSIS

Though it is impossible to trace exact lines of descent, it is certain that the ultimate source of the poetic nature who appears in the Boethian poem and in the works of Statius and Claudian is the Physis of the tenth Orphic hymn, "the age-old Mother of All," in the words of Ernst Robert Curtius, who "is one of the last religious experiences of the late-pagan world," a cosmic goddess of "inexhaustible vitality."[17]

> Nature, all-parent, ancient and divine,
> O much mechanic mother, art is thine;
> Heav'nly, abundant, venerable queen,
> In ev'ry part of thy dominions seen.
> Untamed, all taming, ever splendid light,
> All ruling, honour'd, and supremely bright.
> Immortal, first-born, ever still the same,
> Nocturnal, starry, shining, powerful dame.
> Thy feet's still traces in a circling course,
> By thee are turn'd, with unremitting force.
> Pure ornament of all the Pow'rs divine,
> Finite and infinite alike you shine;
> To all things common, and in all things known,
> Yet incommunicable and alone.
> Without a father of thy wondrous frame,
> Thyself the father whence thy essence came;
> Mingling, all-flourishing, supremely wise,
> And bond connective of the earth and skies.
> Leader, life-bearing queen, all various nam'd,
> And for commanding grace and beauty fam'd.

Justice, supreme in might, whose general sway
The waters of the restless deep obey.
Etherial, earthly, for the pious glad,
Sweet to the good, but bitter to the bad;
All-wise, all bounteous, provident, divine,
A rich increase of nutriment is thine:
And to maturity whate'er may spring,
You to decay and dissolution bring.
Father of all, great nurse, and mother kind,
Abundant, blessed, all-spermatic mind:
Mature, impetuous, from whose fertile seeds
And plastic hand this changing scene proceeds.
All parent pow'r, in vital impulse seen,
Eternal, moving, all sagacious queen.
By thee the world, whose parts in rapid flow,
Like swift descending streams no respite know,
On an eternal hinge, with steady course,
Is whirl'd with matchless unremitting force.
Thron'd on a circling car, thy mighty hand
Holds and directs the reins of wide command:
Various thy essence, honour'd, and the best,
Of judgment too, the general end and test.
Intrepid, fatal, all-subduing dame,
Like everlasting, Parca, breathing flame.
Immortal Providence, the world is thine,
And thou art all things, architect divine.
O blessed Goddess, hear thy suppliants' pray'r,
And make their future life thy constant care;
Give plenteous seasons and sufficient wealth,
And crown our days with lasting peace and health.[18]

Among the treasure of predicates in these thirty lines, enough to supply a number of divinities, some of the most prominent features of the late Latin and medieval Natura are immediately recognizable: creator, nourisher, shaper, presiding power over generation and increase, the whole world, and as in Boethius' poem, the charioteer who holds the reins of the world in her hands.[19]

The tremendous range of her qualities is perhaps what gave her such wide appeal, for she appears under many names and faces, as one of her own descendents informs Lucius in *The Golden Ass*:

Behold, Lucius, I am come; thy weeping and prayer hath moved me to succour thee. I am she that is the natural mother of all things, mistress and governess of all the elements, the initial progeny of worlds, chief of the powers divine, queen of all that are in hell, the principal of them that dwell in heaven, manifested alone and under one form of all gods and goddesses. At my will the planets of the sky, the wholesome winds of the seas, and the lamentable silences of hell be disposed; my name, my divinity is adored throughout the world, in divers manners, in variable customs, and by many names. For the Phrygians that are first of all men call me the Mother of the gods at Pessinus; the Athenians, which are sprung from their own soil, Cecropian Minerva; the Cyprians, which are girt about by the sea, Paphian Venus; the Cretans which bear arrows, Dictynnian Diana; the Sicilians, which speak three tongues, infernal Proserpine; the Eleusians their ancient goddess Ceres; some Juno, other Bellona, other Hecate, other Rhamnusia, and principally both sort of the Ethiopians which dwell in the Orient and are enlightened by the morning rays of the sun, and the Egyptians, which are excellent in all kind of ancient doctrine, and by their proper ceremonies accustom to worship me, do call me by my true name, Queen Isis.[20]

This Great Mother of oriental religion of the second century fails to mention, perhaps by design, the new and rising religion with which her own was in stiff contention. Christian writers and apologists reacted to and vigorously combated this powerful religious figure under her Latin name Natura.

STATIUS AND CLAUDIAN

Out of the philosophical and the broad Orphic and Eastern backgrounds, there emerges in Latin poetry a figure of nature whose currency and characterization grew with successive generations of poets. Statius and Claudian have been represented, a little too narrowly and categorically, as the only relevant sources in the classical background of Natura.[21] Their importance is unquestionable, but the exclusiveness is doubtful, and their contributions must be viewed within a larger frame of reference.

Two of the most prominent poets before Statius and Claudian in whose work are found significant instances of nature as a cosmic power are Ovid and Lucretius. The well-known opening lines of the *Metamorphoses*, for example, explain that the primal chaos was brought to order by god and higher nature ("Hanc deus et melior litem natura diremit").[22] Lucretius, although virtually unknown to the Middle Ages except for a handful of passages, twice refers to *natura creatrix* as the maker of all things.[23] In view of the many personae the goddess could assume, it is not surprising that in the invocation to Venus in the first book Lucretius identifies her as governess of all things ("quae quoniam rerum naturam sola gubernas").[24] Pauly-Wissowa and Curtius have provided ample lists of the personified nature in Latin literature, and Ovid and Lucretius sufficiently indicate not only the currency of the figure but, more important, the common use of the figure regardless of philosophical persuasion.[25]

Statius (45–96), one of the best known Latin poets during the Middle Ages, was something of an innovator in the use of personifications, as C. S. Lewis has shown in his analysis of the *Thebaid*.[26] Although the major instances of personified nature in Statius occur in the *Thebaid*, there are two of some interest in the *Silvae*, a series of ornate and often lengthy occasional poems. Both passages, which say essentially the same things about nature, are descriptions of villas and their surroundings and illustrate the function of Latin personified nature known as *natura plasmatrix terrae et locorum*. In each poem, the villa is set in a spot of incomparable beauty, a place where the goddess has not been sparing with her talents. Describing the setting of the villa of Manlius Vopiscus at Tibur, the poet exclaims: "How beautiful beyond human art the enchanted scene! Nowhere has Nature more lavishly spent her skill."[27]

Contrasting with her very specific and limited function in the *Silvae*, the goddess Natura appears in the *Thebaid* as a figure of cosmic significance. In all six of her occurrences in the poem, she is either referred to or directly addressed, but she never appears or speaks as a character, a fact that makes her more impressive than if she were to appear, for she is twice identified as "princeps Natura."[28] Further-more, every context in which she is mentioned suggests that she represents something very important. When in the eleventh book the fratricidal Eteocles and Polynices come together in a duel to the death, Pietas, the daughter of Natura, is deeply offended by the brothers' breaking the bond of natural affection and complains to her mother: "Why sovereign Nature, didst thou create me to oppose the passions of living folk and often of the gods? Nought am I any more among men, nowhere am I reverenced" (XI.465–467).

Here Natura is not only *princeps* but *creatrix* as well, having brought into being all the human inclinations and affections represented by Pietas. That Natura is her mother is an important distinction between the two personifications, and leads to an even more profound difference between Natura and the other personifications in the poem.

In the twelfth and concluding book, in which the central episode is the intervention of Theseus, Natura is referred to in directly related scenes. Speaking for the Argive women, Capaneus' widow pleads with Theseus to put an end to the strife at Thebes. She asks Athens for a restoration of order and makes her plea in the name of princeps Natura (XII.561–562). Less than a hundred lines later, Theseus exhorts his men in the name of Natura to help him set the monstrous Theban disorder right: "Soldiers, who will defend with me the laws of nations and the covenant of heaven, take courage worthy of our emprise! For us, 'tis clear, stands the favour of all gods and men, Nature our guide and the silent multitudes of Avernus: for them the troops of Furies, that Thebes has marshalled, and the snakehaired Sisters bring forth their banners. Onward in warlike spirit, and trust, I pray you, in a cause so noble!" (XII.642–648).

As the juxtaposition of Natura and Athens in the Argive woman's plea suggests, Theseus decides to make his city the instrument of the order of "Natura dux"; as Lewis maintains, he "claims Natura as his patron."[29]

It should by now be patently clear that the personified Natura of the *Thebaid* cannot be classed with the other personifications in the poem. They represent specific passions, states of mind, religious concepts, such as Bellona, Pietas, and Clementia. But Natura represents something much greater; she is no less than the Stoic "whole," and as J. H. Mozley points out in his introduction, is an example of Stoic syncretism, "the regarding of different deities as so many manifestations of one ultimate Power."[30] To the Stoic, the world is a vast organism governed by an intelligence and divine nature which is itself god, and this organism is variously called the world, god, or nature, as no less an authority than Cicero explains: "Hence it follows that the world possesses wisdom, and that the element which holds all things in its embrace is pre-eminently and perfectly rational, and therefore that the world is god, and all the forces of the world are held together by the divine nature (eoque deum esse mundum omnemque vim mundi natura divina contineri)."[31]

"Princeps Natura," then, manifests the divine order and unity of the world.

Statius' Natura is an important phase in the tradition from which developed the medieval goddess. A deity to whom the characters in the poem can appeal, in whose name the righteous may act, she represents the order of the entire universe, a fact that sharply distinguishes her from the Christian vicaria Dei whose cosmic powers are more limited and subordinated to God. Conversely, because she is all, Statius' Natura remains mute and invisible, while the medieval goddess, for a variety of reasons, is the subject of elaborate allegorical characterization. What is really significant is that here in a work of imaginative literature that was widely read in the Middle Ages is a Natura figure who assumes, if only by invocation, a role in the affairs of mankind,[32] however slight it may seem in comparison with the role of the medieval figure.

While Statius made a significant contribution to the history of Natura, Claudian (c. 370–c. 404), who is generally considered "the last poet of classical Rome," made an even greater one.[33] In his works, Natura speaks, acts, and is the subject of a little description. Curtius has listed the five new functions of Natura that are found in Claudian, the most important of which are *Natura discretix veteris tumultus*, *Natura plangens*, and *Natura pronuba*, although all five are closely related in Claudian's handling.[34]

In the *De raptu Proserpinae*, Proserpina, having been left in Sicily for safekeeping by her mother, occupies herself with sewing a tapestry on which she embroiders pictures of the creation and plan of the universe. One of the first things she depicts there is how Mother Nature made order out of elemental chaos: "In this cloth she embroidered with her needle the concourse of atoms and the dwelling of the Father of the gods and pictured how mother Nature ordered elemental chaos (veterem qua lege tumultum discrevit Natura parens) and how the first principles of things sprang apart, each to his proper place" (I.248–251).

Like Ovid's higher nature, Claudian's is a figure of great power, but the activity of ordering chaos is one that her medieval descendant will never be allowed, for the *mens Dei* alone has that power. The closest parallel in the medieval allegories—and I am not convinced it is merely fortuitous or circumstantial—occurs in Bernard Silvestris' *De mundi universitate*, where in the opening lines of the work Natura describes for Noys the chaotic state of matter and pleads with her to give it the shape of order. Besides the hint of Natura plangens, Bernard's account brings Natura, who in the Neoplatonic hierarchy is closer to matter than Noys is, as near to the first stage of creation as a Christian dare by making her the instigator.

In the second book of the *De raptu Proserpinae*, there is an episode in which Natura plangens and pronuba figure prominently. In their celebration of the marriage of Proserpina to Pluto, the shades of Dis refer to Natura as joyously awaiting the birth of new gods from the union (II.371–372). One critic has suggested that this is the reason Natura, who is marriage-maker of the gods, arranged the wedding.[35] Actually, the affair is more complex. Natura has been something of an instigator, for when Jupiter explains his purpose in allowing the girl's abduction, he indicates that the complaint of Natura about the wild and bestial state of man has moved him to set in motion the events described in the poem. In the reign of Saturn, man had become lethargic, so on Jupiters' accession, he stopped all crops from growing of their own accord and bade mankind search out the hidden ways of things (III.18–32). Man failed to discover these hidden ways, the principles of agriculture, and wandered the earth like an animal, subsisting on acorns. It is because Natura's bountiful gifts were lying in a state of abeyance, Jupiter explains, that she complained to him: "Nature now with ceaseless complaint bids me succour the race of men, calls me cruel tyrant, calls to mind the centuries of my

sire's empery and dubs me miser of her riches, for that I
would have the world a wilderness and land covered with
scrub and would beautify the year with no fruits. She complained that she, who was erstwhile the mother of all living
things (genetrix mortalibus), had suddenly taken upon her
the hated guise of a stepmother" (III.33–40).

Within a few lines, Natura makes clear that she wants
not only her own status restored but that of man, for whom
she has nothing but compassion, because his animal-like
existence opposes his intelligence and his upright posture
(III.41–45). Jupiter, therefore, decreed the marriage so
that Ceres, after having wandered over sea and land in
search of her lost daughter, would be so overjoyed at finding
traces of her that she would grant man the gift of corn,
hence the art of agriculture (III.45–49). A powerful and
dominating figure in Claudian's version of this ancient myth,
Natura acts in her own interest as well as that of man, to
raise him from his low estate by bringing the art through
which he may enjoy her plentiful gifts.

When these features are translated into Christian poetry,
they operate somewhat differently. The medieval goddess,
of course, is pronuba of earthly marriages, as in the *De
planctu naturae* and Chaucer's *Parlement of Foules*. As Natura
plangens, she effects a marriage that will result in a major
change in the lives of men, just as the complaints of the
Natura figures in the *De mundi universitate* and the *Anticlaudianus* raise questions that affect the cosmos. But in the
best known medieval treatments of Natura plangens, the *De
planctu naturae* and Jean de Meun's *Roman de la Rose*, the shift
from pagan to Christian cultural context necessitates that the
goddess complain against man, though still in his interest,
meaning his salvation; Claudian's Natura may complain
to the lord of the gods, but clearly the vicaria Dei has
neither desire nor cause to complain to God the Father,
a thought that would completely shatter her reasons for

being. Though the direction of complaint is completely reversed, there nevertheless remains the significant similarity of Natura as intermediary between man and God.

Scattered in the minor poems of Claudian are various references to Natura. In a rather clumsily conceived poem entitled "Magnes," Natura pronuba presides over a miracle that takes place in a golden temple housing an iron statue of Mars and a lodestone statue of Venus.[36] As priest and choir celebrate the union of opposites, love and strife, the statue of Mars moves across the floor to that of Venus, which clasps him to her bosom. Even an allegorical interpretation of this conquest of Mars by Venus, which recalls the eloquent glorification of the binding love that keeps the warring elements and therefore the world in balance in Boethius' *Consolation* (II, m. viii) and Chaucer's *The Knight's Tale*, cannot rescue it from banality. In another short poem, "Phoenix," Natura acts as the sustainer of life by presiding over the ancient ritual of regeneration in which the bird and Phoebus participate.[37] Of much greater interest is the description of Natura in the second book of *De consolatu Stilichonis*.[38] She sits within the entrance to the cave of Aevum, which is surrounded by a serpent devouring its own tail. Inside the cave is a venerable old man, probably a Father Time figure, who fixes the numbers of the stars and the courses of the planets.[39] When Phoebus' rays strike the threshold of the cave, Natura runs to meet him, and the old man raises his head before the rays. The great door inside the cave swings open of its own accord, the poet explains, and reveals the secrets of time. Phoebus inspects the metals symbolic of the four ages, selects the best of the gold to be marked with the name of Stilicho, and announces an age of nobler ore. Though this allegory is trite, both the close association of Natura with the repository of time's secrets and the way in which she is described are of interest: "Before the entrance sits Nature, guardian of the threshold, of age immense yet ever lovely, around whom throng and flit spirits on every side" (431–433).

Her appearance as a woman of great age but fresh beauty matches the descriptive epithets of Physis in the Orphic hymn and recalls Boethius' description of Philosophia (I, pr. i, 2–8), which clearly implies a continuity in the way that the ancients pictured the figure and the ease of transferring striking descriptive details from one figure to another. Again her creative power is underlined by the spirits (*animae*) that flit about her as she sits guarding the providential cave, for they may be read as unborn souls. When all the fragments pertaining to Natura in the works of Claudian are put together, they give a picture of a profound and active personification, a goddess Natura.[40]

The Consolation of Philosophy reaffirms and clarifies several of the major classical concepts of nature. The references to nature as the power presiding over the continuity and preservation of whatever lives in the world and as a creative principle directly subordinated to the mind and will of God are especially well defined by Boethius and take on added significance in the medieval commentators. It is noteworthy that Boethius nowhere limits the realm of nature to the sublunary world. The medieval goddess rules the whole of the created world, of which the sublunary is the lowest, most volatile part and therefore requires her attention as procreatrix and pronuba. The sublunary world, after all, is the setting in which the crown of creation, man the microcosm, plays out the drama of salvation or damnation in a world that is as it is because of the Fall. Boethius also makes use of the poetic nature that arose from the Orphic hymn, but he does not combine the two traditions, allowing the surrounding philosophical context to qualify the poetic expression.

In the poems of Statius and Claudian, Natura emerges

as a significant and meaningful personification in whose composition both the philosophical and poetic traditions play roles. Their poems, particularly Claudian's, definitely influenced the medieval figure. Yet if their Naturas are placed beside those Bernard, Alan, Jean, and Chaucer, they seem like shadows, vaguer and less detailed. One critical difference between these exceptional illustrations of the figure in classical poetry and their medieval counterparts lies in their radically different philosophical and cosmological characterizations. In the Roman poets, the fact that she represents everything, the whole, made it difficult for Natura to emerge as a singular and arresting poetic figure. This is especially true in Statius, and though less true in Claudian, the variety of roles she plays there, which are sometimes in service to trivial allegory, serve to blur rather than sharpen her image. The medieval poets, for whom Natura was a creation of God and his vicar, whose place in the universe was clearly defined, did not have this problem.[41] At the risk of oversimplifying, classical poetry supplied her with a mode of expression and gave her some features, but Christian philosophy gave her character.

To consider a single detail in her characterization, Alan describes Natura's tunic as having been torn and abused in that part of it which shows man laying aside the sluggishness of his sensuality and, under the direction of reason, penetrating the secrets of the heavens. Most likely Alan borrowed the motif of a rip in the clothing of an allegorical figure from Boethius' description of a similar tear in the robe of Philosophia (I, pr. i, 22–24), just as Boethius borrowed some features from descriptions of the pagan *nature*. The meaning of the torn part of Philosophia's robe is explained by pseudo-John Scotus: "It [her garment] receives the violent force of the damned heretics of warped understanding, who rend sound doctrine with their heresies, who lack perfect wisdom."[42]

Just so the fugitives from Natura's laws, the lustful and unnatural, rend her sound doctrine with their sins. These natures, though fallen, are nevertheless capable of transcending depravity through reason and the guidance of Natura.

III THE LATIN MIDDLE AGES: BERNARD SILVESTRIS AND ALAN OF LILLE

The three major literary works connected with the school of Chartres—the *De mundi universitate* of Bernard Silvestris, and the *De planctu naturae* and *Anticlaudianus* of Alan of Lille—are the seminal works in which the medieval goddess Natura received her essential shape and characterization. These three allegories are of major significance in the cultural history of medieval Europe, for they reflect the intellectual vitality and originality, the love and respect for classical letters and thought, that were distinguishing features of the great cathedral school with which they are associated. Yet the figure that was to play such a dominant role in them owed much to the contribution of the earlier Latin Middle Ages. The importance of these earlier writers lies in their efforts to place the nature of classical civilization within the context of the Christian faith, a step that anticipated and prepared the way for some of the most distinctive characteristics of the allegorical goddess.

PRUDENTIUS, LACTANTIUS,
AND SAINT AMBROSE

Representative of a wide range of concepts in ancient civilization, the term nature had considerable weight in philosophy, religion, and poetry. It could represent the sublunary world, the moment of contact between the world-soul and matter, or the proper movement, both individual and collective, inherent in all creatures in the world of becoming; it could be identified as the creative principle in the universe and thus venerated as a deity, and it could signify the entire universe, the all, as portrayed in Stoic poetry, which was the most direct poetic antecedent of the medieval Natura. For the early Christian, who could not ignore the legacy of philosophy and literature that had come to him—indeed, surrounded him—from the pagan world and who yet had to defend and uphold the true faith, these various concepts of nature were very threatening.[1] Early Christians, therefore, took measures to place definite limitations on the potency of nature which they accomplished largely through making nature the creation and servant of God.

The Christian poet Prudentius (348–405), who is generally thought of in connection with the development of allegory because of the influence of his *Psychomachia*, carefully stressed three things about nature in his *Contra orationem Symmachi* (402).[2] In praising Theodosius I for forbidding pagan worship, unlike some of his predecessors who had tolerated it, Prudentius asserts that the emperor had acted to the benefit of humanity when he outlawed belief in the old gods and the worship of nature, which is, in fact the work of the Father who created everything (I.9–13).[3] The true God, who created the universe, governs it ("Deus verus . . . qui praesidet omni naturae," I.325–327). As the work of God, nature serves Him ("Dei serva") by furnishing her services for the creation of men, whom she in turn serves by providing them with sustenance ("altrix hominum"). To this definition of nature as procreatrix and altrix, which anticipates the allegorical figure of the later Middle Ages, Prudentius adds a third characteristic: nature has no moral force. She can only serve, not judge, a function that God ("summus naturae Dominus") reserves for Himself: "Nature, then, while furnishing her services for the creation of peoples, is indifferent and cannot distinguish between the different merits of living, because her only duty is to feed them. For the world is our servant, not our judge; this function the supreme Lord of nature reserves for Himself at the appointed season"(II.794–798). Perhaps in reaction to the Stoic concept and literary treatment of the term, Prudentius never treats it allegorically and denies it moral judgment. The need to limit and subordinate nature to God helped establish her relationship to Him as serva, but it would take a positive, intellectually aggressive, and speculative, rather than an essentially defensive, view of nature to establish her as vicaria Dei.

That Prudentius' view, based on a reaction to pagan concepts, was not unique is well attested by a passage from Lactantius (250–317), in which this distinguished Church Father vigorously attacks pagan beliefs and stresses the subservience of nature to God:

For they, either not knowing by whom the world was made, or desiring to persuade others that nothing was completed by the divine mind, said that nature was the mother of all things, as if to say all things were born of their own accord: by which word they clearly reveal their ignorance. For nature, removed from divine providence and power, is absolutely nothing. But if they call God nature, what perversity it is to use the name nature rather than God! But if nature is the order, or the necessity, or the condition of birth, it is not itself capable of sense: but it is necessary that there be a divine intelligence which by its providence supplies all things with the basis of their births. Or if nature is heaven and earth, everything that is created, then nature is not God, but the work of God.[4]

These examples of the corrective measures taken by early Christian writers against the pagan nature must be understood in the context of apologetics: they were defending the true God and the faith in Him against the hostility of pagan philosophy and religion. A work like the *Hexaemeron* of Saint Ambrose (337–397) may place the same restrictions on nature, but since the hexameral tradition involves the interpretation of "truth" as revealed in Divine Scripture, the appreciation of nature as the work and law of God takes precedence over limiting her power. The restrictions are merely given, for in this context there is no need to argue them.

Written as nine sermons which were preached on six days during Lent, the *Hexaemeron* of Ambrose was one of the most renowned and highly influential exegetical works of the Middle Ages.[5] References to nature are scattered throughout the work, and though it is difficult to ascertain whether or not its various senses were meant to be understood as aspects of a single concept, these senses can be definitely linked with those found in other authors. As in Prudentius and Lactantius, for example, nature is unquestionably the work of God ("opus Dei natura est"). And since it was God who created nature, it is God who gives her her law. In addition to the subordination to God, uses of the term in the *Hexaemeron* are reminiscent of some of her other qualities in both pagan and Christian writers. Nature is said to have provided man with nourishment, and the following passage presents a feature that is by no means uncommon in Christian and Stoic literature: "For nature is a better guide of truth. Without any director, she infuses our senses with knowledge of what is sweet and healthy, and she teaches us to avoid the bitterness that brings pain. Thereby life becomes sweeter, thereby death more bitter."[6] This sense of nature as teacher and guide of truth clearly anticipates the allegorical goddesses, especially those of Alan and Chaucer. Her concern with life also suggests natura procreatrix, especially in another passage in which Ambrose explains that since Creation, all creatures have perpetuated themselves according to their aspect and kind. The succession of generations follows the law of nature, which was ordained by God, and that which was once commanded by God ("Crescite et multum reddite fructum") becomes in nature a habit for all time ("Semel praeceptum in perpetuum inolevit naturae").[7] The point is not that these uses of the term are necessarily sources for the character of the later goddesses, but rather that many details of her characterization have a long history in Christian tradition.

Throughout the *Hexaemeron*, Ambrose seems to be personifying nature. Were it not for one passage in which the personification is clearly realized, his handling of the word would merely show a strong tendency toward grammatical personification. The first chapter of the sixth homily, however, deals with the fourth day of Creation, the day on which the sun, the moon, and the stars were created. Before explaining the movements of the heavens, Ambrose insists on clarifying the fact that the sun, though it is possibly the single most beautiful and glorious object in creation, is only a part of all created nature and in itself has no creative power. He then ingeniously proceeds to have nature explain the role of the sun, which is subordinate to her and in turn to God, in a speech: "Indeed, the sun is good, but as one that serves, not as one that commands; good as one that assists my fecundity, but not as one that creates; good as nourisher of my fruits, but not as their maker . . . Standing by me, it praises the Creator, it sings a hymn to our Lord God."[8]

Rhetorically, this is an obvious device, possibly intended by Ambrose to shed light on some of the other passages in which nature appears rather than to to be read merely as a grammatical personification. If a claim of novelty can be made for it, it must be based on its being a very early instance in a Christian work of the personification of nature by speech, a feature that is absent from the classical antecedents, but which is indispensable to the allegorical Natura.

BERNARD SILVESTRIS

The literary career of the goddess Natura, for all practical purposes, did not begin until the middle of the twelfth century.[9] The intellectual setting was the school of Chartres, representing the culmination and climax of several centuries of medieval Neoplatonism. Among the remarkable men who made up this community of scholars and thinkers were two individuals of unusual literary genius and originality, to whom the goddess Natura owes her existence as the most significant allegorical figure of medieval Latin and vernacular poetry. In the works of Bernard Silvestris and Alan of Lille, Natura assumes a central position in the poetic expression of the Chartrian vision of the universe, a vision based on the conviction that man is capable of interpreting and understanding the natural and moral order of a universe which, like its transcendent model, is a single, harmonious whole, a sensible, concrete world that participates in the divine reality which gave it being. The nature of the cosmos reveals the nature of man; to know the macrocosm is to know the microcosm, man, in whom "the immense unity of all things was knotted up together . . . who stands at the paradoxical borderline of matter and spirit."[10]

The *De mundi universitate*, Bernard's poem of the cosmogony, laid the foundations for subsequent poets to explore man's relation to nature and to God in a world shaken by the Fall, an event which, though strongly foreshadowed and implied, could not be explicitly included in the action of his work. Bernard's poem not only stands at the beginning of the medieval tradition of Natura but, by virtue of its subject, also sets forth the medieval notion of the beginning of the history of the universe itself. His cosmogony and cosmology established a frame of reference to which every subsequent Natura poet—Alan, Jean de Meun, Chaucer, and even Spenser—was in one way or another indebted.

Composed between 1145 and 1156, the *De mundi universitate* reflects its author's wide scope of learning and interests.[11] His basic philosophical sources range from Chalcidius, Macrobius, and the Hermetic *Asclepius* to the investigations of his Chartrian contemporaries. His literary as well as philosophical models are Boethius and Martianus Capella, with the work being composed in the prosimetrum form that those popular and authoritative authors bequeathed to the Middle Ages. Bernard knew astrology and something of geomancy.[12] Familiar with the Latin poets, he wrote commentaries on the first six books of the *Aeneid* and on Martianus' *De nuptiis Philologiae et Mercurii*, and it is quite certain he composed the no longer extant *Summa dictaminis* and *Liber de metrificatura*.[13] Though there is no indication he ever taught at Chartres, there are many reasons to believe he had close ties with that school, the most obvious being the dedication of his creation allegory to Thierry of Chartres: "Terrico veris scientiarum titulis Doctoris famosissimo Bernardus Silvestris opus suum."[14] His extensive learning and the variety of his literary activities earned him the respect not only of his contemporaries but also of medieval intellectuals for at least the next two centuries.

Like many Latin poems of the twelfth century, *De mundi universitate* is a difficult work for the modern reader. Indeed, some sense of the work's content and structure is necessary to an appreciation of its historical importance. Readers of this work are therefore referred to the Appendix for a summary that is somewhat fuller than those offered previously. Although the role and characterization of Natura are of primary concern here, a word on the work's intellectual background and milieu should help to elucidate its literary nature. A brief review of *De mundi* criticism raises some of these questions.

The earliest modern judgments of Bernard's allegory were for the most part brief and disapproving, accusing Bernard of being more pantheist and pagan than Christian. This is basically the opinion of Ernst Robert Curtius, while Etienne Gilson and Theodore Silverstein offer more enlightened readings of the poem. All three interpretations agree on the obvious point that the work is a fabulous account of the *ornatus elementorum*, but disagree not only on several important issues but also in their approaches to the poem. Gilson attempts to rescue Bernard from the paganist view by arguing that his work is essentially Christian in character. It combines, he claims, the Platonism of the time, which reaches back to the Chalcidian *Timaeus*, with the hexameric exegetical tradition of Genesis in an effort to supply a rational justification for the revelation of scripture. Yet despite its Christian character, Gilson believes the work is finally dualistic, for Bernard never explicitly mentions the Christian doctrine of God's creation of matter *ex nihilo*. It seems to Gilson, therefore, that there are two irreducible principles in Bernard's system, God and matter. Curtius, in contrast, directly opposes Gilson's understanding of the work as an interpretation of Genesis. In fact, he sees very little that is particularly Christian in it. To him, "The whole is bathed in an atmosphere of a fertility cult, in which religion and sexuality mingle." Since Bernard's poem is related to the philosophical and literary traditions examined in the first two chapters, then Curtius' *Geschlecht* theory falls wide of the mark. Though the *De mundi universitate* deals with generation, it does so not in a fertility cult atmosphere, but rather in an atmosphere of philosophical and scientific exploration of the nature of the universe and man's place in it. Bernard's concept of Natura depends largely on the Neoplatonic theory of emanations and the astronomical view of nature as a celestial generative principle. There is little that suggests she is a *Geschlechtsfigur*.

Silverstein, in the most thorough treatment of the work to date, convincingly repudiates Curtius' reading, agrees with Gilson as to the Christianty of the *De mundi*, clarifies some of the difficulties Gilson found, and presents the sources Bernard worked with. Though many of the sources have been recognized for some time he adds some new titles to the list. Perhaps the most significant and influential feature of his study is Silverstein's insistence that the *De mundi* be read as a work of literature. He makes the important point that by writing an allegorical fable, Bernard managed to avoid many of the serious difficulties that had arisen in Chartrian speculation.[15]

The advantage, not to mention the validity, of reading the *De mundi* primarily as a poem, which is to accept it as an allegorical fable or, to use Bernard's medieval term, an *integumentum*, is illustrated by examining two theological problems in light of Bernard's "poetic" handling of them.[16] The dualism of God and matter which Gilson complained of is one such problem. Silverstein points out that matter exists as a condition prior to the opening of the work and that at no point does Bernard suggest he believes in the eternity of matter. A further defense of Bernard's obscurity on this question is the view that matter, with its evil propensities, supplies a thematic correspondence for the doctrine of original sin.[17] Bernard's reluctance to refer outright to the creation ex nihilo can be justified, then, in terms of narrative time and a desire for consistency with the Timaean pattern, a consistency which seeks not to contradict but to reveal a correspondence between God's two books, his scripture and his creation. Such apologies, which I believe are thoroughly consistent with Bernard's intentions, are perhaps more necessary for modern readers than they would have been for the poem's contemporary audience. A hint that this suspicion is correct may be found in the *Tractatulus super librum Genesis* by Clarembald of Arras, a student and disciple of Thierry. Although he clearly establishes that God created the entire world, including matter, Clarembald's argument that the world has a maker emphasizes not so much the authority of the Bible as it does the very existence of that world.[18] The effort to accept and experience the world as real and concrete, as a manifestation of a transcendent reality with an actuality of its own, is characteristic of Chartrian thought, and such speculation raised serious difficulties in thinkers more original than Clarembald. But if he could accept the actuality of the physical world as his basic premise, there was nothing to prevent a poet, who could take for granted that his readers understood who created matter, from starting his narrative at the point at which that matter is about to be shaped into an intelligible, sensible universe by the agents of the God who created all.

Among the numerous doctrinal difficulties that arose in the course of Chartrian speculation, one that has definitely left its stamp on the *De mundi* is the identification of Neoplatonic emanations with the persons of the Trinity. Again, Silverstein points out how Bernard the poet saw his way clear of this problem. Through the use of integumenta, "he was able to show how God's power, wisdom, and goodness work in the world, as Abelard and Guillaume had tried to do, but without involving himself in their dilemma."[19] The figures of Noys, Natura, and Endelechia correspond to divine wisdom and the Holy Spirit, but never are they identified as such. Instead, they are allowed to operate in the poem without being specifically connected with the Trinity, which is separately introduced at a critical moment in the action. This occurs when Natura and Urania pray for success to the triple-shafted light in the mansion of Tugaton before they descend to earth to complete the work Noys has assigned them: "Illic Urania pariter et Natura cuidam trinae maiestati plurima precum devotatione auspicium propositumque itineris commendarunt" ("In that place Urania and Natura together committed the direction and purpose of their journey to a certain majestic trinity by means of a very ardent offering of prayers"; II.v.41).[20]

By having them pray, Bernard manages to keep these agents of Noys under the proper sponsorship of the Christian God and Trinity, although it is impossible to determine their relationship. By writing an allegorical fable, Bernard was able to free himself from certain difficulties that he might not have been able to avoid had he been writing a philosophical tract: Noys has strong parallels to but is never identified with the *Verbum Dei*, and Natura, whose function partially involves the activity of the Chartrian world-soul, which had been identified with the third person of the Trinity, becomes for the first time the unique cosmic goddess of medieval allegory.

Subordinate to the figure of Noys, the role of Natura in the *De mundi* involves four activities. First, Natura complains of matter's shapelessness and disorder and pleads with Noys to put it in order, natura plangens. Second, she provides bodies for the souls that are produced by Endelechia, the world-soul. Third, she makes a celestial journey. Finally, Natura joins the soul of man, furnished by Urania, to the body fashioned for him by Physis, in which joiner's work she must emulate the order of the heavens. The first and third activities present less in the way of difficulty than the second and fourth, possibly because they stem from well-known literary conventions. The complaining Natura and her persuasive power to move divinity are quite prominent in Claudian. Translated into the cosmogony setting of the *De mundi*, the complaining Natura admits her helplessness in the face of chaos, for, as in the commentary of William of Conches on Boethius (III, pr. xii), Natura's creative power involves things that are alike, not contrary. This feature is tellingly stated by Clarembald when he considers the nature of the world and the question of who made it.[21] "Silva rigens" requires the shaping hand of God, represented in the fable by Noys, the intellect of the supreme God and born of his divinity ("Ea igitur noys summi et exsuperantissimi Dei intellectus et ex eius divinitate nata natura," I.ii.13). The celestial journey is a common convention in works with cosmological themes or settings, the best known of those that precede Bernard being the *Somnium Scipionis* of Cicero and the *De nuptiis Philologiae et Mercurii* of Martianus Capella. The heavenly journey of Lady Philology in the latter is particularly relevant, for her journey, like Natura's, provides her with the knowledge of the divine and celestial that is necessary to the fulfillment of her destiny. Of much greater importance to Bernard, and more difficult for the modern reader to ascertain, are Natura's second and fourth activities.

At the end of the first book, where the realization of the physical world is described, Natura's participation is identified as producing bodies out of matter, and her title in this context is that of artifex. The process follows a descending series of stages: Noys passes the divine ideas to Endelechia; Endelechia in turn endows the souls with substantia and transmits to them the ideas received from Noys; the souls are then passed on to Natura, who has provided bodies for them; and finally, to Imarmene falls the responsibility of the regulation of their continuation in time (I.iv.32).[22]

In general terms, this process sounds familiar. It is basically related to the animating and perpetuating function of the Timaean world-soul and its derivatives: the world-soul animates the universe, that is, brings the world of nature into being by its contact with matter, in Macrobius; nature unites anima and mundus into one living whole in the *Asclepius*; and it is nature, acting upon silua, "quae ... exordium et fons est corporum," that is the vivifying power of the world-soul in the lower regions of the universe in Chalcidius. In these authors, as in Bernard, nature acts as an intermediary between the worlds of being and becoming. But it is difficult to determine her role with exactness. She is an active principle as artifex, but she also has ties with Plato's third nature, the nurse and mother of all becoming; she is, in the words of Noys, "uteri mei beata fecunditas" (I.ii.9). Bernard's obscurity may have an advantage, for it helps him avoid the error committed by some of the masters of Chartres in assimilating nature to the Timaean world-soul, which, in their effort to unite Platonism with Christian doctrine, often resulted in the identification of the world-soul with the Holy Spirit.[23] Bernard does not, in fact, identify the world-soul, his Endelechia, with the Holy Spirit, and he separates Natura from Endelechia, though she is closely associated with it.

The Neoplatonic background of Bernard's Natura is complemented by the concept of a generating celestial nature found in astronomical writings, particularly the medieval Hermetic book *De vi rerum principiis*. In this work, nature passes on to the lower, sublunary world of generation the essences that have their source in racio (*noys*), and thus she establishes each thing's being and nature. Nature, according to the astronomers, is identified with the superlunary world, while the sublunary world is identified as the work of nature. This conception of Natura, which is described in a passage in the first book of the *De mundi* (I.iv.30–31), should be taken along with her function of providing bodies for souls as her chief activity in the shaping of the macrocosm. Thus, in the fashioning of bodies, Natura acts as intermediary to Noys and to the heavenly principle according to which these bodies operate.[24] Along with Endelechia and Imarmene, Natura participates in the ordering and perpetuating of the created world as a minister of Noys.

In the creation of the microcosm in the second book, Natura's role again has ties with the astronomers' nature, for in her share of that act she joins the soul, provided by Urania, to the body, formed by Physis, in emulation of the order of the heavens. Once more Natura performs a critical function between the worlds of being and becoming, for she joins the soul, the image of the divine image of man, to the body; she connects the earthly with the heavenly, the divine with the material. The little world thus made, this image of the greater world because it is a union of the heavenly and earthly, may live in man's body on earth, but his soul will be capable of reaching heaven:

> Mentem de caelo, corpus trahet ex elementis,
> ut terras habitet corpore, mente polum.
> mens, corpus diversa licet iungentur ad unum,
> ut sacra conplacitum nexio reddat opus.
>
> (II.x.15–18.55)

(He will derive his spirit from heaven, his body from the elements, that he might dwell on the lands in his body, in heaven in his spirit. The spirit and body, though different, will be joined into one, that this sacred bond might render the work pleasing.)

The unity of the microcosm is further indicated by the fact that Urania's *speculum providentiae* and Natura's *tabula fati* share the image of the heavens. Bernard, therefore, carefully distinguishes between the two: "Ea speculi tabulaeque differentia, quod in speculo specialiter status naturarum caelestium indeflexus, in tabula quidem quam maxime temporales qui permutantur eventus" ("This is the difference between the mirror and the tablet: namely, that in the mirror there is a particular unalterable state of celestial natures; in the tablet, however, are those events which are altered to the greatest possible degree in time" II.xi.57–58).

The difference is between the immutable and the mutable, for the tabula reflects the world of change and history, the destiny of all that is contained in space and time.

The microcosm, though the sensible and intelligible are united in him, still shares with the entire created world the common denominator of silva, a point Noys significantly makes by referring to the indivisible (*unitas*) and the divisible (*diversum*), the two principles of being, just before Physis shapes man's body out of what is left of the four elements after the creation of the macrocosm.[25] Matter may be ordered and beautified in the macrocosm and ennobled in man, but its essential character has serious implications for the moral history of mankind. This qualification notwithstanding, Bernard's description of man, the crown of all creation, reflects what Chenu has called the "optimistic intellectuality of Chartres," and "the Dionysian and Erigenist theme of a 'continuity' between man and the cosmos."[26] John Scotus had described all nature as being divided into five parts: first, that which is created (the cosmos) by that which has not been created (God); second, the created is divided into the sensible and the intelligible; third, the sensible is divided into heaven and earth; fourth, earth is divided into paradise and the sphere of the earth; and fifth, mankind is divided into masculine and feminine. And all creation is put together in man: "In quo, videlicet homine, omnis creatura visibilis et invisibilis condita est."[27] To Bernard's goddess Natura belongs the honor of uniting these in man.

The various functions of Natura in the *De mundi* suggest that she was conceived out of a wide and rich erudition. No single work has been discovered that adequately covers all of the features Bernard assigns to his figure. The suggestions that parallels can be found in Hugh of Saint Victor's

Didascalicon, written in the late 1120s, and that the *De vi rerum principiis* was an actual source are reasonable.[28] Yet neither work offers definitions of nature that encompass all of her activities in the *De mundi universitate.*[29] There is, however, a strong resemblance between the *De vi rerum principiis* and Bernard in the former's distinction between noys as an originating power and nature as an operating power and in the subordination of nature to noys. The Hermetic work also mentions nature as composer of man in imitation of the macrocosm.[30] Conversely, there is no mention of nature's joining man's soul to his body in emulation of the heavens, though this idea and the tabula fati might have been inspired by the astronomical coloring of her conception in that work. Also, Endelechia and Imarmene do not appear in the Hermetic book. Though it is likely that Bernard did draw certain conceptions of nature from the *De vi rerum principiis,* it would be a greater credit to his mind and method to think of his Natura, along with his work, as "un singulier mélange d'éléments d'origines diverses."[31]

To say at this point that the *De mundi universitate* is an unusually original work, the product of a notable intellect and an imagination of the first rank, might seem unnecessary. But it is a good idea to keep in mind while considering the work from a more strictly literary viewpoint. Rhetorically, the major figures—Noys, Natura, Urania, and Physis—are all personified abstractions.[32] But unlike the *Psychomachia* of Prudentius, one of the earliest and most influential models of medieval allegory, and the later Natura allegories, personification in the *De mundi* operates on a minimal level. Bernard's use of the devices of *amplificatio* is virtually limited to that of *prosopopeia* in its strictest sense, the attribution of speech.[33] In terms of the wider meaning of prosopopeia, which includes description of physical form,[34] Bernard's personification of Natura and other figures merely suggests the physical presence that is the logical extension of their ability to speak and move. Unlike Boethius, Prudentius, or Alan, to name a few, Bernard does not use the device of *descriptio*, or *ecphrasis*, in his handling of personified abstractions. Natura is never described; there is no suggestion of what she looks like. One might surmise that Bernard was not interested in her appearance, or that he did not relish the kind of rhetorical flourishes involved in such descriptions. But such assumptions would be deceptive. If Bernard was deliberate in this omission, then the question is no longer one of rhetoric but of poetry. As poet, Bernard is describing a cosmic event that *ends* with the creation of man; he is writing about that which no man has witnessed but which he knows to be true. Its truth rests, as for all Christians, on the account in Genesis. To write of this truth, or any other truth that is part of the whole truth revealed in Holy Scripture, the Christian poet-philosopher, following his understanding of classical predecessors, uses the method or mode of integumentum. According to Bernard in his commentary on the *Aeneid*, integumentum is a kind of demonstration wrapping the thing understood under a fabulous narration of the truth ("Integumentum vero est genus demonstrationis sub fabulosa narratione veritatis involvens intellectum, unde et involucrum dicitur").[35] The scriptural truth of Genesis, God's creation of the universe, is therefore presented *sub fabulosa narratione*, wrapped in the Timaean myth of creation, the inspired philosopher's truthful vision of that which God's book revealed absolutely.

Just as the philosophers of old, according to Macrobius, used fabulous narratives to avoid the open exposition of nature's secrets, Bernard uses the integumenta of Noys and Natura, the fabulous figures of God's wisdom, power, and goodness, while the entire action of the *De mundi* is enveloped in the Timaean setting, which becomes not only the mode of expressing but also an analogy to the traditional Christian view of the universe.[36] These two authorities, then—the rationalist, philosophical truthful wrapping which contains the eternal, divinely granted truth—become the vehicle through which Bernard gives his vision of the origins that man has accepted by both faith and understanding. Descriptio, therefore, is not only irrelevant but illogical in a poem that purports to describe what men may know but have never seen. If this view contributes to an understanding of Bernard's rhetorical conservatism, it is even more important in helping one to understand that his employment of the Platonic cosmic setting does not contradict or dilute the essentially Christian character of his perspective.

Just as there is explicit reference to the Trinity when Urania and Natura pray before it in the mansion of Tugaton, the virgin birth of Christ is referred to in a passage early in the first book where the history of mankind is described as it is written in the stars (I.iii.53–54.16). The coming of Christ, the central event in human history, gives to the ages the true divinity, for without the Incarnation, the restoration of man after the Fall is impossible. The Fall and its results are consciously woven into the fabric of Bernard's narrative, at times through reference to the inferiority and instability of the sublunary world, a common feature of the philosophical tradition, and at the conclusion of the poem through specific reference to the direst consequence of the Fall, death. Thus, the idea that the evil propensities of silva provides a parallel to original sin is manifested in several passages. For example, in Noys, as in a clear mirror, can be seen the destiny of all things created out of matter: the vicissitudes of the human condition can be read in the providential "dispositio saeculorum" (I.ii.13). So too is the mutability and impermanence of the world reflected in Natura's tabula fati (II.xi.58). During their cosmic journey, Urania and Natura observe or have pointed out to them by Noys several signs of the inferiority and volatility of the sublunary world. In the house of Cancer, the souls destined to descend to earth weep at the sight of the blind and dull habitacula that await them (II.iii.37). The spheres of Mercury and Venus, immediately above that of the Moon, are both sexually active, and Venus, the power that excites man's desire for pleasure ("voluptas"), holds the infant Cupid at her left breast, almost as if Bernard intended a parodic parallel to the figure of the Incarnation in the stars (II.v.45). Finally, at the sphere of the Moon, the traditional dividing point between the upper and lower worlds, of ether and air, of stability and mutability, Noys explains that the nature of all below is changeable and turbulent, given to passion and confusion (II.v.45–46).

The effects of the Fall are suggested through details in the Neoplatonic declension of the creation, and they act as a significant background to Bernard's description of the paragon who enjoys, presumably, a moment of prelapsarian splendor. Yet even as the three goddesses create man, Bernard makes one aware of his fate. Particularly in the passage in which the sexual organs are praised, one is made aware of man's mortality, for these organs are praised precisely because they will aid man in his fight against death:

> Cum morte invicti pugnant genialibus armis,
> naturam reparant perpetuantque genus.
>   (II.xiv.161–162.70)

(Unconquered the genial weapons [suggesting also the marriage bed?] fight with death, they restore nature and perpetuate the race.)

In the next few lines, one learns that the penis battles Lachesis and skillfully renews the threads cut by the Parcae, whose cosmic function had been described in the tabula fati (II.xi.58). Natura, despite the assignment of the responsibility of continuation to Imarmene in the first book, is back in her role of procreatrix, for it is she who skillfully forms the seminal fluid so that ancestors are revived in their children.

She survives herself, streaming into the world even as she flows out of it.

These consequences of the Fall, so artfully insinuated into the argument of the poem, demonstrate Bernard Silvestris' concern with the moral status of man in the universe. Although the cosmogony theme of his work did not allow for wider development in this area, it was undertaken by his great successor, Alan of Lille.

ALAN OF LILLE

In his two allegories, the *De planctu naturae* (1160–1172) and the *Anticlaudianus* (1181–1184), Alan of Lille made what is without doubt the single most significant contribution to the history of the goddess Natura in medieval literature.[37] It would be impossible, or at best foolhardy, to undertake the study of Jean de Meun's continuation of the *Roman de la Rose* or Chaucer's *Parlement of Foules* without paying serious attention to the poet who did more than any other writer to establish Natura as the most heroic figure in medieval personification allegory. Aside from the fact that Alan's work occupies a pivotal position in this literary and intellectual tradition, elaborating on what he had found in Bernard Silvestris and exerting a still unmeasured influence on subsequent generations of poets, the *De planctu* and *Anticlaudianus* are deserving of study on their own merits, as Winthrop Wetherbee and Richard Hamilton Green have shown.[38]

The *De planctu naturae*—like Boethius' *Consolation*, its chief model, and the *De mundi universitate*—is written in alternating sections of verse and prose, the already familiar prosimetrum or satura.[39] The goddess Natura appears before the poet in a kind of vision, in order to complain to him of man's delinquency from her laws. She explains to him that she is God's vicegerent and that she has fashioned man as a mirror of the world. To clarify the correspondence between microcosm and macrocosm, she points out that just as the planets move in countermotion to the movement of the fixed stars, so too in man there is a conflict between his reason, which has a heavenly source, and his lust, which has an earthly source. Just as the world he lives in is subject to change, so is man also subject to change. Though her work bespeaks her great power, she makes clear that she is still the lowly disciple of the supreme God, that her power is small compared with His. Asked by the poet why she appears so full of grief, she charges it to the unnatural acts of man, which are allegorically represented by a tear in her tunic. The gist of her complaint is that of all her creatures man alone does not act in accordance with her laws. Whereas all other terrestrial creatures propagate themselves in obedience to her, man performs acts of fruitless and vicious perversion. She had been ordained by God to give to the world of mutability its continuity through procreation, and to this end had enlisted the aid of Venus, Hymen, and their son Cupid, so that the line of mankind might persevere despite the destructive activities of the Fates. At this point she is interrupted by the poet, who is anxious to learn about the power of Cupid, to which she answers that his power is so great that flight is the only way to escape the madness it brings. Resuming her story, Natura explains that at first Venus had followed her instructions, properly using the hammers and anvils given her by Natura, obeying the grammatical constructions prescribed by the goddess for marital coition, and laboring faithfully to mend that which the Fates had cut. But then Venus became weary of her continued labor and committed adultery with Antigamus. She bore him a son, Mirth (Jocus), who is as like his gross, ignoble father as Cupid is like his noble, courteous father Hymen. Thus was loosed on the world intemperate, adulterous, and unnatural love. Other vices, identified as the daughters of old Idolatry, soon followed, and the reason of man became the servant and slave of his flesh. When Natura has finished her complaint, the virtues in her retinue appear—Hymen, Chastity, Temperance, Generosity, and Humility—all of whom reflecting in their faces Natura's sorrow. Natura tells them of a letter she is writing to Genius, her priest and other self, which Hymen will deliver. In her letter she asks that Genius come and banish from her congregation all those who defy her laws. Shortly Genius arrives, his long white hair and smooth, unwrinkled face giving him the simultaneous appearance of age and youth. After exchanging greetings with the goddess, he dons his sacerdotal robe and pronounces as excommunicate all those who practice unlawful love or other vices of intemperance. Thereupon the entire mystical vision disappears, and the poet remains in a deep sleep.

The character and meaning of Alan's cosmic heroine, the nature of her complaint and her response to its causes, are much more complex than this simple summary can convey, for they depend both on Alan's method as a poet and on the intellectual foundations of its themes. The significance of Natura, the dominant but not exclusively important figure in the poem, gradually unfolds not only through the fabulous account of the poet and the narrative sections of Natura's speeches, but through a highly sophisticated series of relationships between the goddess and the poet, and between Natura and the other allegorical figures. Thus, Natura may identify herself as vicaria Dei and procreatrix of the sublunary world, but her relation to Hymen and Venus suggests that Alan also intended her to be understood as pronuba. The relation between Natura and the poet, which is established immediately and continues throughout the poem, provides the mode by which the theme of man's corruption and loss of communion with Natura may be expressed.

The poem is organized into three major parts—the arrival of Natura who reveals her identity and cosmic role, the goddess' explanation of the causes and consequences of man's fall from his intended condition, and the conclave of Natura and the virtues which ends with the excommunication by Genius. The first of these parts is itself organized into three closely related stages: the allegorical description of the divine figure who has appeared to the poet, the exposition of her character and functions in the universe by Natura herself, and a hymn of praise to her by the poet. In his descriptive portrait of Natura, Alan represents almost every significant detail in her cosmological aspect. Following the example of a number of earlier poets, particularly Prudentius, Alan, unlike Bernard, uses the device of descriptio, or ecphrasis, in his handling of personified abstractions. Descriptio, which is a separable decorative description, as Alan uses it to introduce Natura is not quite so conventional as has sometimes been thought.[40] The portrait is highly functional in terms of the meaning veiled beneath the literal level; in terms of the poet's initial failure to recognize Natura; and in terms of its clear-cut reference to the opening of Boethius' *Consolation*.

Just as suddenly as Philosophia appears to the distraught Boethius, Natura comes before Alan, who in the opening meter has been lamenting the ruin brought about by *Venus monstrosa*, the monster of sensual love. And just as Boethius had done earlier, Alan immediately begins to describe the figure before him.[41] After giving an idealized description of the face and form of the lady who has glided down from the inner palace of the impassable heavens, Alan shifts the mode of his description to the technical device per vestimentum. On her head she wears a crown in which are set sparkling jewels. They represent the firmament, the twelve signs of the zodiac, and the planets. On her robe are pictured the creatures of the air, from the eagle to the hermaphroditic bat, as if they were holding a parliament.[42] On her mantle all the creatures of the waters are depicted. On her tunic all the animals of the earth can be seen, each one behaving according to its natural instincts. But the main part of the garment is torn and abused, that part which shows man laying aside the sluggishness of sensuality and, under the direction of reason, penetrating the secrets of the heavens ("In hujus vestis parte primaria, homo sensualitatis deponens segnitiem, directa rationis aurigatione, coeli penetrabat arcana," 441).

Of the pictures on her undergarment the poet is not certain, but it seems to him that they are of herbs and trees. On her shoes, he says, are delicate flowers. As she approaches in her chariot, he can see her drawing pictures of various things on tablets with her pen. But the pictures will not adhere to the material and quickly fade away. Though she often gives them life, they are unable to persevere in the plan of her composition ("tamen in scripturae propositio imagines perseverare non poterant," 445).

In this fullest of portraits of Natura, Alan has incorporated all of her major cosmological features. Her coming from the heavens beyond the firmament not only represents her celestial nature but also implies her relation to God as second cause. Her costume represents the entire created universe, from the fixed stars to the lowliest herb, her domain as vicaria Dei, and in its depiction of the macrocosm provides a parallel with the microcosmic form of man, whom she shaped to correspond with perfect symmetry to the greater world.[43] Her drawing on the tablets represents her function as procreatrix of the transitory sublunary world, guaranteeing the generational persistence of the species in matter through procreative activity.

All of this is to be delineated in greater detail and more directly when Natura explains her nature to the poet, who, being overcome by the delirious ecstasy of his vision, has failed to recognize her. His failure, in fact, foreshadows Natura's narrative of the cause for man's falling away from her and from God and, as such, is itself a symptom of the disease that prevents man from realizing the heights of understanding of which he is capable. The poet has seen man's fall depicted in the torn part of her tunic, but he has not grasped its meaning. Only after she identifies herself and is well into her complaint, does he interrupt her to ask why her garment is torn. Her answer is that through the wrongful thrusts of man her garments of modesty suffer outrages of division ("Hoc autem integumentum hac scissura depingitur, quia solius hominis injuriosis insultibus mea pudoris ornamenta discidii contumelias patiuntur," 467).

Natura has been the victim of a metaphorical assault by the viciousness of man, from his unnatural sexual practices to his general propensity to seek satisfaction for the lusts of his eyes and flesh.[44] This single example illustrates the thematic relevance of Natura's portrait to the rest of the work and subtly reveals that even a poet-theologian who is aware of the goddess' existence suffers from the same malady and ignorance that afflict the entire human race. Just how far man has fallen from his intended condition of self-control and rational perception is emphasized by the brief description of Natura's charioteer, in whom the ideal condition of man is depicted. Like the microcosm of Bernard Silvestris, he transcends the earthly aspect of his being. He assists Natura with his godlike masculine virtue and guides her chariot on a steady course (445).[45] But man's alienation from Natura and the rest of her realm is delicately implied by the description of all the created world, from the firmament to the animals of this earth, responding joyously to the approach of Natura's chariot, an elaboration of an episode in the *De mundi universitate* in which all the flora in Physis' garden sensed the approach of Natura.[46]

Unlike the rest of created nature, the poet-narrator experiences a delayed recognition of the goddess Natura and does not demonstrate his joy and appreciation until after she has revealed herself to him. Her exposition of her place and operation in the universe and the original nature and constitution of man, which are the main topics of her lecture, remains faithful to the fabulatory mode of the rest of the poem. Even here, where she is revealing her secrets, Alan is conscientious in maintaining a fictional narrative that is meant to convey truth beneath its covering. Macrobius' remark about Natura's distaste for too open an exposition of her secrets lest they become the undeserved property of the vulgar, controls and justifies Alan's method. Like his poet-narrator, who is Natura's audience within the fiction, the audience of Alan's poem must use their intelligence to get at the truth contained in his metaphor and myth. This aspect of the work requires close attention, particularly where Natura introduces the subject of the defection of Venus.

Irked at the narrator's blind ignorance in failing to recognize her, Natura asks him if he does not know the one who as vicegerent of God has ordered the course of his life ("quae a tua ineunte aetate, Dei auctoris vicaria rata dispensatione, legitimum tuae vitae ordinavi curriculum," 450). After identifying herself as man's nurse ("nutrix")—possibly echoing, the natura altrix hominum of Prudentius and Saint Ambrose—Alan's Natura explains her subordination to God. It is significant that Alan has removed Noys, to whom Natura was subordinated in the *De mundi*, perhaps because he wished to give his cosmology a more Christian context by suppressing the Neoplatonic emanative hierarchy.[47] Natura's absolute dependence on God is a point she wishes to stress, lest her account of her power be misunderstood as arrogant detraction from God:

Ejus operatio simplex, mea operatio multiplex; ejus opus sufficiens, meum opus deficiens; ejus opus mirabile, meum opus mutabile; ille innascibilis, ego nata; ille faciens, ego facta; ille mei opifex operis, ego opus opificis. Ille operatur ex nihilo, ego mendico ex aliquo. Ille suo operatur numine, ego operor illius sub nomine (455).

(His operation is simple, my operation is multifold; His work is sufficient, my work is deficient; His work is marvelous, my work is mutable; He cannot be born, I was born; He is the maker, I was made; He is the creator of my work, I am the work of the creator. He works from nothing, I beg [work] from another [God]. He works by His divine will, I work under His name.)

Yet her power as vicaria Dei is far greater than that of man, and making a three-way comparison, Natura explains that the power of God is the superlative, her own power the comparative, and the power of man the positive ("Et sic in quadam comparationis triclinio tres potestatis gradus possumus invenire, ut, Dei potentia potentia superlativa, naturae comparativa, hominis positiva dicatur," 456). Reflecting the Aristotelian threefold classification of creative power found in medieval commentaries from Chalcidius to William of Conches, and specifically repeating William's claim from his gloss on the *Consolation* (III, m. ix) that his description of the opus naturae in no way detracts from God ("nichil detraho Deo"), Natura's exposition anticipates the much fuller account of her work as procreatrix in the next major part of the poem. The distinction between God's work, the creation of the universe ex nihilo, and Natura's, the sustaining of the world of becoming through procreative activity, is one that Alan makes here, in the *Anticlaudianus*, and in several other works.[48]

Natura's emphasis on the less than perfect quality of her work extends to her explanation of man as microcosm and provides the basis for her moral indignation and powerlessness to do anything about man's errors. As in the *Consolation* where Philosophia speaks for nature, Alan's Natura informs the narrator that she has endowed man with the special gift of reason. His rational faculty is in constant conflict with his lust, just as the firmament and the planets move in motions counter to each other. The exercise of his reason raises man to angelic heights, but his lust drags him downward to the level of the beasts. The one raises his mind to a state of serene virtue, while the other causes it to fall among vices so that it is destroyed ("Haec igitur, sensualitas, mentem humanum in vitiorum occasum deducit, ut occidat; illa, i. ratio, orientem, ad serenitatem virtutum ut oriatur invitat," 451).

Man was made with this conflict so that his reason could defeat his lust and he would thereby receive his proper reward. Continuing her microcosm-macrocosm analysis of man's nature, the goddess points out that government of man, just like government of the universe or of a great city, involves the correct subordination of the lower to the higher parts. In the head resides wisdom, which gives commands. In the heart dwells magnanimity, which administers the commands of wisdom. And in the loins abides passion, which submits to the will of magnanimity. Wisdom commands, magnanimity administers, passion obeys (453–454). This pattern for the proper ordering of the life of man, which may be taken as a moral pattern for the matrimonial state, is exactly what man has willfully betrayed. Reason, Natura's greatest gift to man, which enables him to understand the purpose of her laws, should dictate to him the proper way in which to express the passionate side of his nature. The inversion of this moral pattern, the enslavement of reason to lust and unbridled passion, will become the explicit cause of the goddess' complaint.

Between this expository passage and Natura's *planctus*, Alan offers as fine a piece of poetry as occurs in the entire work in the form of a sapphic ode that serves as both a hymn of praise and a recognition speech. In the concluding two stanzas, the narrator asks Natura to reveal the reason for her coming and to explain why she is weeping. The first four stanzas amply illustrate the verse's quality:

O Dei proles, genetrixque rerum,
vinculum mundi, stabilisque nexus,
gemma terrenis, speculum caducis,
    Lucifer orbis.

Pax, amor, virtus, regimen, potestas,
ordo, lex, finis, via, lux, origo,
vita, laus, splendor, species, figura,
    regula mundi.

Quae, tuis mundum moderans habenis,
cuncta concordi stabilita nodo
nectis, et pacis glutino maritas
    coelica terris.

Quae noys puras recolens ideas,
singulas rerum species monetas,
rem togans forma, chlamidemque formae
    pollice formas.

(458)

(O child of God and mother of things, bond and steadfast knot
of the world, jewel among earthly things, mirror of the perishable, the sphere's morning star. Peace, love, power, guidance,
might, order, law, end, way, leader, source, life, light, brilliance,
beauty, form, rule of the world. Who, guiding the world with
your reins, uniting all things in stability with concord's knot and
with the bond [lit. paste or glue] of peace, marry the heavens to
earth. Who, reflecting on the pure ideas of the divine mind, coin
every species, and clothing matter with form, shape with your
thumb the cloak of form.)

A good deal of the preceding history of Natura is concentrated in these lines, but more significant at this point is the
indication that once he has been informed of her identity,
Alan's poet-narrator is able to sing her praises with knowledgeable accuracy and a fund of information. This interpretation is supported not only by the general awareness
of the tradition of Natura displayed in the poem but also and
especially by its specific correspondence to Boethius' poem,

"Quantas rerum flectat habenas/Natura potens," the second meter of the third book of the *Consolation*.[49] Alan's poet is something of a philosopher-theologian, worthy of Natura's visitation in similar way to Boethius' worthiness of Philosophia's coming. And yet, like Boethius, he is in need of instruction, for, like all men since the Fall, despite his learning he is severely limited. His failure to recognize Natura at the beginning is a telling illustration of that limitation. Natura's fabulous account of the cause and effects of man's fallen condition is an attempt to respond to a problem that has affected not only the human race but herself as well.

Among the number of significant lessons contained in the goddess' narrative of the divinely ordained nature of her operation and destruction of its integrity is the idea that once the inner unity of the created world, of which the figure of Natura is the image, has been subverted by man's willful disobedience, Natura has no power to correct it.[50] Her law itself, provided by God, has not been altered by the Fall, but neither before the Fall nor subsequent to it has Natura had any way of enforcing it. The process of human history, determined by mankind's moral choices (specifically in this context the deposition of reason in favor of the passions), has divorced man from his original bond with Natura, a bond that neither man, with his rational power debilitated and diminished, nor Natura is capable of restoring. But through the myth of Venus the goddess does try to enlighten the narrator on the subject of the process that has tainted human experience since Adam's sin. Her audience within the poem represents human consciousness limited and obscured by the continuous warfare between sensuality and reason—the condition in varying degrees of all men and, therefore, of Alan's audience in general. The narrator, notwithstanding his learning and even his awareness of the eroding effects of sensuality set down in the introductory meter of the *De planctu*, is inextricably bound by this lowest common denominator to all men. The allegorical method of the poet, therefore, becomes the method of Natura's narrative discourse, the integument that veils (and thereby protects) a truth which is accessible only to those whose reason can penetrate the surface. In Natura's own words:

Aut in superficiali litterae cortice falsum resonet lyra poetica, interius vero auditoribus secretum intelligentiae altioris eloquitur, ut exterioris falsitatis abjecto putamine, dulciorem nucleum veritatis secrete intus lector inveniat (465).

(The poetic lyre resounds with falsehood on its surface literal shell, but in fact it expresses interiorly to those who listen a deep, hidden meaning, so that the reader who casts aside the outer shell of falsehood discovers the sweet kernel of truth hidden within.)

If there is irony in man's reduction from his original state of penetrating the secrets of the heavens to having to perceive truth through literary and mythological integumenta, it is nevertheless true that the poetic method calls to action and makes demands upon the better side of his nature. By listening to Natura, man can gain a certain amount of understanding, though the fact remains that his restoration requires a power beyond that of Natura.[51]

Preceding her complaint against man's perversion and abuse of the rules of love and providing a moral backdrop against which man's lapse may be depicted, Natura supplies the narrator with a complete account of the divine plan she serves. His bountiful and limitless goodness overflowing into the creation of the physical world, God brought the warring elements into harmony, and all things were joined in peaceful agreement by the invisible bonds of union; plurality returned to unity, diversity to identity, dissonance to consonance, discord to concord. Introducing the principles of plentitude and replenishment, the goddess then explains how God brought her into the scheme of things so that perishable things might be given stability and continuity in a sure and lawful way:

Me igitur tanquam sui vicariam, rerum generibus sigillandis monetariam destinavit, ut ego in propriis incudibus rerum effigies commonetans, ab incudis forma conformatum, deviare non sinerem, sed mei operante solertia, ab exemplaris vultu, naturarum nullarum dotibus defraudata exemplati facies deviaret (469).

(Me, therefore, He appointed as His deputy, a coiner for stamping the classes of things, so that I, minting the copies of things on the appropriate anvils, would not allow the shape to deviate from the shape of the anvil, but that through my operating skill the face of the copy would deviate in no way from the face of the exemplar, defrauded by the endowments of any other elements.)

Because she needed help in this work, and because she wished to remain in the pleasant, changeless palace of the ethereal region, she appointed Venus as her subvicar in the lower world ("in mundiali suburbio"), where, assisted by her husband and her son, Hymen and Cupid, she does Natura's work against the counter activities of the Parcae.[52]

The articulation of Natura's position as vicaria Dei and of her role as procreatrix, with its employment of Macrobius' image of natura artifex working her skill in the mint where man is coined and its application of the Boethian explanation from the *Consolation* of nature's dependence on the One who orders and disposes all motions (II, pr. xii), prepares the way for the moral aspect of Alan's characterization of Natura, which has deep roots in the classical tradition, especially Cicero and Seneca, and in such early Church Fathers as Tertullian and Saint Augustine.[53] With such precedents behind him, Alan develops the moral side of Natura out of her function as procreatrix, with the primary reason for her coming being her desire to make bitter attack on homosexuality and other vices. The moral value and activity of Natura, furthermore, is established by the association of Venus monstrosa with the vices of Drunkenness ("Bacchilatria"), Gluttony, Avarice ("Nummulatria"), Pride, Envy, and Flattery (484–501), which are opposed—though not quite symmetrically, as they would be in a psychomachia—by Hymen and the virtues of Chastity ("Castitas"), Temperance ("Temperantia"), Generosity ("Largitas"), and Humility ("Humilitas"), all of whom travel in Natura's company (502–509).

For Natura's account of the cause of the disintegration of man's original moral condition, Alan employs one of the most prominent themes of medieval mythographic tradition. The concept of two Venuses, one defined as the goddess of chaste, legitimate love and the other as the goddess of lechery and fornication, had become by Alan's time a commonplace of medieval culture, the double definition having been repeated over and again—with minor differences—in the works of Fulgentius, Remigius, John Scotus, the third Vatican Mythographer,[54] and Bernard Silvestris, who defines the two Venuses in his commentary on the *Aeneid*: "We read there are two Venuses, a legitimate goddess and a goddess of lechery. We say that the legitimate Venus is *mundana musica*, that is, the equal proportion of wordly things, which some call Astrea and others natural justice. For she is in the elements, in the stars, in times, in animate things. But the shameful Venus, the goddess of sensuality, we call concupiscence of the flesh because she is the mother of all fornication."[55]

But Alan's use of this tradition reveals an originality for which he has not frequently been credited. Unlike the mythographers and commentators of the past, he does not posit two separate figures of Venus. Retaining the sense of *Venus impudica* as the mother of all vice, sexual and otherwise, and subsuming *Venus legitima* in the cosmic function of Natura, being named her subvicar in procreation, Alan attributes both sets of qualities to one Venus. What he does, in other words, in Natura's account of man's rejection and fall from a state of natural virtue and grace, is to combine both senses of Venus as two dispositions within a single figure, a characteristic of his Venus that is suggested even on the level of verbal play by the opposition of heavenly and wicked in the pairing of *Venus caelestis—Venus scelestis*. Natura, therefore, is describing the career of one Venus when she explains that the goddess of love rebelled against her and betrayed Hymen with Antigamus.

This novel and ingenious variation of the tradition was unquestionably intentional, for it enriches and deepens the perspective on the theme of man's seemingly irreparable falling away from his original bond with Natura. First, it indicates the impossibility of man's art to convey truth in a manner that is free of the corrupting influence of his fallen nature, since Alan has shown at a number of points in the poem that human perversion is manifested in language as well as in sexuality. With nothing better than the mytho-logical integuments of poets at her disposal for educating the narrator, who failed even to recognize her, Natura gives an account of the Fall and its consequences that seems to incorporate inconsistencies in the traditional careers of Venus and Cupid. On the one hand, this inconsistency reinforces the theme of the pervasiveness of man's corruption. On the other hand, the implication that this allegorical method, which is consistent in its inadequacy with man-kind's degeneration, can be instructive but not corrective, points ahead to the resolution of the problem in the character of Genius. On the other hand, the fusion of two Venuses into one is a literary innovation that provides an appropriate metaphor for the confusion in human psychology that came about as the result of man's willful abuse of the passions with which he was originally entrusted. Once it has been corrupted, human nature's experience of love involves a blurred apprehension of Venus and the difficult demand upon its intelligence to distinguish between Venus caelestis-scelestis, a pattern of deceptive antithesis that extends to Cupid and Mirth as well. As the representation of the condition of love in the world, this myth supplies the basis for a discussion of the confusion and perversion that man's weakness and immoderate sensuality has imposed on love.

Natura's first target in her complaint against man's subversion of her laws is sodomy, the most heinous of all vices to her, for it is a complete distortion of the love that populates the world. Condemned as *contra naturam* long before Alan, homosexuality draws the attack of the goddess because it renders the organs that were intended for the continuation of the human race utterly fruitless.[56] This breach of her law is expressed by Alan's Natura through metaphors in which the sodomites are pictured as committing monstrous perversions of the rules of the grammatical arts (429–430, 462–463), grammar having been elevated in the twelfth century to the status of a major discipline and being commonly thought to imitate nature.[57]

Despite the forcefulness of her attack, sodomy plays a relatively secondary role in Natura's complaint about the state of love; it is merely the violation *in extremis* of her law. Of far greater significance to the work and to the subsequent history of the goddess Natura are her pronouncements on heterosexual love. On this subject Natura makes two major points: that the only lawful coition takes place within the state of marriage, and that sexual passion, while serving a useful end in God's plan for the world, must be controlled and checked by moderation.

Natura's advocacy of marriage as the proper and holy bond through which her procreative law may be expressed becomes apparent in her relation to Hymen and through her account of Venus' departure from the rules given her upon her appointment as subvicar of procreation.[58] When Venus committed adultery with Antigamus (literally, "against marriage") as a result of boredom with her daily labors, she not only defiled her marriage bed but also allied herself to Atropos, against whose destructive sword she had formerly defended the continuity of the human race. The issue of her excessive fornication was a son whom she named Mirth (Jocus), as if by antiphrasis, for he is characterized by the absence rather than the presence of that disposition. This bastardization and perversion of Cupid, who had been defined by Saint Augustine as "irrationabilis et instabilis amor," symbolizes the uncontrollable, mad pursuit of sexual pleasure, the base and destructive aspect of man's sexuality, which Natura fears and warns against elsewhere in the work. Moreover, the wronged Hymen appears later on the right hand of Natura, attended by the virtues Chastity, Humility, Temperance, and Generosity, the last of which has been described as "a natural virtue . . . and a quality essential to sexual and moral fulfillment."[59] Complementing the pattern of virtue associated with Hymen is the doctrinal pattern of the sacramental faith ("sacramentalem matrimonii fidem"), the peaceful unity, the equal yoke and indissoluble bond of marriage as pictured on his garment (503). This characterization of Hymen, along with his role as Natura's messenger to Genius in the crucial last episode of the poem, clearly establishes that Alan thought of Natura as pronuba as well as procreatrix. Alan wished not only to defend the orthodox doctrines of marriage against heretical sects but also to present Natura as affirming the institution of marriage, which was the way in which sexual passion, ruled by reason and virtue, might serve the ends that she and God had ordained for it. To this end, Alan assigned the classical function of pronuba to his Natura, a function that was stripped away from Natura by Jean de Meun and restored by Chaucer in his *Parlement of Foules*.

However sincere his aspirations to attain the original dignity and virtue for which he was intended, man, since his Fall, must constantly struggle to control that which in his original nature was unequivocally ruled by his rational faculty. Through marriage he can seek to emulate the uncontaminated natural virtue that once was his. For this reason, I believe, Alan's Natura refuses to deny honor altogether to passionate love; as she says with reference to its regulation within the marital state, it may be kept honorable providing it is restrained by the bridle and reins of modesty and temperance ("si circumscribatur frenis modestiae, si habenis temperantiae castigetur," 474) and providing it does not overheat. What she is describing represents in her own words the original nature of Cupid, but the degeneracy of man is such that when the narrator asks her advice, she has no choice but to speak of the perverted Cupid, who holds so great a power over the minds of men that he easily turns instinct into a dishonorable activity. So powerful, contradictory, and maddening is this love that the only medicine Natura has to offer is flight:

> Si vitare velis Venerem, loca, tempora vita;
> et locus et tempus pabula donat ei.
> Prosequitur, si tu sequeris; fugiendo fugatur;
> si cedis, cedit; si fugis, illa fugit.
>
> (474)

(If you wish to shun Venus, shun her places and occasions; place and occasion give her nourishment. She attends if you follow, she is put to flight by fleeing; if you retreat, she retreats; if you flee, she flees.)

Similar warnings would later be made by Jean de Meun's Raison and in the inscription on the garden gate in Chaucer's *Parlement*, but here Natura procreatrix herself is uniquely proposing complete abstinence from the form of love that operates beyond her law and auspices. The descriptio

Cupidinis poem of Natura, therefore, represents the prevailing state of love on earth, for while man may do her work according to his reason, her noblest gift to him, the control of sexual passion lies not within her power but in the complex, fallen nature of man, which is prone to succumbing to his lower nature, ignoring the lawful purpose and pleasure of his sexuality, and giving himself over to the satisfaction of his wanton, sometimes perverse desires.

The concluding episode of the *De planctu naturae*, in which Genius excommunicates those who disobey Natura's laws, provides a resolution to the problems raised in the poem on two levels of meaning.[60] First, it represents Natura's response to the offenses of man's uncontrolled sensuality, that depravity which has marred his image on her tunic. More a matter of reaction than of true resolution, this episode contains in its descriptions and its actions imagery and allusions that point toward a resolution beyond its own narrative context: the possibility of restoration. Alan's characterization of Genius, therefore, requires close attention.

In the letter delivered by Hymen in which the goddess asks Genius to come and anathematize all offenders, Natura describes her relation to him by referring to Genius as her other self ("sibi alteri"). So marked is their resemblance that she sees herself in him as if she looked in her own mirror. They are bound to each other by a knot of love, so closely that they must fail or succeed together (511). These words are echoed by Genius in his address to Natura on his arrival: it is no wonder to him if in the union of their wills he discovers the melody of concord, for one idea and thought conforms his will to that of Natura and brings them to the same mind (520). The resemblance is conveyed more concretely in the description of Genius as he approaches: on his robes the images of things appear for a moment and then vanish, a sight barely perceptible to the viewer. In his left hand he carries an animal skin that he has scraped clean of hair, and in his right hand he holds a fragile papyrus reed with which he constantly draws images on the skin. These images, like those Natura drew, fade away, and as they fade, he draws others to replace them (517). Finally, and most significantly, the Natura-Genius relationship is summed up in the descriptio Veritatis in which it is stated that Natura and Genius have a daughter, Truth, who assists him in the execution of his pictures. She was begotten, not by the carnal passion of Aphrodite, but by the loving kiss of Natura and Genius at the moment the eternal idea greeted matter ("yle"): while meditating on the mirror of forms, the idea kissed matter though the intermediary image ("iconia"). The assisting activity of Truth is opposed by the undermining activity of Falsity who perverts and deforms that which Truth has helped Genius produce (518–519).

This characterization of Genius provides several broad features that help explain his identification both as a kind of double to Natura and as her priest. First, the subject of the goddess' complaint, the conflict between Venus caelestis-scelestis and Cupid-Mirth, extends to the work of Genius, where the struggle between good and evil is represented by the opposition of Truth and Falsity. It is also evident that though none of Natura's celestial features have parallels in his description, he shares with her those features that pertain to her as procreatrix of the sublunary world. Thus, when he lays aside his common garment and puts on his sacerdotal vestment in order to pronounce excommunication, he is acting as the priest of Natura, for according to her own account he assists her in the priestly office ("Genium vero qui mihi in sacerdotali ancillatur officio," 510). In this connection, it has been suggested that Alan introduced Genius because he could not possibly assign to Natura the priestly office of excommunication.[61] This is certainly logical, for she is goddess and vicaria Dei as *signum* but a woman as *res*, yet, like the preceding aspects of his characterization, it does not fully explain the essential relation between Natura and Genius.

The crucial feature of this relation, out of which all its other aspects develop, is the cosmic kiss of Natura and Genius, a poetic image for one of the most significant elements in Chartrian thought. The doctrine of secondary forms, the positing of intermediary images of divine ideas as the substantial embodiments of those ideas in matter, has already been noted in Bernard Silvestris, in Boethius' *De Trinitate*, and in Chalcidius.[62] Alan's portrait of Genius kissing Natura as the eternal ideas meet with matter through the intermediate iconiae identifies Genius' office with that of the secondary forms, "the transmission of the Divine Wisdom into the sphere of Nature," and along with the other details of his characterization he is established as Natura's priest in administering "the 'mystical' union of form and matter."[63] The various elements in Genius' character depend on this motif for their meaning, particularly in connection with the significance of his relation to Natura and to human nature. The unity of Alan's figure in this sense, as Wetherbee has demonstrated, is a result of the successful conflation of the two Genius figures represented in Bernard's *De mundi universitate*: the cosmic Genius (Pantomorphos), who assigns forms to individuals in the world below (II.iii.38), and the two genii who reside in the male genitals for the purpose of preserving the human race (II.xiv.70), whose role resembles that of Genius both as god of generation and as tutelary guide. By virtue of his cosmic office associated with the secondary forms, Genius acts as intermediary between God and Natura. The highly allusive kiss with Natura also refers to the birth of the virtue Generosity (Largitas) out of the "divine bounty by the generative kiss of *Noys*" (518), providing thereby a correspondence to the birth of Truth.[64] Furthermore, the description of the kiss, with its reference to the birth of Generosity, brings into focus the relation between Natura and Genius in the incarnation of original man and Genius' office of preserving the natural order and process of creation according to its divine ideal. Since the original integrity of the natural order over which he presides has been rent by man's irrational rejection of it, symbolized by the activity of Venus scelestis, her son Mirth, and Falsity, Genius arrives at the behest of Natura to condemn the abominators of natural virtue, who are theologically the product of the Fall and philosophically the product of the resurgence of the evil inherent in matter, and to reassert the original dignity and justice of both his cosmic role and "his special role in human nature, where he effects the 'incarnation' of a type of the divine *Noys* and the transmission of his likeness from generation to generation, thereby ensuring the survival of man and affirming the ultimate continuity of human marriage, *largitas*, and the moral integrity with cosmic order."[65]

Further implications of the Natura-Genius relation that reinforce the conceptualization of Genius as priest of Natura and as holding a special role in human nature may be found in typological associations. Natura has figural affinities, as Wetherbee has shown, with the Synagogue and the Church.[66] A most interesting expression of this and of Genius as her priest may be found in the respective descriptions of their robes. Whereas the images of the universe on Natura's vestments are fixed (the only change being the tear that represents the Fall), the images on Genius' robes are in constant motion, appearing, disappearing, and reappearing. The translation of these details to the typological level of Natura as Church, descending to the world from the heavens at the beginning of the vision, and Genius as priest, pronouncing excommunication on those who disobey her laws at the end of the vision, suggests the difference between doctrine and action, *episteme* and *moralia*. Like God's church, Natura reveals to man as much as He permits, and enough for his salvation. Man's acts, which are the consequences of his will, either conform to or stray from the dictates of that doctrine, represented by Genius as individual human nature whose activity is characterized by the struggle between Truth and Falsity. When Genius removes his robe and puts on his priestly garb, he is acting in the interests of his mistress by enforcing the moral order that is her divinely established due and which lies within man's intellectual and spiritual reach.

Shifting perspective to the interaction between Natura and the narrator that operates throughout the poem, one finds a significant pattern emerging. The troubled poet is granted a vision of the vicaria Dei, whom he fails to recognize until she reveals her identity to him. Once he recognizes her, his own cognitive faculty is brought into play, and though he sings her praises, his questions and their dialogue is betrayed by the confusion that has beset man since the Fall. But this does not prevent Natura from explaining as much as she can as well as she can; nor does it prevent the narrator from witnessing the coming of Genius, which reveals both man's original, ideal condition and the present depths to which he has sunk, apparently beyond salvation. The redemptive function of Natura, like that of the church, is severely limited without the divine gift of grace. The resolution to this problem is offered in the concluding episode in which Genius plays the central role.

To appreciate fully Alan's accomplishment in his characterization of Genius, one must consider the profound implications of that figure for the tradition of the goddess Natura. The extent to which Alan's Genius is the product of an active, innovative poetic imagination can be gauged by a comparison with corresponding figures in Bernard Silvestris and others. Even more revealing of the magnitude of Alan's contribution is the difference between his Genius, who has a complex moral, cosmological, and religious relationship to Natura, and the kind of Genius described in twelfth century mythography. In William of Conches' commentary on the *Consolation* (III, m. xii), for example, Genius is defined in Horatian terms as "a good and bad god who is in every mortal head (deus albus et ater mortalis in unumquodque caput)."[67] William also defines Genius as "naturalis concupiscentia," a term he applies to Euridice as well, for her name means "judgment of the good (boni iudicatio)" in the same sense that "naturalis concupiscentia" is said to judge everything it desires to be good, whether it is or not. However adequate such a definition may be for interpreting the story of Orpheus and Euridice, it is a far cry from what Alan meant by Genius and provides an excellent, if somewhat extreme, example of the difference between allegory as a way of reading and allegory as a way of creating. The essential distinction between the conventional Genius of medieval commentary and Alan's figure is that Alan's reflects developments in twelfth century theology in which Alan himself, being both poet and theologian, played a part. These developments, primarily the result of the influence of Greek Christian thought, have been summarized by Wetherbee, who quotes from Chenu:

[Certain twelfth century intellectual developments displayed] a growing tendency to conceive the *opus restaurationis* as essentially a return to the condition of man before the Fall. Inspired largely by the cosmic determinism of the pseudo-Dionysius and other Christian Neoplatonists, this approach tended to deemphasize the events of sacred history in favor of a cosmic process of emanation from and return to the divine Unity which, like the Chartrian preoccupation with the *anima mundi*, obscured the precise relations of nature and grace by effectively identifying cosmic and providential order . . . The restoration or *recreatio* of fallen man becomes a return "au régime paradisiaque, état idéal et vraie 'nature' de l'homme, point de départ du mouvement cosmique autant que lieu où a été commis le péché; au terme, c'est la reintégration de tout le genre humain dans l'unité primordiale." Rather than resulting from an intervention of God in history, grace is present in man "comme une nature, selon laquelle l'homme est *imago Dei*. Suivre cette nature, c'est s'assimiler à Dieu." Restoration thus involves a double movement, a rediscovery of the divine likeness within and a renewed sense of participation in the harmony of the cosmos.[68]

The intent of both the complaint and appeal of Natura as well as the condemnation by Genius is therefore to summon up a vision of man's original virtue and integrity, a kind of golden age of human nature. The delineation of this original nature of man through presentation of the activities of Natura and Genius establishes the character to which man may return through the effects of grace. Founded on the Chartrian rationalist perspective of the *ordo naturalis*, the restoration of man through the presence of grace within evolves from recognition and contemplation of the transcendent meaning of the divine order of nature (*Theophania*), the way of knowing God which, though imperfect, will be perfected in the future, as opposed to natural philosophy, which does not go beyond the recognition of the order and coherence of natural things. The resolution, then, to the confusion of human experience, manifested in Natura's speeches and in the characterization of the narrator, is offered in the poem's final scene, after which the narrator is left in a deep slumber: Genius returns to Natura, Hymen, and the company of the virtues to restate the conditions of man's restoration. By following his reason, which is to follow Natura, man may seek to emulate his first condition and thereby return to the state of grace that means salvation, or he may continue in his renegade ways subsequent to the Fall, obfuscating his reason and perverting his ideal image until he is more beast than man, earning him the anathema of Genius and damnation. Alan's narrator, by whom all men are to be measured, has been granted a vision of Natura;

when he returns to consciousness, his true reawakening will
be at issue.

The central event in Alan's later poem, *Anticlaudianus*, is
the creation of a new man, a *novus homo*, who fulfills the ex-
pectation of returning to the state of perfection foreshadowed in the *De planctu*. He is the perfect man, who may
attain to the imitation of Christ; in the words of the anony-
mous author of the summary appended to the poem, he is
"such a man as he would come to be, if he had erred in no
way (qualis futurus esset homo, si in nullo errasset)."[69]
Despite the continuation of this theme and the dominant
role of the goddess Natura, *Anticlaudianus* differs greatly from
De planctu naturae. Through a skillful combination of several
previously established allegorical themes, the assembly of
virtues, the cosmic journey, the creation of man, and the
psychomachia, Alan originates a new poetic genre, which
Curtius has described as "the philosophical-theological
epic." Within its framework there is ample room for the
treatment of subjects ranging from the moral and doctrinal,
the encyclopedic and literary, to the scientific and metaphysical.[70] The poem deals with such various subjects as
man's place in the universe, the purpose of Natura in the
universe, the influence of the goddess Fortuna and of the
vices on man's life, and the progression from sense to reason
to faith in the quest for knowledge, as illustrated by Prudentia's journey to heaven, which culminates in a vision of
the court of heaven, the nature of the seven liberal arts,
and to a lesser degree, the causes of natural phenomena.
Green has summed up this journey as an exploration of
"the directions and limits of human knowledge, and the
implications of what man knows for what he is and how he
ought to act."[71] Alan's awareness of the necessary complexity
of his work is shown by his comments in the prose prologue:
he wants as readers only those who are able to transcend the
senses, who seek reason's truth, lest his holy work be defiled

by dogs, the pearl be trampled by the feet of swine, and its secrets be dishonored by being divulged to the unworthy (56). The study of his allegory, he promises, will sharpen the intellect. The range and complexity of the work recommend it to a high place in the history of medieval Latin literature, and its influence on later literature, a subject that has not yet been fully investigated, was probably considerable, even though *Anticlaudianus* must play a secondary role to *De planctu naturae* in the history of the goddess Natura.

As the title suggests, and as the author of the summary points out, Alan intended the perfect man of his poem to be the antithesis of the vicious character attacked by Claudian in *In Rufinum*. Just as the vices thoroughly pervert Rufinus in Claudian's poem, the virtues in Alan's inform his man with blessedness, and thus he should be properly named Antirufinus (201).[72] The creation of this perfect man and his triumph over the vices give the nine books of hexameters their main narrative line, representing a successful synthesis of a number of allegorical themes. Dissatisfied with her works, Natura calls a council of her sisters, the virtues, in order to make a proposal to them. Concord, Plenty, Goodwill, Youth, Laughter, Shame, Moderation, Reason, Honor, Beauty, Prudence, Piety, Faith, Generosity, and Nobility all convene at Natura's home, a high-columned building set on an elevated plain in the middle of a grove or garden of perpetual spring surrounded by a forest and graced by a silver stream. On the palace itself are painted the images of famous philosophers and heroes. Natura proposes to her sisters that they redeem their hitherto defective creation by making a perfect man. Prudence (Prudentia) thinks it a good proposal but points out that the soul for such a perfect being will have to come from a power higher than they. Reason (Ratio) then suggests that they send Prudence (who is called Fronesis here and will later be called Sophia) to the court of heaven to present their petition to God. Prudence, out of modesty, does not immediately agree, but Concord finally persuades her to make the journey. The seven liberal arts, Prudence's daughters, construct a chariot for her: Grammar builds the shaft, Logic the axletree, and Rhetoric gilds and decorates them; Arithmetic, Music, Geometry, and Astronomy each make a wheel. Concord then assembles the chariot. Reason brings the five senses, the team, while she herself becomes the driver.

During the first part of their journey up through the heavenly spheres they observe various natural and spiritual phenomena, but when they reach the fixed stars, Reason can no longer guide the team and the horses refuse to obey any command. At this moment a maiden appears in the highest heaven. She is Theology, who understands all the secrets of the universe and all the mysteries of revelation and has access to truths inaccessible to Reason. This heavenly queen, *poli regina*, having heard the purpose of Prudence's coming, offers to guide her the rest of the way, but Reason and the chariot must remain behind. Now Alan, who at the beginning of the poem had invoked Phoebus, asks God the Father for divine inspiration. Proceeding with her new guide, Prudence comes into the supernal region, where one mystery after another is unfolded to her. But when they reach the sanctuary of God, she faints, only to be revived by Faith. She then presents the petition of Natura and the virtues to God, who sends Noys to seek out the idea of a perfect soul. Noys returns with the idea of the soul, in which all the graces are summarized: the form of Joseph, the wisdom of Judith, the patience of Job, the simplicity of Jacob, the faith of Abraham, and the piety of Tobias. God then creates the soul and puts his seal upon it. He warns Prudence not to let any harm come to it during the descent to earth, and to this end Noys anoints it with a celestial balm that will protect it from possible damage by the planetary influences. When Prudence returns to her sisters,

Natura marvels at the beauty of the new soul and fashions an appropriate body as its habitat. Concord joins the soul to the body, and all the virtues and the seven arts lavish their gifts upon the homo novus. But Alecto, having heard of the virtues' achievement, musters her vices to make an immediate attack. Natura is unafraid, as are the virtues with whom the man is equipped. In a series of individual combats, the virtues, now qualities in the man's character, defeat the vices, and a new era or golden age begins.

The victory of Natura and the virtues through the new man represents not only the restoration of man to his original condition but also the restoration of Natura to her original authority as described in the *De planctu*. In short, the complex action of the poem, with its emphasis on the attainment of divine wisdom through the role of Prudence, on the endowment of man's character with the virtues and the triumphant response to the attack of the vices, repairs the disfiguration of man in the goddess' tunic. In the new dispensation, man's renewed integrity is closely allied with the renewal of Natura's authority, for in anticipation of the psychomachia, Honor instructs man to overcome the vices by following Natura ("Vt uicium fugiat, Naturam diligat," VII.208.163). Through a reunion with Natura, man may return to God, though Natura's status as vicaria Dei, as indicated early in the poem, has always remained intact:

> Quod Natura facit diuinus perficit auctor;
> diuinum creat ex nichilo, Natura caduca
> procreat ex aliquo; Deus imperat, illa ministrat;
> hic regit, illa facit; hic instruit, illa docetur.
>
> (II.71–74.75)

(That which Natura makes the divine Author perfects; the divine One creates from nothing, Natura breeds perishable things from something; God commands, she serves; He rules, she acts; He instructs, she is taught.)

In fact, it is the moral order associated with Natura even after the Fall, as indicated in the final episode of the *De planctu*, that enables her to instigate the action which results in the consolidation of her sisters in the new man.

But the process that Natura has begun depends for its fulfillment largely on the characters Reason, Prudence, and Concord. The former two in particular represent the two stages of human cognition that lead to wisdom and salvation. Reason, the charioteer who resembles the unimpeded rational control and percipience figured in Natura's charioteer and in the original nature of man presented in the *De planctu*, guides the mind to the limits of created nature. The description of the three mirrors of Reason—in the first she distinguishes between form and subject, in the second she sees the pure forms separate from matter, and in the third she looks upon the pure, uncontaminated forms—indicates her role as mediator between substantial images and the forms or ideas they reflect (I.450ff., 70–71). But Reason cannot go beyond the abstract comprehension of physical reality. At this point, Prudence is taken over by Theology, who reveals to her the eternal truths that only faith and love can comprehend.[73] This process was described by John of Salisbury in the *Metalogicon*: "Thus when love of reason, which concerns earthly things, ascends with prudence to the hidden secrets of eternal and divine truths, it becomes transformed into wisdom, which is in a way exempt from mortal limitations."[74] Embodied in the narrative of the poem is this progress from natural philosophy to Theophania, which is the way to the summit of man's knowledge of God and himself and to the future perfection of his whole nature.[75]

When the virtues return with the soul of the new man, Natura performs the function of preparing the body, which Alan again describes with his favorite image of Natura as coiner (VII.34–36.158). It is Concord, however, who unites soul to body, not Natura as in Bernard's *De mundi universitate*, for this incarnation, unlike that in the earlier work, has a figural relationship to Christ, the Incarnate Redeemer who is exemplar for redeemed man.[76] This contrast between analogous scenes in the two works points up a significant and essential difference. Whereas the soul that Urania brings when she and Natura descend to the earth must be educated in the laws of the fates and the vicissitudes of fortune because it must one day return through the heavens to its true home (II.iv.39–40), the soul of the new man that Prudence brings to Natura and her sisters is protected from the influence of the planets by the unguent of Noys (VI.452ff., 154). Unlike the soul in the *De mundi*, which journeys *de splendore ad tenebros*, this soul descends in the guardianship of a Prudence who has attained divine wisdom, to be united in perfect harmony with the body in which it will vindicate divine justice in man and cosmos. The story has come full circle in a sense, from the cosmogony of *De mundi universitate* with its ambivalence between glorification and pessimism for the great and small worlds, to *De planctu naturae* with its sorrowful recognition of man's corruption qualified by awareness of the possibility of restoration, to *Anticlaudianus* in which that possibility finds realization.

In historical perspective these three works of Bernard and Alan appear to form a kind of trilogy, which I do not believe is an accident or an illusion born of a seven-hundred-year distance. The phrase "allegory of doctrine" fits all three poems, for their central concerns are deeply rooted in Christian doctrine and the providential history of man. Although they have much to do with human experience, they deal with it in a unique way. Compared with the Chartrian poems, the works of Jean de Meun and Chaucer might be called—as indeed they have been called—"allegories of love," which is not to say that they have nothing to do with doctrine. Rather, the central concerns of Jean and Chaucer are the problems of love as viewed by thirteenth and fourteenth century men in a secular context imbued with the Christian doctrine of the Middle Ages and consciously adapted from the Latin literary tradition of the High Middle Ages.[77]

If the history of man as it unfolds in the works of Bernard and Alan can be said to have a beginning, a middle, and an end, then *De planctu naturae* was in the position to have the greatest influence on subsequent Natura poems. This influence has been measured in terms of source studies and the adaptation of lines, passages, images, and the poet's own references.[78] Moreover, the *De planctu* contains implicitly and explicitly the beginning and end with which the two other works are concerned while it also deals with the condition of man in this life.

That even before the medieval vernaculars reached their poetic maturity in Jean and Chaucer the goddess Natura had become a significant figure in a poetry emphasizing experience and the search for knowledge and purpose is evidenced by Jean de Hauteville's *Architrenius* (c. 1184), a satirical poem in nine books, whose youthful hero sets out through the world to find Natura in order to learn from her the way to correct his weaknesses and give life a purpose.[79] His searching takes him to the palace of Venus, the house of gluttony, the schools of Paris, the mount of Ambition and the hill of Presumption, all of which provide material for satire. He finally arrives at Thule, the philosophers' paradise, where after hearing the philosophers, he sees the goddess Natura. She gives him a lecture on the heavens and natural philosophy and then marries him to the maiden Moderation. Jean de Meun and Chaucer narrow and sharpen the focus on the issue of the role of earthly love in the universe.

IV JEAN DE MEUN

Despite its celebrity, the *Roman de la Rose*, especially the continuation by Jean de Meun (c. 1275), has evoked comparatively little criticism. The much shorter *Parlement of Foules* enjoys a considerably longer bibliography, which continues to grow at a rate faster than that of the *Roman*, although recent publications indicate that this poem is on the threshold of a period of intense study. Over the last twenty-five years, the major critical studies of the *Roman* have centered upon a controversy over the *significatio* of Jean's work, with much of the disagreement involving the interpretation of his goddess Natura.[1]

In the *Roman de la Rose*, Natura appears along with a number of other allegorical figures in the context of a grand debate on the meaning and end of sexual love. As in Chaucer's *Parlement*, she is placed at the center of the poet's attempt to investigate the meaning of human sexuality. Introduced at a late point in the narrative of the Lover's quest of the rose, Natura's description, her confession to Genius, and his exhortation to Love's barons constitute the last major suspension of the narrative action before the rose is finally taken. This section of the poem, which is just short of five thousand lines in length, contains Jean's view of Natura as well as what some students of the poem believe to be the definitive statement of Jean's personal conviction on the question of love.[2] Indeed, whether or not Natura and Genius speak for Jean is one of the crucial questions that has been raised in interpretations of the poem.

In Jean's presentation of the two figures, Natura first comes on the scene after the God of Love and his barons, reinforced by the arrival of Venus, have sworn an oath to do their utmost to overcome Love's adversaries. Natura is described as busying herself in her workshop with the forging of individual beings—a familiar image—in order to sustain the continuity of life against the destructive assaults of Death. The principle of perpetuation is illustrated by the story of the phoenix, an example of the way Natura assures continuity to all creatures who live in the sublunary world. After describing Art's futile competition with Natura, Jean tells his readers that Natura grieved and wept in repentance over a former deed, which remains unexplained until she confesses to Genius. Invoking the inexpressibility topos, Jean refuses to describe Natura, for since she is entirely the work of God, her beauty exceeds his power of expression. Her grief partially relieved when she hears Cupid's barons swear their oath, but still wary of being deceived, the goddess proceeds to her chapel, where Genius, her priest, celebrates mass. She wishes to confess to him the deed that now weighs heavily on her conscience. After a comically ironic passage in which Genius ridicules woman's inability to keep a secret, the priest promises her absolution. Natura's confession, which is essentially a complaint against man's imperfect keeping of her law, begins with an account of God's creation of the universe and His appointment of her as His chamberlain. The order of the universe and the perpetuation of all living things within it are her responsibility. Natura continues with a series of lectures on destiny and free will, on the influence of the heavens, on the properties of mirrors and glasses, on dreams, and on gentility. She absolves of any wrongdoing all the constituents of the universe, from the heavens to the insects, except for man, whom she denounces as a recreant, because he alone refuses to obey her law. She enjoins Genius to go before the God of Love and his followers to inform them that she has sent him to excommunicate those who oppose her will and law and to absolve those who obey her commands.

Having dictated this decree to Genius, Natura returns to her forge, and the priest goes before Love's forces to deliver Natura's message. After exhorting them to use the instruments Natura has given them in order to propagate and thereby undo the work of Death, and after threatening those who refuse with damnation, Genius delivers a sermon in which he describes the paradise that is to be the reward of those blessed ones who practice Natura's law. This paradise, Genius preaches, is the Good Shepherd's Park, wherein all who obey Natura will live in eternal bliss, a place where the hour is always noon and the season ever spring. Even the Golden Age, Saturn's reign, cannot compare with this paradise, a point that gives rise to an account of Jupiter's usurpation of his father's throne and the decline of the ages of history. Genius concludes his sermon by contrasting the Good Shepherd's Park with the Garden of Deduit (Diversion), which had been described by Guillaume at the beginning of the poem. The Good Shepherd's Park, Genius maintains, is the true paradise, while the other is nothing but a fable, a vain delight that is doomed to fade away.

Even so brief an account of the narrative reveals elements from the earlier Natura tradition. Particularly prominent are natura plangens and natura procreatrix. The immediate source is Alan's *De planctu naturae*, which had a profound influence on the *Roman*.[3] But Alan's poem is by no means the only work put to use by the well-read Jean in this part of his poem. In addition, there are clear indications that Jean was influenced by the contemporary scholasticism of thirteenth century Paris.[4] Thus, he had at his disposal not only the Platonically inspired works of the Chartrian allegorists but also the most current philosophical investigations of the nature of the universe. Like Bernard and Alan, he incorporated in his work the latest intellectual concerns of his time.

The features of Jean's Natura that link her with Alan's figure are scattered throughout her portion of the *Roman*. In introducing the goddess, Jean borrows many features from Alan and, as Ernest Langlois has pointed out, translates many lines verbatim.[5] It is in this section of the poem that Natura appears working at her forge in her constant war against Death, striving to ensure continuity:

> Mais Nature douce e piteuse,
> Quant el veit que Mort l'envieuse,
> Entre li e Corrupcion,
> Vienent metre a destruccion
> Quanqu'eus treuvent dedenz sa forge,
> Toujourz martele, toujourz forge,
> Toujourz ses pieces renouvele
> Par generacion nouvele.
>
> (IV.16005–16012)[6]

(But when Nature, sweet and compassionate, sees that envious Death and Corruption come together to put to destruction whatever they find within her forge, she continues always to hammer and forge and always to renew the individuals by means of new generation.)

When Natura begins her confession to Genius, she speaks in a close paraphrase of Alan on the subject of God's boundless goodness and beauty, His creation of the universe, and His naming of her as "chamberiere" and "vicaire" and entrusting her with the perpetuation of all things in the golden chain of creation (IV.16729–16813). Similarly, Jean appropriates from Alan's goddess that part of Natura's confession in which she absolves the heavens and all creatures of guilt but complains bitterly of man's failure to live according to her law (IV.18947–19334).

These three parallels to Alan's figure are of critical importance to understanding Jean's conception of Natura. They represent three features of Natura's cosmological role: Natura as the vicaria Dei, the exalted subordinate of God the Father of all things; as His representative, working in His name to sustain life and preserve the plenitude of creation through continuity; and finally, as a moral judge of the behavior of all things that come within her domain as vicaria Dei. Indebtedness to Alan for these features, however, did not necessarily require that Jean follow Alan's characterization on other points as well. It is even possible that Jean regarded these cosmological features as poetic motifs. How far it was possible for Jean to depart from Alan's presentation of Natura is nicely illustrated by the goddess' long lecture on the nature of her domain. Although the three basic motifs are present, and although some passages are straight out of Alan, Jean begins to show here that he conceives of Natura and her realm in an individual way.

The many subjects Natura touches on in the course of her confession give her an authority that befits her title of queen of the world ("dou monde reine"), as Genius addresses her, echoing Alan's "mundanae regionis regina," for she knows the operations of her domain. Her systematic exposition of the world, one of the earliest instances of the use of a vernacular in the treatment of philosophical ideas, serves to magnify man's sin against her law by depicting on a vast canvass the orderly operations of every heavenly body and of every living thing save man.[7] Although Alan's Natura had also described the operations of the world according to her law, Jean's figure does not repeat only what her predecessor taught. While her description of the creation follows the *De planctu* and is characteristically Platonic, her discussion of the sublunary world is greatly indebted to contemporary thirteenth century Aristotelianism.[8] Similarly, her discussion of the properties of mirrors shows close affinities with current works on the subject, combining the scientific consideration of optics with the Neoplatonic metaphor of the mirror as symbol of the generative process. Finally, Natura's lecture on destiny and free will (IV.17039–17874) is based on Boethius' *Consolation*, which Jean himself had translated. This lecture in particular illustrates Jean's application of sources other than Alan to the theme of Natura's complaint. Near the end of the lecture, the goddess states that she must explain herself fully on this subject in order to prevent man, her enemy, from excusing his actions as the result of a binding destiny over which he has no control, claiming he had no free will to choose the course of his life (IV.17737–17762). Again, at the conclusion of the lecture she reiterates her purpose in speaking at such great length on the existence of free will and on man's obligation to use it and to take responsibility for his actions: she does not want to leave him any room for argument or defense (IV.17871–17874). Thus, by anticipating the excuse man might plead in self-defense, Natura allows him no ground on which to stand when some fourteen hundred verses later she accuses him of cheating her. She denounces those of whom the God of Love also complains, condemning their refusal to pay her tribute for the tools she has given them. For the gift of sexuality, Natura claims, man owes her an eternal debt (IV.19327–19334).

From this point on the differences between the figures of Alan and Jean become more pronounced.[9] Two are of extreme importance to an understanding of the Natura of the *Roman*. First, unlike the goddess of the *De planctu*, Jean's Natura never refers to the sacramental state of marriage as the only acceptable avenue of sexual expression. Her interest lies in procreation only, and her plangens fundamentally involves the condemnation of man for his resistance to the fulfillment of her law—though she makes clear that she is acquainted with his other vices as well. Whereas Alan's Natura had sanctioned procreation only within the marital state, Jean's admits no limitations or qualifications whatever to her law. She is a beautiful and limitless fount of creative energy, as described in a passage that further displays Jean's unwillingness to follow in the footsteps of Alan by subjecting his goddess to the formal rhetorical descriptio (IV.16165–16248,16233–16238). Although she shows acquaintance with Christian doctrine at various points in her confession, when she speaks as procreatrix, she speaks simply as the creative force assigned by God to attend to the continuation of life in the sublunary world. In a second major departure from Alan's Natura, who had been closely associated with reason and indeed, like Boethius' nature, was identified as the giver of reason, Jean's Natura explains that man's reason and understanding were not provided him by her, for her jurisdiction does not extend so far:

> Senz faille, de l'entendement,
> Quenois je bien que vraiement
> Celui ne lui donai je mie;
> La ne s'estent pas ma baillie.
>
> (IV.19055–19058)

(Certainly I know truly that I did not give him his understanding; that is not my area of responsibility.)

By virtue of these conspicuous and deliberate differences, Jean disengages from his Natura two concepts that were central in Alan's figure.

It is clear that Jean wishes his Natura procreatrix to be taken as a personification of the reproductive power with which God endowed His creation in order that it might

perpetuate itself. This is Natura's exclusive duty as vicaria
Dei in the poem, and neither reason, morality, nor religious
orthodoxy and ceremony concern her, provided her law is
observed. Perhaps Jean thought that such a limitation on
her character made her a more striking, concentrated allegorical figure. Perhaps, as Alan M. F. Gunn argues, her
allegorical role in the debate of the poem is to give voice to
the divinely ordained principles of replenishment, continuity, and plenitude within the complex of ideas that finally
express the Lover's striving toward an Aristotelian entelechy,
from sexual and social immaturity to maturity and fulfillment as man and lover[10] In any event, not only is Jean's
Natura significantly different from Alan's, but another of
Jean's characters, Raison, teaches a doctrine of natural love
much closer to that expressed by Alan's Natura.

The realization that the Natura of the *Roman* operates as
procreatrix outside the Christian context within which
Alan's Natura acts leads to a proper appreciation of the
significance of Genius' sermon to Love's barons, for Genius,
despite Jean's occasionally ironic treatment of him completes
the expression of Natura's position in the poem. Before the
goddess receives her absolution and returns to her forge, she
informs Genius that she wishes him to go before Love and his
retinue to deliver a message, namely, that those who refuse
to abide by her law will be excommunicated and that those
who observe her law and strive to multiply the race will
receive pardon. She then dictates the decree to him and retires
to her shop to continue her work in the service of God
(IV.19369–19436). In addition to the plot elements borrowed
from the *De planctu*, there is an echo here of the sentiments
expressed by Natura in Alan's *Anticlaudianus*, for just prior
to her charge to Genius, Natura expresses regret at ever
having made man ("Mout me repent don ome fis,"
IV.19210). This correspondence, however, functions as an
indication of the differences rather than the similarities

between the two poets. Both goddesses experience regrets, but they each offer extremely different remedies. Unlike the Natura of the *Anticlaudianus*, who proposes the creation of the novus homo and sees her proposal victoriously fulfilled, and unlike the goddess of the *De planctu*, who sends Genius to excommunicate the unnatural and vicious at the same time as she offers the narrator a view of man's original honor and integrity, Jean's Natura sends her priest to urge Love and his barons to victory in their quest of the rose. This difference in their reactions not only shows how far Jean has departed from his models, but also shows the careful consistency with which he developed his characterization of Natura.

Delivering his sermon with the authority given him by his mistress, Genius promises pardon to all who will follow their natural inclinations. To those who refuse, he promises a curse and excommunication. He especially warns Love's barons against following the example of those who neglect to use the styles and tablets, hammers and anvils ("Grefes, tables, marteaus, enclumes"), those instruments that God has made with His own hand and given to Natura so that she may impart to mortal creatures eternal being. If everyone followed the evil example of these recreants to Natura's law, the human race would disappear within sixty years, and a significant part of God's creation would be undone. Genius' rather lengthy exhortation is forcefully epitomized in these urgent lines:

> Arez, pour Deu, baron, arez,
> E voz lignages reparez;
> Se ne pensez forment d'arer,
> N'est riens qui les puist reparer.
>
> (V.19701–19704)

(Plow, for God's sake, my barons, plow and restore your lineages. Unless you think on plowing vigorously, there is nothing that can restore them.)

For those who will listen to him and will plow for the repair of their lineage, who will enlist in the fight against Death and Atropos, and who will consent to preach Natura's law just as they have heard it preached by Genius, Natura's priest promises eternal life in the Garden of Paradise, a fair park in which flowers and grass grow forever. Its flocks live idyllic lives under the care of the Good Shepherd ("Dou bon pasteur"), who is most likely based on the shepherd in Christ's first parable in Luke 15, in this blissful paradise where time stands still, glorious day endures forever, and it is always spring (V.20027–20031).

But the aim of Genius' sermon is not simply to describe the paradise that awaits those who are Natura's faithful. It is not enough to win converts by depicting the Good Shepherd's Park when another park exists that resembles it superficially but which differs drastically in its effect on those who enter it. Genius' mission, therefore, is in part to warn Love's barons against this dangerous place of fables and vanities. His target, ironically, is Guillaume's Garden of Deduit, a place well-known to Cupid and his host, and Genius takes great pains in the next two hundred lines to make the differences between the two gardens clear (V.20369–20596). The central contrast lies in their fountains: the perilous fountain of Narcissus in the Garden of Deduit is not, like the Fountain of Life in the Garden of Paradise, the source of its own waters. Furthermore, the fountain of Narcissus is a deceptive mirror, reflecting only half of the garden it occupies. It is, in short, a perilous fountain. But the carbuncle of the Holy Trinity that shines from within the Fountain of Life reflects both the truth and the entire garden. Independent of the sun, it is everluminous. Drawing to a close, Genius asks his listeners which of these two gardens sounds better. Surely, if they wish to act wisely, they will drink from the holy fountain in the Garden of Paradise.

In completing the case for Natura, Genius brings to bear on her doctrine of love some of her own learned observations on the subject of optics. Gunn has suggested that the object of Natura's discussion of mirrors is to present "a symbol of the whole generative process as well as a symbol on the one hand of love's birth in the mirror of the eye," as in the case of true mirrors, and to show on the other hand "that there goes on in the world a sort of false generation which parodies the process of faithful reproduction or reflection," as in the case of distorting mirrors.[11] If this is indeed true, then Genius has applied the "scientific" truth of Natura's discussion of mirrors to his own description of the two fountains. It is a neat assimilation of contemporary physics to the old and well-known Neoplatonic tradition of picturing the Chain of Being as a chain of mirrors, an idea best known in the Middle Ages through Macrobius' commentary on Cicero's *Somnium Scipionis* (I.xiv.15). Thus, Genius associates the Fountain of Life, which reflects the whole truth about the garden that represents true generation, with Natura's truthful mirrors; and he associates the perilous fountain of Narcissus, which obscures and distorts the truth about the other garden that parodies true generation, with Natura's false, distorting mirrors. Furthermore, and this point is crucial, the goddess Natura is herself a reflection of the mirror of God. Genius states this clearly in a passage that epitomizes the metaphorical concept of the Chain of Being as a series of mirrors, only Genius sets the focus entirely on Natura as the reflection of the *speculum Dei*, the only cure of body and soul, the mirror of Natura, who would know nothing were it not for that beautiful mirror. He governs and rules her, for she knows no other law. Whatever she knows, she learned from God when He made her his chamberlain:

> Cil est saluz de cors e d'ame.
> C'est li beaus miroers ma dame.
> Ja ma dame riens ne seüst

Se ce bel miroer n'eüst.
Cil la gouverne, cil la regle;
Ma dame n'a point d'autre regle;
Quanqu'ele set il li aprist
Quant a chamberiere la prist.

(V.19899–19906)

(He is the salvation of body and soul and the beautiful mirror of my lady, who would never know anything if she did not have this beautiful mirror. It is he who governs and rules her, and my lady has no other rule. He taught her whatever she knows when he took her for his chamberlain.)

Genius has bound together the substance of Natura's lecture on optics, which precedes this passage, and his own description of the true and false fountains, which succeeds it. The Fountain of Life, symbolic of true generation, is the future reward of those who are willing to drink from it, that is, to follow unstintingly the procreative urge given them by Natura, the vicaria Dei and procreatrix who reflects the mind and will of God.

There is some controversy over whether the teachings of Natura and Genius may be regarded as the definitive expressions of Jean de Meun's own philosophy of love, for although they come last in a series of lectures by a number of allegorical figures, all the others claim to speak with authority as well. This is one of the crucial issues in *Roman* criticism, for behind the question of whether or not Jean's Natura is his own spokesman lies a conflict over the orthodoxy of the pronouncements of the goddess and her priest. To Edmond Faral, Jean was no skeptic but a man of faith who preached a strange sort of religion with the enthusiasm of a prophet calling men to the will of Nature.[12] Curtius, in contrast, argues that Natura in the *Roman* "has become the servant of rank promiscuity, her management of the life of love is travestied into obscenity."[13] This view of Natura's doctrine as immoral if not downright heretical has been most thoroughly presented by Gérard Paré, who sees the speeches of Natura and Genius as virtual repudiations of those made by Alan's figures. For him, Jean's goddess and priest aim their attack at practices that oppose procreation and the perpetuation of the species, with Genius in particular emphasizing the idea that chastity and continence are vices.[14] Both Curtius and Paré believe that this modification of the doctrines of Alan's Natura and Genius came about largely as a result of the popularity among Paris schoolmen of doctrines related to Averroism, which were among the 219 theological propositions condemned on March 7, 1277, by the bishop of Paris, Étienne Tempier.[15] It is clear that there are some resemblances between views expressed in the *Roman* and the condemned propositions. Genius' apparent belief in the eternity of the world is one example. However, such a relationship between the poem and Latin Averroism is not corroborated by any historical document connected with the condemnation of Averroistic heresies. The tendency to assume such a connection has been nourished by the popular misconception that the *Roman* caused a furore when it was published and that Natura's position is necessarily the stand of the poet.[16] Most important, such a view completely ignores the possibility that Jean's characterizations of Natura and Genius are the results of a poet's reworking of traditional figures in order to suit the particular conflict and theme of his work.

Although he seriously doubts that the poem was influenced by Averroistic thought, Gunn asserts that Natura essentially expresses Jean's own views. He sees the poem as a series of conflicting views on love, which presents an allegorical picture of youth's progress toward maturity. This debate on the central theme of love is what gives the poem unity. The resolution of the debate among love's doctors comes in the argument of Natura and Genius, which holds that the chief end of man is "to glorify God by the perpetuation of his earthly image" and thereby to attain the fulfillment of sexual love. Rather than dismissing the arguments of the other major characters, Natura and Genius subordinate them to their own purpose, for the partial truths of the other discourses have contributed to the fulfillment of that purpose. The other figures have brought the lover to the brink of victory, but Genius, speaking for Natura, makes the pronouncement that incites Love's barons to final action. In short, all the doctors of love have been made to serve Natura's aim. Gunn's interpretation, however, does not resolve the conflict between what he calls the "other-worldliness" position of Raison, who opposes the lover's quest, and the "this-worldliness" position of Natura, which triumphs. That the conflict is never fully resolved, Gunn believes, is perhaps to be accounted for by the fact that it was the fundamental conflict of the poet's age, as well as that the poem is dominated for the most part by a question of behavior in this world.[17]

Disputing Gunn's interpretation of the poem, D. W. Robertson, Jr., argues that carnal love is the poem's subject and that Jean's allegory illustrates man's imperfect manner of loving. For Robertson, Jean's opinions are represented by the "Boethian" Raison. Once the main themes are established by Raison, "the rest of the poem is an elaborate, but not a digressive account of what happens to those who disobey Raison's counsels."[18] Natura and Genius, who are interested in replenishment, are not to be blamed for the outcome of the poem: they speak for natural desire, but Cupid and Venus, who represent willful desire and sexual delight, subvert their purpose by making Genius' sermon serve their own end, the taking of the rose. Natura and Genius neither tolerate nor even make use of the discourse of the other allegorical doctors of love. Understanding the conclusion of the poem as the triumph of Venus and of cupidinous desire rather than as the triumph of Natura and procreation, Robertson concludes that it is Natura and Genius who are being used.[19]

Despite their antagonism, both these interpretations of the poem raise a subject that directly pertains to the question of Jean's indebtedness to Alan, that is, the role of Raison in the poem. Less than two hundred lines after the beginning of the poem, Jean introduces the figure of Raison, who holds center stage for the next three thousand lines (II-III.4221–7231). Her argument, long recognized as a systematic and unified expression of the doctrine of rational love, touches on many subjects.[20] The relevant portions of her discourse are concerned with the God of Love and with procreation and continuity. In her pronouncements on these subjects can be found her position on the meaning of sexual love. Fundamentally, Raison espouses the doctrine of natural love that was taught by Alan's Natura, and like that goddess, she has no use whatsoever for the brand of love taught by Cupid and Venus, both of whom are identified throughout the *Roman* with the evil Venus and Cupid of medieval mythography and with the forces of cupidity and destruction—Venus scelestis, Mirth, and Falsity—in the *De planctu*. Raison's attack on the God of Love, in fact, consists largely of a translation of the descriptio Cupidinis that Alan's Natura had delivered to the narrator (II.4279–4358). Replete with oxymoron, Raison's condemnation, like that of her predecessor, emphasizes the confusion at the heart of such loving:

> Amour ce est pais haineuse,
> Amour c'est haine amoureuse.
>
> (II.4293–4294)

(Love is hateful peace and loving hate.)

The point she wants to make is that the God of Love can subdue even the stoutest of men once he has him in his power. And just as Alan's Natura had advised against fruitless love, and just as the black inscription on the gate in Chaucer's *Parlement of Foules* was to warn, Raison states that the Lover's best defense against this powerful lord is flight; in Chaucer's words, "th'eschewing is only the remedye":

> Se tu le suiz, il te suira,
> Se tu t'en fuiz, il s'en fuira.
>
> (II.4357–4358)[21]

(If you follow him, he will follow you; if you flee, he will flee.)

Summing up her attack on him, Raison accuses the God of Love of caring only for delight and having no concern for procreation:

> Amanz autre chose n'entent
> Ainz s'art e se delite en tant.
> De fruit aveir ne fait il force;
> Au deliter senz plus s'efforce.
>
> (II.4385–4388)

(A lover so burns and is so enraptured that he thinks of nothing else; he takes no account of bearing fruit, but strives only for delight.)

Raison, like Alan's Natura before her, condemns Venus and her son because they mislead man and undermine the real purpose of sexual attraction, which in the argument of Raison, as in the complaint of Alan's Natura, is a means for the provision of a home for a new soul in order to ensure the succession of the human race (II.4403–4414). According to Raison, the natural love provided by Natura has but one purpose, to perpetuate the race. Natura's law, Raison instructs the Lover, is common to man and beast. But this natural love is not the kind of love the Lover has involved himself in; he has embraced a kind of madness that he should quit for his own good.[22]

Raison's doctrine of love, which is no more "otherworldly" than that of Alan's Natura, corresponds to that of the twelfth-century goddess in two important points. First,

cupidinous desire, or sexuality unguided by reason, is fruitless. Jean's Natura, in contrast, is concerned only with procreation. She admits that reason is beyond the sphere of her
influence, and neither she nor her priest appear to be concerned with the manner in which they achieve their goal.
Natura, therefore, sends Genius before Love's barons to
urge them to act in the cause of procreation, an exhortation
that results in the taking of the rose. Whether this means a
victory for Natura or for Venus, one thing is certain: Alan's
Natura could never have participated in such a "co-
operative" effort, for in her view, Venus and her son were
responsible for the waywardness of man. Second, being the
source of man's reason as well as his sexuality, Alan's Natura
had warned against the madness, confusion, and fruitlessness that attend cupidinous desire. This is exactly what
Raison does. Raison's position, then, more closely approxi-
mates that of Alan's Natura than does the position of Natura
herself in the *Roman*. While Jean's Natura personifies the
procreative urge, his Raison represents a view of rational
love which acknowledges the necessity and goodness of procreation but condemns the willful confusion and distortion
of it that Venus and the God of Love have brought about.

The fact that Raison's doctrine of love is closer to Alan's
Natura than is Jean's own Natura indicates something
about Jean's use of the Natura tradition. To begin with, one
of the most striking differences between his treatment and
that of Alan appears in his characterization of the goddess.
Alan had taken considerable pains to give his Natura a
majesty and eloquence approaching that of Boethius'
Philosophia. She is a divine goddess, a powerful representative of God, who commands profound respect and reverence
from man as well as from her priest and her attendant
virtues. Even in righteous sorrow, she complains with a
dignity and nobility that is commensurate with her cosmological status as vicaria Dei. Jean de Meun, in contrast,

concentrates on the human quality of a macrocosmic force that he had personified as a woman. His goddess Natura is identified as vicaria Dei, the queen of the world, but at times she speaks more with the petulant and distraught voice of a betrayed woman than with the tones of an outraged, majestic goddess. The episode in which Natura goes to Genius to confess her fault in making man, the only creature who disobeys her law, illustrates this aspect of Jean's characterization. Before hearing her confession, Genius delivers a mock sermon on the loquacity of women (IV.16347–16706), its point being that one should not tell women anything that can be used against one when they are angry. Besides its relevance to Natura's own lengthy and angry exposure of man's deviation from her rules, the passage provides a moment of ironic humor when Genius graciously excepts Natura from this criticism of the female character. Such treatment from her priest, while it is certainly the opposite of that which Alan's Genius gave to Natura, is not surprising or inappropriate because of the extent to which Jean has "humanized" this character.[23] In addition, the other figures in the poem, in their treatment of her representative Genius, do not offer her the respect that figures in the *De planctu naturae* showed for the goddess and her priest. All these features, along with his concentration on the function of procreatrix in Natura's cosmological role, indicate Jean's intelligent and purposeful alteration of the figure he had inherited.

Natura complains against man's failure to procreate, and she accounts for this failure by referring to his stubborn waywardness and selfishness. Nowhere does she show awareness of the possibility that it is the God of Love who thwarts her purpose by frightening and charming the Lover into becoming his vassal; neither does Genius show any such awareness when he speaks to the assembly of Venus, Cupid, and the barons in Natura's behalf and attacks sexual abstinence and chastity as the enemies of procreation. Their failure to recognize the basic enmity of Venus and the God of Love is quite appropriate for a Natura and her priest who represent a procreative instinct and inclination that has been separated from the guidance of reason. It is Raison who is aware of this danger to natural love, but not Natura and Genius, who are blind to any kind of opposition except the obviously antithetical ones of chastity and abstinence. Natura, in fact, believes that Cupid loves and wishes to serve her and that Venus is her friend (IV.19336–19344). It is with this understanding that she sends Genius to them, for she believes their efforts to win the rose have aligned them with her. But she misunderstands their motives and ends, a failure that is entirely in keeping with Jean's characterization of her.

That Jean meant Natura and Genius to be unaware of the intentions of Venus and her son is emphasized and clarified by the details of Genius' preparations to go before Love's company and of his reception there. Before leaving with Natura's charter, Genius exchanges his priestly garments for secular clothing, exactly the opposite of what his counterpart in the *De planctu naturae* did prior to reading the excommunication before Natura and her virtues (IV.19428–19438). If this is an instance of Jean's ironic use of details from Alan, it is also a deliberate artistic tactic in the poet's preparation for Genius' ironic treatment by the God of Love and his mother. Having put aside his priestly robes, which signify his office in the religion of Natura, he comes, appropriately dressed in secular clothes, before Love's host, only to be newly arrayed by the God of Love:

> Tantost li deus d'Amours afuble
> A Genius une chasuble;
> Anel li baille e croce e mitre
> Plus clere que cristal ne vitre.
>
> (V.19477–19480)

(Straightway the God of Love put a chasuble on Genius. He gave him a ring, a crosier, and a miter clearer than crystal or glass.)

The God of Love has thus made Natura's priest into his own bishop, and Venus, who is unable to restrain her laughter, gaily places in his hand a candle, which is described as not being made of virgin wax (V.19484–19490). The priest of procreation has unwittingly become the priest of Love, and his message and promise of paradise become the means by which Venus and Cupid inspire the barons to begin their victorious assault on the castle. The natural inclination for sexual reproduction is made to serve a cause that has as object only the act of love and not its proper end.

Jean de Meun's vision of Natura as procreatrix who gives man his sexual but not his rational power, who struggles against Death in order to ensure continuity to God's creatures in the mutable world, who finds man's unwillingness to obey her law regrettable and offensive, and who regards chastity and abstinence with suspicion and fear, is the result of the poet's careful and deliberate modification of the figure handed down to him by Alan and other writers. In humanizing the august goddess of the twelfth-century poet and in limiting her moral sphere to a demand for fruitful procreation, Jean produces a strikingly novel figure of Natura. Her position in his poem, which it must be remembered is a continuation of a love vision whose major purpose is to describe the psychology of *fin amor*, is a candid and forceful argument for the perpetuation of the human race through sexual reproduction. If the quest of Guillaume's Lover, and for that matter of Jean's as well, is motivated by a desire to possess the rose, Natura's hope is that this possession will result in fruitful issue. But unlike Raison, who is rejected by the brainwashed Lover, she does not understand that the doctrine of Cupid and Venus makes no provision for the accommodation of her purpose. She is seeking help from a camp that by definition has no concern whatsoever for her teaching, even though—and this is the great irony of Jean's poem—the God of Love and his mother depend on that natural urge over which she presides not only for their ultimate success but also for their initial enchantment of the Lover when he feels the first stirrings of love for the rose.

Natura, therefore, is morally neutral in Jean's poem. She can be used by Venus because the instinct to procreate is at the basis of the power of Venus. Jean's Raison, unlike the Raison of Guillaume de Lorris, does not condemn love as foolish and valueless; rather, she represents the mental force behind, but not of, the procreative love that Natura stands for. And since Natura is neutral in the conflict between Raison and Venus, it is difficult to see how she could be the poet's spokesman. It is not that Natura, as Jean conceives her, is imperfect and faulty per se; it is that man is imperfect and faulty since the Fall. Jean himself does not challenge the virtue of chastity; rather, his Natura feels threatened by it. The poet's allegory is a demonstration of the way that natural love can be thwarted by an over-refinement and exaggerated exaltation of man's sexual passion, which ignores the God-given reasons for its existence. Jean's Natura and Genius know why and how they serve God, and they sincerely try their best to do so. Raison, too, knows their purpose; but she also knows that it can be perverted and misused and that the greater danger to Natura's purpose is not man's chastity but his cupidity. Although Raison essentially takes this position in her discourse, it is never fully realized as the meaning of the poem until the poet has shown the basic conflict and resolved it through the action, which distinguishes the narrative poem from a simple statement. In the last analysis, it is not what any one character in the poem says that represents the poet's attitude but the meaning of the entire poem that indicates his beliefs.[24]

V CHAUCER'S
THE PARLEMENT OF FOULES

Chaucer's love vision *The Parlement of Foules*, a poem that has provoked a great deal of criticism and disagreement, is the last medieval work in the tradition of the goddess Natura. A complex poem that shows a remarkable awareness of European literary tradition, it has its strongest ties with the works of Jean de Meun and Alan of Lille. The diverse and numerous opinions of Chaucerian critics on this poem reflect for the most part a failure to perceive just how important the Natura tradition was to Chaucer when he composed the poem. Consequently, much of the critical canon on the *Parlement* concentrates on aspects of the poem, from the historical identity of some of its birds to its apparent lack of unity and coherence, which become irrelevant once the poem is placed in proper literary context. Even the critics who have recognized the importance of Natura to the poem's meaning have not adequately explored the relationship between Chaucer's poem and the Natura tradition. A close reading of the poem, however, must take cognizance of the fact that it is also rich in literary allusion and quotation. One therefore has to deal with the poet's use of materials that are not part of the Natura tradition in order to investigate the total context in which Chaucer placed his view of the goddess.[1]

The poem opens with a statement by its first person narrator that he is astonished and confounded with the "wonderful werkynge" of the God of Love. In the second stanza, however, it emerges that the narrator's response to the power of Love is based not on experience, "For al be that I knowe nat Love in dede," but on the narrator's reading in books that describe "his myrakles and his crewel yre." In the third stanza, the narrator explains that since he habitually reads for pleasure and for learning, he began to read a book not long ago that "was write with lettres olde" because he wished "a certyn thing to lerne," presumably on the subject of love. There follows a transitional stanza in which the narrator explains *per sententiam* why he was seeking knowledge in an old book:

> For out of olde feldes, as men seyth,
> Cometh al this newe corn from yer to yere,
> And out of olde bokes, in good feyth,
> Cometh al this newe science that men lere.
> (22–25)[2]

The next eight stanzas are occupied with a summary of the old book, "Tullyus of the Drem of Scipioun." In the following stanza it develops that Africanus, who had appeared to Scipio in his dream, also appeared to the narrator in a dream, which he had soon after putting down the book and going to sleep. The following two stanzas (99–112) explain why the narrator has dreamed of Africanus. Since the book in which Africanus plays a prominent role has occupied his waking thoughts, his reading can be said to have caused the narrator to dream of Africanus. The narrator interrupts his account of the dream in order to invoke "Cytherea! thow blysful lady swete" to give him the power to write his "sweven." The description of the dream, which is the *narratio* section of the poem, then resumes.[3]

The *praefatio* of the poem (1–119), according to the conventions of the love vision, contains both a statement of the poem's theme, *propositio*, and an *invocatio* to Cytherea. The poem's theme, according to the first two stanzas, is love, more specifically at the outset, the seeking to learn a certain thing about love in an old book, since the narrator is apparently confined to learning about the subject from books alone. The book, since it is the possible source of the knowledge the narrator seeks, is then summarized. Before describing his own dream, however, the narrator appropriately invokes Cytherea, the celestial Venus and goddess of love, for love is his theme.

The point of the story of Scipio's dream is that man must win salvation through service to "commune profit" ("patriam" or "rem publicam" in Cicero's words). Africanus teaches his descendant this lesson by appearing to him in a dream and by taking him to "a sterry place," a vantage point from which Africanus can show Scipio "the blysful place" that is the reward of every man, "lered other lewed/ That lovede commune profyt, wel ithewed" (44–45), and from which to show him the entire created universe.[4] By pointing out how small the earth is, Africanus can emphasize his warning that Scipio "ne shulde hym in the world delyte." That the universal lesson of the *Dream of Scipio* did not furnish the information the narrator has been seeking is made clear by the narrator's description of his state of mind after having put down the book and begun to prepare for bed:

> And to my bed I gan me for to dresse,
> Fulfyld of thought and busy hevynesse;
> For bothe I hadde thyng which that I nolde,
> And ek I nadde that thyng that I wolde.
>
> (88–91)

His predicament, expressed through *contentio*, is that his reading has given him something he did not want and that he still does not have the thing that he does want. Although he has studied the book all day, the narrator feels he has learned nothing about love. Several details of the narrator's summary of the *Dream of Scipio* are related both directly and indirectly to the scenes that follow. "Commune spede" (507) will be an issue in the raucous parliament of birds, which includes both those who are "lered" and those who are "lewed" in the ways of love. The mention of "likerous folk" (79) can perhaps be related to the temple in the park. Most important, the language used to describe the music of the spheres and the phrase "blysful place," which occurs three times in the summary (48, 76–77, 83), reappears in the later scenes. Although the narrator does not see any connection between his book and love, his description of the harmonious sounds in the "grene mede" (184) and his reintroduction (*traductio*) of the word "blysful" and the phrase "blysful place" suggest connections made by the poet behind the persona of dreamer/narrator.

After the narrator's dream has begun and Africanus is standing at his "beddes syde," and after it becomes apparent that the Roman has come to help the narrator ("sumdel of thy labour wolde I quyte") because the narrator has borne himself so well in studying his "olde bok totorn," the narrator pauses to invoke Cytherea before continuing an account of the dream:

> Cytherea! thow blysful lady swete,
> That with thy fyrbrond dauntest whom the lest,
> And madest me this sweven for to mete,
> Be thow myn helpe in this, for thow mayst best!
> As wisly as I sey the north-north-west,
> Whan I began my sweven for to write,
> So yif me myght to ryme and ek t'endyte!
>
> (113–119)[5]

That Chaucer uses the name Cytherea in the invocatio is of great significance, for he is here not simply addressing a pagan goddess but "the benevolent planet of a christianized cosmology."[6] This heavenly "blysful lady swete" is the powerful star of love, a heavenly body that acts as inter-mediary of God's decrees, and therefore a goddess of legiti-mate love. The fact that Chaucer refers to her "fyrbrond" does not necessarily identify her as the Venus of the *Roman de la Rose*, nor is the invocation meant ironically.[7] To the medieval mind, this "blysful" goddess was a part of those heavens that Africanus showed to Scipio. Above all, Cytherea must not be identified with the Venus figure described in the temple in the garden of love some hundred and fifty lines later.

The narration of the dream resumes with the next stanza, in which it appears that Africanus has guided the narrator to the gate of "a park walled with grene ston." Over either half of this gate are two inscriptions "of ful gret difference." The first is in gold letters:

> "Thorgh me men gon into that blysful place
> Of hertes hele and dedly woundes cure;
> Thorgh me men gon unto the welle of grace,
> There grene and lusty May shal evere endure.
> This is the way to al good aventure.
> Be glad, thow redere, and thy sorwe of-caste;
> Al open am I—passe in, and sped thee faste!"

The second is in black letters:

> "Thorgh me men gon," than spak that other side,
> "Unto the mortal strokes of the spere
> Of which Disdayn and Daunger is the gyde,
> Ther nevere tre shal fruyt ne leves bere.
> This strem yow ledeth to the sorweful were
> There as the fish in prysoun is al drye;
> Th'eschewing is only the remedye!"
>
> $(127-140)$[8]

Standing before this entrance to the allegorical garden of

earthly love, the narrator is unable to decide whether or not to enter, for this double inscription is something he is "astoned to beholde." These two inscriptions juxtapose two extreme possibilities of love. The first ("That oon me hette") is an invitation to enter the park because it is a happy, healthful, and fertile place, the way to good "aventure." The second ("that other dide me colde"), is a warning to keep away, for in some part of the park those traditional figures of courtly love allegory "Disdayn" and "Daunger" cruelly rule; there the trees are doomed to barrenness; there the "strem," counterpart to the "wey," leads one into a trap, a prison, for which the only escape is avoidance.[9] The narrator stands before the gate in a state of stunned confusion. But in the light of the Natura tradition, one should recognize that the double inscription reflects elements from the conflicts between Natura and Venus-Cupid in the *De planctu naturae* and Jean's *Roman de la Rose*. In both these works, man was counseled to follow Natura and to avoid Venus-Cupid; in both, the way of Natura promised felicity and goodness and the way of Venus-Cupid promised pain. Both Alan's Natura, in her descriptio Cupidinis, and Jean's Raison, in Jean's translation of that descriptio, reveal that flight is the only escape from the trap, sorrows, and pain of the love taught by Venus and Cupid. In examining how Chaucer uses this conflict in his own poem, one should note that the first line of the gold inscription indicates that there is within the park of earthly love a "blysful place," just as there was another "blysful place" in the heaven of the *Dream of Scipio*.[10] What this repetition of the phrase implies, with the adjective "blysful" applied to Cytherea in a stanza coming between the phrase's appearances in the dreams of Scipio and the narrator, becomes clear after the narrator has toured the park.

Lest the narrator's dilemma cause undue delay, his guide shoves him "in at the gates wide" and explains to him that he has nothing to fear. The inscriptions do not refer to him, for he has lost his taste for love; the writing applies only to those who are love's servants. In the last words he speaks in the poem, Africanus tells the narrator that although he is "dul" and cannot do, still he may see:

> "For many a man that may nat stonde a pul,
> It liketh hym at the wrastlyng for to be,
> And demeth yit wher he do bet or he.
> And if thow haddest connyng for t'endite,
> I shal the shewe mater of to wryte."
>
> (164–169)

In other words, though he is incapable of love, he may still enjoy looking on, just as a spectator at a wrestling bout enjoys looking on. To follow the analogy further, the narrator may be capable of making a judgment about what he sees, just as the spectator in the analogy is capable of judging which wrestler is the better. Africanus then rather ironically tells him that if he has any ability to write, his guide will certainly show him something to write about.

The first two lines of the following stanza are the last reference to Africanus in the poem; immediately after the narrator mentions the comfort he felt in his guide's taking him by the hand, he suddenly seems to be aware only of the great beauty of the scene before him:

> With that myn hand in his he tok anon.
> Of which I confort caughte, and wente in faste.
> But, Lord, so I was glad and wel begoon!
> For overal where that I myne eyen caste
> Were treës clad with leves that ay shal laste,
> Ech in his kynde, of colour fresh and greene
> As emeraude, that joye was to seene.
>
> (169–175)

The rich abundance of trees clad in leaves that shall last forever is the first description of the earthly garden that the narrator gives. The "fresh and greene/As emeraude . . .

leves that ay shal laste" suggests the quality of immortality
that was expressed in the words of the gold inscription,
"There grene and lusty May shal evere endure." It would
seem that the narrator is near, if not already in, "that
blysful place" mentioned in the first inscription. But since
the two inscriptions describe two extreme estates of love, the
one characterized by joy and fruitfulness, the other by pain
and sterility, it is also possible that there is between these
extremes a territory of love that the inscriptions do not
explicitly chart. This likelihood is borne out during the
narrator's progress through the park, when he describes
scenes that suggest the great variety of the estates of love on
earth rather than a simple opposition between fruitful and
fruitless love.

The single-stanza catalog of trees and their functions that
follows emphasizes the abundance and variety of nature,
and it prepares for the longer five-stanza catalog of birds
when the narrator returns to this particular locale within
the park. As a forest (*silva*), it also suggests the traditional
meaning of chaotic matter which requires the ordering
faculty of Nature.[11] The description of the "grene mede"
initiates a series of short scenes that are characterized by
subtle transitions rather than by sharp divisions. That this
segment of the poem (183–294) is based largely on Boccaccio's *Teseida* and partially on other works, including
the *Roman de la Rose*, is a well-known fact, despite several
differences between Boccaccio's scene and Chaucer's rendi-
tion. In Chaucer's poem, the emphasis in the description of
the "grene mede" is on the harmony of sounds within it:

> On every bow the bryddes herde I synge,
> With voys of aungel in here armonye;
>
> .   .   .   .
>
> Of instruments of strenges in acord
> Herde I so pleye a ravyshyng swetnesse,
> That God, that makere is of al and lord,

Ne herde nevere beter, as I gesse.
Therwith a wynd, unnethe it myghte be lesse,
Made in the leves grene a noyse softe
Acordaunt to the foules song alofte.
(190–91; 197–203)[12]

When the narrator returns to this place "that was so sote
and grene" (296), he will find Nature, the cause of its order
and harmony, presiding over the mating of the birds. Two
key words in the presentation of her activity in the world,
including her guidance of the birds, will be "ordre" and
"acord," and the joyous song in her honor that the birds
sing after having mated will parallel the birds' singing that
the narrator hears in this scene. As well as pointing ahead,
the lines in this scene direct attention back to the description
of the harmony of the spheres in the *Dream of Scipio*:

And after that the melodye herde he
That cometh of thilke speres thryes thre,
That welle is of musik and melodye
In this world here, and cause of armonye.
(60–63)

That the music in this earthly place has some correspondence
to the heavenly music is underscored by the poet's *comparatio*
that the birds sang with "voys of aungel" and by the suggestion that God himself never heard better harmony.
This correspondence, along with the repetition of the words
"blysful place" in an earthly context, suggest an analogy to
be made more explicit later in the poem.

After describing the perfection of the air, the wholesome-
ness of the herbs and grasses, and the quality of agelessness
that the place enjoys, the narrator comes to a well where he
sees the God of Love:

Under a tre, besyde a welle, I say
Cupide, oure lord, his arwes forge and file;
And at his fet his bowe al redy lay;

> And Wille, his doughter, temprede al this while
> The hevedes in the welle, and with hire file
> She touchede hem, after they shulde serve
> Some for to sle, and some to wounde and kerve.
>   (211–217)[13]

The narrator has here finally seen the powerful God of Love of whom he spoke in the opening stanzas of the poem. Based in part on the Ovidian figure who shoots two different kinds of arrows, this lord was popularly depicted in medieval love allegories as a handsome young prince rather than a blind, mischievous infant.[14] Perhaps, as J. A. W. Bennett remarks, there is no good reason to give any signification to this "Cupide, oure lord," other than the "traditional *l'amour du coeur*, the civilized courtly emotion."[15] Certainly he is later represented by the three "tersel egles" in the parliament scene and is therefore symbolic of a form of love that is acceptable to the goddess Nature. Moreover, in the immediately following series of courtly love figures that are based on the *Teseida*, the lord Cupid appears at the farthest remove from the Venus described inside the temple. That these positions follow Boccaccio's text does not make them meaningless, for Chaucer significantly altered his source material to suit his purpose, and the positions of Cupid and Venus in the source happen to fit that purpose.[16]

As the narrator continues, he sees "Plesaunce," "Aray," "Lust and Curteysie," "Craft," "Delyt, that stod with Gentilesse," "Beute, withouten any styr," "Youthe," "Foolhardynesse, Flaterye, and Desyr,/Messagerye, and Meede." It is important to note the mixed nature of this series. They are traditional courtly love personifications, representing the pleasure, the physical and social aesthetics, and some of the less noble elements of such loving. The worst of them are not in the same class as "Disdayn and Daunger," and the best of them, for all their social worth, are not directly related in any way to procreative love. They cannot, therefore, be aligned with either of the inscriptions, though courtly behavior in love will have a place in the climactic scene of the poem.

The narrator then comes to "a temple of bras." The transition to this temple, whose description will occupy the next nine stanzas, is smooth and unobtrusive. But it is in this scene that Chaucer most significantly alters his source by the addition of details and the transposition of Boccaccio's descriptions of the figures within the temple.[17] The narrator sees "Dame Pees" sitting before the temple, and by her side "Dame Pacience" sitting upon a "hil of sond," which contrasts with the "hil of floures" upon which Nature sits in the subsequent scene, and implies not only the unstable and shifting circumstances that the lover must endure with patience (a patience that is sometimes never rewarded) according to the code of courtly love, but also suggests the sterility implicit in the black inscription. The suggestion of sterility, highlighted later by the contrast with Nature's "hil of floures," subtly indicates the character of the temple, which represents excessive sensuality and fruitlessness. The dominant sound within the temple is that of "sykes hoote as fyr" (perhaps to be contrasted with the harmonious music in the "grene mede"), which fan the flames burning on the altars. The narrator then sees the cause of all the sorrowful sighs, "the bittere goddesse Jelosye." This personification, who is not called a goddess in the *Teseida*, is one of the great obstacles to successful courtly love, along with "Daunger" and "Disdayn." The figure of the "god Priapus" comes next. In this instance Chaucer has transposed the stanzas of the *Teseida* so that Priapus appears immediately before the appearance of Venus; the intervening stanzas in which Boccaccio had described the broken bows of Diana hanging on the wall and the murals depicting the stories of famous lovers are shifted by Chaucer to a position immediately following the description of Venus. The figure of Venus in the *Parlement* is thus preceded by "Jelosye" and Priapus, and is followed by trophies of chastity overcome and stories of unfortunate lovers.

With regard to the figure of Priapus, Chaucer has made some important alterations:

> The god Priapus saw I, as I wente,
> Withinne the temple in sovereyn place stonde,
> In swich aray as whan the asse hym shente
> With cri by nighte, and with hys sceptre in honde.
> Ful besyly men gonne assaye and fonde
> Upon his hed to sette, of sondry hewe
> Garlondes ful of freshe floures newe.
>
> (253-259)

Chaucer's direct reference to the story in Ovid's *Fasti* of Priapus' thwarted attempt to make love to the nymph Lotis clearly marks the temple as a place of sexual frustration. Moreover, just as "Jelosye" was made a goddess, Priapus is assigned a "sovereyn place" in the temple. Neither attribution will be assigned to Venus, who is not called a goddess and who occupies "a prive corner" in the temple. Unlike the personified prayer of Palemone in the *Teseida*, who simply notices the presence of Priapus on her way to Venus, the narrator stops to watch a scene in which the votaries of the phallic but frustrated god bedeck him with flowers—perhaps because he is also traditionally the "god of gardyns."[18]

As the narrator proceeds, he finds, "in a prive corner in disport," Venus attended by "hire porter Richesse." The place is dark, but after a while he sees Venus reclining on a bed of gold:

> Hyre gilte heres with a golden thred
> Ibounden were, untressed as she lay,
> And naked from the brest unto the hed
> Men myghte hire sen; and, sothly for to say,

> The remenaunt was wel kevered to my pay,
> Ryght with a subtyl coverchef of Valence—
> Ther nas no thikkere cloth of no defense.
>
> (267–273)[19]

This languid Venus, titillatingly covered with only a small bit of thin cloth, who lies in an atmosphere of "a thousand savours sote," is attended on either side by Bacchus and Ceres, symbolizing two other desires of the flesh that lead to the sexual act.[20] On their knees before Venus are two young people (not in the *Teseida*) beseeching her help, who will very possibly end up as did those lovers whose stories are depicted on the wall. With the comment, "But thus I let hire lye," the narrator continues his walk. This comment, along with the ironic statement that Venus was partially covered to the narrator's satisfaction, "The remenaunt was wel kevered to my pay," strongly suggest that the narrator has not been impressed either with Venus herself, the transparency of her garment, or with her artificial, voluptuous surroundings. He continues walking through the temple, noting that many a broken bow is hung upon the wall "in dispit of Dyane the chaste" and that the stories of famous lovers "and in what plyt they dyde" are depicted on the wall. That Chaucer augmented the list in Boccaccio with the names of additional lovers reinforces the impression that the temple, which accords the highest status to "Jelosye" and Priapus and sets Venus in a dark corner, is a place of thwarted, painful, and ultimately destructive love.[21]

The Venus inside the temple is not the goddess that the poet invoked earlier. The details of Chaucer's presentation of her indicate that she is to be identified with the Venus who stands for excessive sensuality, with Venus-Luxuria, goddess of enticement and lasciviousness. However, Cytherea, the planet Venus, is always identified in Chaucer as the goddess of legitimate love, a love that functions in accordance with the love that binds together the entire universe in harmony. This Venus is also identified with marriage, as in a passage from *Troilus and Criseyde*:

> "O Love, O Charite!
> Thi moder ek, Citherea the swete,
> After thiself next heried be she,
> Venus mene I, the wel-willy planete!
> And next that, Imeneus, I the grete."
> (III.1254–1258)[22]

These words, which Troilus speaks in joy at having his Criseyde in his arms, are followed by Chaucer's translation of Dante's hymn in the *Paradiso*, "Benigne Love, thow holy bond of thynges."[23] Troilus' praise follows a strict order. First he speaks of heavenly love (*caritas*), then of Venus, the well-willing planet, and finally of Hymen, the patron of marriage.[24] Venus-Cytherea in Chaucer, therefore, has the best of credentials and can be associated, in the context of the Natura tradition, with the Venus who was Natura's faithful subvicar in Alan's *De planctu naturae*. By the same token, the Venus in the temple can be associated with the adulterous Venus who betrayed Hymen with Antigamus. When Chaucer invokes Cytherea, he has in mind the Venus who serves the chain of love, who, as the celestial aspect of Venus in Alan, serves directly under Natura *pronuba et procreatrix*. This definition might well explain why Chaucer placed the God of Love as far as possible from Venus in the temple. Chaucer's description of this Venus figure conforms to the picture of the evil Venus of medieval mythographic tradition and associates her with the Venus of the *Roman de la Rose*, whose son descends from the perverted Cupid that Alan names Mirth. But Cupid is also the legitimate son of Venus and Hymen in *De planctu naturae*. It is possible that Chaucer's careful placement of his Cupid figure away from the Venus of the temple and his acceptance of the courtly ceremony of love (which Cupid often symbolized) in the Nature scene of his poem reflects this double tradition, even though the moral significance of Cupid seems deliberately ambiguous when compared with Chaucer's use of the double Venus tradition.[25] Recognition of this distinction between Cytherea and the Venus in the temple is absolutely necessary if one is to understand Chaucer's poem.

The most sudden and dramatic transition in the narrator's progress through the park occurs between the stanza in which he lists the names of the lovers on the temple wall and the next stanza:

> Whan I was come ayeyn into the place
> That I of spak, that was so sote and grene.
>
> (295–296)

He is back in the place that had delighted him when he first entered the park, a world of green and light. The contrast between the temple and this place is skillfully heightened by the juxtaposition of the words "sote and grene" with the last words of the previous stanza, "in what plyt they dyde." The narrator, who walks forth in this place to console himself, comes upon a scene in which there sits a queen more beautiful than any other creature he has ever seen, just as the summer sunshine surpasses that of any star:

> And in a launde, upon an hil of floures,
> Was set this noble goddesse Nature.
> Of braunches were here halles and here boures
> Iwrought after here cast and here mesure;
> Ne there nas foul that cometh of engendrure
> That they ne were prest in here presence
> To take hire dom and yeve hire audyence.
>
> (302–308)

Abundant life announces the *domus Naturae*, with the goddess herself "upon an hil of floures," just as "Dame Pacience" atop her "hil of sond" announces the sterility and instability that characterize the scene in the temple. The words "engendrure" and "mesure" and the great number of birds

that press about their goddess announce the themes of procreation, plenitude, and moderation:

> For this was on Seynt Valentynes day,
> Whan every foul cometh there to chese his make,
> Of every kynde that men thynke may,
> And that so huge a noyse gan they make
> That erthe, and eyr, and tre, and every lake
> So ful was, that unethe was there space
> For me to stonde, so ful was al the place.
>
> (309–315)

So great is the plenitude of creation over which Nature
presides ("so ful" appears twice in as many lines), that there
is scarcely room for the narrator to stand.

In the next stanza, the narrator, who is a habitual reader,
refers to Alan's *De planctu naturae*, a book in which one might
find a description of this noble goddess:

> And right as Aleyn, in the Pleynt of Kynde,
> Devyseth Nature of aray and face,
> In swich aray men myghte hire there fynde.
> This noble emperesse, ful of grace,
> Bad every foul to take his owne place.
> As they were woned alwey fro yer to yeere,
> Seynt Valentynes day, to stonden theere.
>
> (316–322)

The description of Natura in Alan's poem was basically a
descriptio per vestimentum of the goddess' domain as
vicaria Dei: the heavens were symbolized by her crown, the
animal world and man were depicted on her vestments, and
the vegetable kingdom was pictured on her shoes. While
reference to this passage enabled Chaucer to identify his
figure with that of Alan, he also stood to gain advantages by
not repeating the description outright. Like Jean de Meun,
Chaucer may well have been impatient with the kind of
lengthy rhetorical descriptio that characterized medieval
Latin allegory, and he therefore chose not to suspend the

action in order to include a description that would interrupt the flow of the poem. Also, it would seem reasonable to expect that the more learned individuals in his audience were familiar with the work or with the traditional depiction of Natura that originated in it. More significant is the fact that Natura's description in Alan's poem focused on the rip in her tunic, which represented mankind's failure to abide by her law. This detail, important to Alan's theme, would have been inappropriate to Chaucer's work, which is a study of man's eagerness—not without its own problems—to follow Nature's decree rather than of his reluctance to behave according to her law.

The plenitude and variety of creatures over which Nature presides is then demonstrated by a social classification of the birds and by a catalog of avian species. Representative of the various estates of human society and temperament, this section of the poem (323–364) not only stresses the wondrous variety and fullness of the human race, but also indicates the wide spectrum of human behavior over which Nature watches and anticipates the problem that is to arise in the parliament scene as a result of such great variety, where it is demonstrated that human, or avian, behavior needs to be controlled and kept in check by Nature lest it turn Nature's purpose into a chaotic, confusing situation.[26] This earthly confusion is certainly one of the reasons that Chaucer is careful to characterize Nature in this part of the poem as a force operating in the service of harmony. Soon after her appearance, one learns that the birds have come to mate "By hire acord" (371), which after all the arguments have ended will indeed be the result. Nature, however, is not depicted simply as a force for harmony in the microcosm, because her activity is necessary in the macrocosm as well:

> Nature, the vicaire of the almyghty Lord,
> That hot, cold, hevy, lyght, moyst, and dreye

> Hath knyt by evene noumbres of acord,
> In esy voys began to speke and seye,
> "Foules, tak hed of my sentence, I preye,
> And for youre ese, in fortheryng of youre nede,
> As faste as I may spak, I wol me speede.

$$(379\text{-}385)^{27}$$

"The vicaire of the almyghty Lord," a designation that Chaucer could have gotten from either Jean or Alan or from both rules the macrocosm as well as the microcosm. Not only does Nature knit the elements together "by evene noumbres of acord," but she also gives the birds their mates "By evene acord" (668) when they pay heed to her "sentence," which is intended to give them "ese" (ease and delight) and to assist them in their biological need.

The four stanzas that follow contain the conditions which Nature expects her birds to observe on this traditional day of mating. Her "sentence" is of great significance to the meaning of the poem and to an understanding of the place of Chaucer's Nature in the goddess Natura tradition. As Nature says, the birds have come, "By my statut and thorgh my governaunce," to choose their mates, "as I prike yow with pleasaunce." She is speaking here as pro-creatrix as well as pronuba, for she acknowledges that their instinct to mate is governed by her law, and she candidly refers to the pleasure with which she spurs them to the occasion. Because their mating precedes procreation, how-ever, she insists that they observe the order of social de-corum, and therefore the "tersel egle," he who is most worthy, will begin. After him, the rest will follow according to rank and kind. Then in the next stanza she states her last and perhaps most important condition:

> "But natheles, in this condicioun
> Mot be the choys of everich that is heere,
> That she agre to his eleccioun,
> Whoso he be that shulde be hire feere.

> This is oure usage alwey, fro yer to yeere,
> And whoso may at this tyme have his grace,
> In blisful time he cam into this place."
>
> (407–413)

In this extremely important passage, Chaucer has restored to Nature the function of pronuba that Jean de Meun had omitted from his figure. Chaucer's Nature directs sexual love in the way prescribed by her predecessor in the work of Alan. Procreation, which ensures continuity and plenitude, takes place within the marital state.[28]

In addition to its clarification of Chaucer's view of Nature as pronuba as well as procreatrix, this stanza includes a statement that completes the poet's presentation of his philosophy of love. As already suggested, there is in the garden of earthly love a kind of "blisful place" that is analogous to the "blisful place" in heaven which rewards those who serve the "commune profyt" in the *Dream of Scipio*. Natura's statement, "And whoso may at this tyme have his grace,/In blisful tyme he cam into this place," relates directly to the kind of love represented by "Cytherea, thow blysful lady swete," for those birds who successfully court their ladies in this place have won for themselves earthly bliss. It was Cytherea, the goddess of legitimate love, who had inspired the narrator's dream, and he now has seen and heard the goddess whom the celestial Venus serves. Obedience to the decrees of Nature pronuba et procreatrix, who is the vicaria Dei, brings happiness and fruitfulness. Although the goddess accepts almost as many forms of courtship as there are birds in her kingdom, those who seek sensuality for its own sake have been relegated to the temple and are excluded from the "grene mede," just as "likerous folk" were excluded from heaven in the *Dream of Scipio*. The domus Naturae, then, is that "blisful place" on earth where one may find felicity by following her decrees, and if the great multitude of birds pressing around her is an indication, most of her creatures wish to find their earthly bliss through taking their mates "by hire acord."

These conditions laid down by Nature complete the statement of the poet's doctrine of love, but the attempt by Nature's creatures, in all their variety, to put that doctrine into practice is quite another matter. From the very beginning of the courting, with the competition of the three tersels for the hand of the formel, difficulties arise that the birds' parliament fails to solve. It is Nature, the principle of order and harmony in the world, who will finally resolve the conflict that leads the birds to the brink of chaos when they are left to their own devices. In this section of the poem the sterile and destructive perversion of love that was warned against in the black inscription and symbolized by the temple is no longer a significant issue. That the tersels plight their troth in courtly language and according to the manners of court is appropriate to their class and does not mean that they are practitioners of the illicit, adulterous love described by Andreas Capellanus. To be sure, their courtliness will confuse the formel, but that confusion is as much a result of her own inexperience as it is of the mode of the tersels' courtship. If the tersels were in fact "courtly lovers," they would not be in this place where marriages are made and where they have to speak of their love in full view of the lower classes. The issue of this climactic scene of the poem is that the cause of "commune spede" with which the birds hope to resolve their difficulty can be achieved only through submission to the judgment of Nature, which will in fact lead to a happy conclusion of the poem.

The birds' attempt to practice Nature's doctrine of love begins in the competition of the three tersels for the formel. The first and worthiest, the royal tersel, argues that since he loves her better than anyone else does, she ought to be his "thourgh hire mercy" (437), even though she may have not promised her love to him. The young and inexperienced formel blushes at this protestation of love and is unable to make any reply. As soon as she is reassured by Nature, "Doughter, drede yow nought, I yow assure" (448), another tersel of lower rank enters the plea that since he has loved her longer than anyone else, he deserves her love. Then the third tersel announces that, although the other birds are getting impatient, he must nevertheless take the time to make his plea, for if he does not, he "mot for sorwe deye" (469). He reveals that length of service means nothing to him and that since he is "hire treweste man" (479), he should have her love. The argument, which has taken up most of the day, is at a stalemate, and the other birds, no longer able to contain themselves, break out with exclamations of their impatience and disapproval: "Have don, and lat us wende!" (492).

It has been argued that the three eagles show little concern for "commune profyt."[29] Against this allegation, there is little defense for the tersels, except that the other birds' concept of "commune profyt" is equally motivated by selfish concerns. The cuckoo, who represents the worm fowl, first explains that he is moved to speak for the cause of "commune spede" (507), but when he speaks again in the parliament, he reveals a position that runs counter to Nature's purpose: "Lat ech of hem be soleyn al here lyve!" (607). As long as he can have his mate, he does not care whether or not the others marry and procreate. The proposals of the other birds of the lower classes are equally beside the point. The practical goose says simply, "But she wol love hym, lat hym love another" (566); the best the duck can do is to say, "There been mo sterres, God wot, than a payre!" (595); and the turtle, speaking for the lowest social class, expresses a view that is more relevant to fin amour than anything the three tersels have said:

> Though that his lady everemore be straunge,
> Yit lat hym serve hire ever, til he be ded.
>
> (584–585)

Not one of these statements offers a real solution to the problem of getting a mate for the formel, and in fact they contribute to greater chaos, for they provoke the scornful derision of the other noble birds. Clearly, none of Nature's creatures has the answer to any kind of "profyt" except his own, and the comedy of the scene is owing to this failure of all of them and is not exclusively owing to the *demande* involving the three tersels.[30] That the noble birds are not the only culpable party is shown by the solution offered by the "tercelet of the faucoun," which is identical with that of Nature. He suggests that the formel choose the suitor who is:

> the worthieste
> Of knyghthod, and lengest had used it,
> Most of estat, of blod the gentilleste.
>
> (548–550)

This suggestion shows that the nobles are capable of good judgment. That the tercelet's solution is not accepted by the other birds when it is proposed by him is owing to the fact that he does not speak with the same authority that Nature commands.

Having seen that the birds cannot settle the question of whom the formel should accept, Nature finally intercedes so that the issue can be settled and the other birds may finally choose their mates. Nature states:

> That she hireself shal han hir eleccioun
> Of whom hire lest.
>
> (621–622)

In order that the formel might make the right choice, she offers her some advice:

> "But as for conseyl for to chese a make,
> If I were Resoun, certes, thanne wolde I
> Conseyle yow the royal tercel take,
> As seyde the tercelet ful skylfully,
> As for the gentilleste and most worthi,
> Which I have wrought so wel to my plesaunce,
> That to yow hit oughte to been a suffisaunce."
>
> (631–637)

The fact that the formel does not take this advice and asks for a year to think the matter over does not mean that Nature is not in control of the situation. This assumption stems from the idea that Chaucer, like Jean de Meun, separated reason and nature.[31] That the emotion of love is indeed irrational in her creatures has been amply demonstrated both to Nature and to the audience of the poem. So when Nature says, "If I were Resoun," she does not mean that she herself is devoid of reason but that, as F. N. Robinson suggests, if she were the same kind of counselor as Reason had been in other allegorical works, she would give this advice to the formel.[32] She can do no more than offer a bit of guidance, for according to her own condition, the choice must be left entirely to the formel. When the formel asks for a year's respite to make her decision, Nature willingly grants the request. That the inexperienced formel has in fact been confused by the situation is patently clear in her final statement:

> "I wol nat serve Venus ne Cupide,
> Forsothe as yit, by no manere weye."
>
> (652–653)

This refusal is as irrelevant to the issue as the statements of all the other birds save the tercelet's, for no one had asked her to serve Venus or her son. Rather, she has misunderstood the courtly ceremoniousness of the three tersels' suits as meaning that kind of service. Since she does not yet understand, she is allowed by Nature to take another year before mating, presumably in the hope that she will mature sufficiently to be equal to the occasion in the following year. After encouraging the three tersels to "Beth of good herte" and to continue their service, for "A yer is nat so longe to endure," Nature gives mates to every other bird "By evene acord." The cause of "commune spede" has thus been served by Nature's intercession and by the birds' acceptance of her judgment. The narrator's dream finally ends with the singing of a "roundel" by the happy birds in honor of the goddess who has brought them out of chaos into a harmonious acceptance of and active participation in her law, which assures the triumph of life over the darkness of death. The form of the "roundel" itself affirms the harmony of this closing scene:

> Now welcome, somer, with thy sonne softe,
> That hast this wintres wedres overshake,
> And driven away the longe nyghtes blake!
> (680–682)

Throughout this interpretation of the *Parlement*, a direct relationship has been implied between the *Dream of Scipio* and that of the narrator. The correspondence between the dreams, each describing a "blysful place" and explaining the way a man might make his way into it, leads to a unified reading of Chaucer's poem. Frequently, the apparent opposition of heavenly and earthly love in the two dreams has led critics to express the view that the juxtaposition of the two dreams is ironic, that the irrelevance of Scipio's dream to the narrator's dream is an expression of Chaucer's dissatisfaction with the conventions of the love vision, and that the figure of Nature—who has been taken here to be the unifying factor in the poem—offers no solution to the conflict between a philosophy that excluded love and another that included "erotic sensuality."[33] The messages of the two dreams are not, however, irreconcilable; rather they are meaningfully analogous. Africanus, who guided both Scipio and the narrator, promised to supply the narrator with a subject to write about: "I shal the shewe mater of to wryte." Both dreams teach lessons about how to achieve felicity, the one concentrating on salvation through service to "commune profyt," the other concentrating on the achievement of earthly bliss in marriage through obedience to Nature.[34] The concern in the parliament scene for the cause of "commune spede" and its ultimate realization through Nature strengthens the analogy. So, too, is the distinction between Venus-Cytherea in the invocation and Venus-Luxuria in the temple central to an interpretation of the poem, for the love with which the poet is primarily concerned is an integral part, though not the most exalted manifestation, of "the faire cheyne of love."

The figure of Nature, "vicaire of the almyghty Lord," is seen through the eyes of the narrator as pronuba et procreatrix, just as she had appeared in Alan's *De planctu naturae*. Though this aspect is traditional in the Natura allegories, it is not a limitation on her characterization, for in Alan the goddess descends from the heavens when duty calls her to attempt to set the sublunary world right, and in both Alan and Jean, Natura is described as presiding over the entire created universe. The goddess Natura, in short, should not be equated with the sublunary world, which is a part, indeed the most troublesome part, of her domain as vicaria Dei. Thus, the view of her given by Chaucer's narrator as pronuba et procreatrix presiding over the mating of birds on Saint Valentine's Day should not restrict one's comprehension of her kingdom. The celestial harmony that Scipio heard in his dream is also in her kingdom. Just beyond those heavens is "the blysful place" that Africanus spoke of, which is eternal. The "blysful place" on earth, symbolized by the "grene mede" that is the home of Nature as well as the earthly reward of those who follow her decrees for the orderly perpetuation of the mutable world below the moon, is a positive though inferior part of her orderly kingdom, which strives to emulate the eternity that gave it being.

APPENDIX
A Summary of Bernard Silvestris'
De mundi universitate

The work is divided into two parts, "Megacosmos" and "Microcosmos," the second of which is considerably longer. These are preceded by a dedication to Thierry of Chartres and a *breviarium* giving a general account of what is to follow. The first book opens with a meter in which Natura makes an entreaty to Noys, who is explicitly identified as God's providence. Tearfully complaining of the confused state of matter (*hyle* and *silva* are used interchangeably), Natura beseeches the wise Noys to refine it into a more beautiful world. She argues forcefully that the chaotic and rude state of matter needs the order of number and of the chain of music which Noys can give it, for matter is "neque pax neque amor nec lex nec cognitus ordo."

In the prose section that follows, Noys readily assents to Natura's petition and begins to fashion matter into an ordered universe. She separates the four elements, informs matter with copies of the divine ideas, and generates the world-soul.[1] Noys' relation to Natura is graphically represented by her opening words, in which she addresses the other goddess as "natura, uteri mei beata fecunditas."

Natura is below her. Noys proceeds to explain her relation to that which is above her. Generated by God, she is his eternal and divine reason; she is not in time. In her are situated the eternal ideas and the intelligible world; the destiny of all God's creation is mirrored in her. Because she is the intellect of the supreme God, born of his divinity, she cannot be separated from the nature and substance of God. Such is the character of Noys, the major character of the work and the chief artificer of the cosmos, whom Natura often addresses as Minerva.

Bernard interrupts the metaphysical aspect of his cosmogony narrative with a poetic interlude of 480 hexameters in which to celebrate the sensible and visible universe that has been created. The heavens, stars, planets, signs of the zodiac, and angelic hierarchy, all fill the upper universe. Noys views the preordained succession of the ages. She sees a parade of heroes, mostly from classical culture and literature, though the list ends with the Virgin and Pope Eugenius III (under whose pontificate Bernard wrote the work). The earth is situated in the middle of creation, and Bernard rapidly runs through its mountains, rivers, animals, birds, and plants. It is teeming with life.

The next prose section returns to the metaphysics of the Creation. Here Bernard explains the order, harmony, and goodness of the universe. The universe is a living animal, just as in Plato's *Timaeus*, for it is animated by the world-soul, which Bernard calls Endelechia,[2] the immediate life-giving source of the sensible world. Endelechia fills the earth with living things and holds all together in indissoluble bonds.

The emanative process described thus far proceeds from Deus, the one, to Noys, his divine and eternal mind, to Endelechia, the world-soul, who animates the universe. But there are two more stages in the process of fashioning the world from matter, those of Natura and Imarmene, whose roles are explained at the conclusion of the first book.

Imarmene is a Greek term roughly equivalent to the Latin *fatum,* and it is used by Bernard to name the law that regulates the order of succession of corporeal things in time.[3] The position of Natura stands between Endelechia and Imarmene. Natura produces the bodies that will house the souls provided by Endelechia. To Imarmene belongs the responsibility of their continuation in time. Weaving and reweaving all that the universe holds, Imarmene provides for the continuation of things, while Natura as artifex brings them to corporeal life by providing bodies for the souls.

The second book, "Microcosmos," concentrates on the making of man, the climax of the entire creative process since he reflects the whole of the created world. In the first prose and verse sections of the book, Noys rejoices over the newly made world and asks Natura to look over her handiwork. But this beautiful world, molded out of the ancient confusion of matter, though it is full of life, is still incomplete. Its creation must be consummated with the birth of man.

Noys charges Natura with this task and bids her seek out Urania, who is situated in the uppermost sphere of heaven, and Physis, who inhabits a lower place. Natura journeys upward through the heavens until she finally reaches the aplanes, the outermost and uppermost circle of the heavens, which is composed of ether, the fifth and most perfect element. At this traditional outer limit of the created universe, before meeting Urania, Natura encounters the figure Pantomorphos, also identified as "oyarses" and "genius."[4] He assigns forms to the lower world according to the heavenly pattern, but also so that each form will be different, for though individuals are alike in being of the same kind, they all differ circumstantially in the time and place of their birth.

When Natura finally reaches the seat of Urania, she finds that her arrival has been expected. After greeting Natura, Urania reveals that she knows why Natura has come and that she is prepared to do her part. She will bring man's soul with them as they descend to earth so that it may become wise with knowledge of the ineluctable laws of fate and the variability of fortune, for the soul will one day have to return to the heavens from whence it came.[5] Urania bids Natura lead them on the journey, but before they begin their descent, they ascend to the mansion of light, the holy place that is the temple of the highest God—if one can believe the arguments of the philosophers, Bernard editorializes. There they come before the infinite and eternal light of the supreme divinity, Tugaton (*to agathon*, "the good"). This light, in one of the few direct references to Christian doctrine in the work, is triple-shafted: out of its divine splendor flows a second ray of light, and out of these two a third. The two goddesses pray for success to the majestic light.

Their prayers to the Trinity finished, Natura and Urania begin their descent to earth. On their way, they pass all the heavenly bodies, and each is fully described. The descriptions of Mercury and Venus are of particular interest. In the sphere of Mercury, they find Cyllenius (who is not specifically identified as Mercury himself), occupied with forming hermaphrodites. The neighboring planet Venus is described as the power that influences man's desire for pleasure (*voluptas*). She looks upon the two travelers with a face that is full of light and grace, and at her left breast hangs the infant Cupid ("Sinistro super ab ubere Cupido parvulus dependebat"). It is noteworthy of the unstable character of the lower universe that these two planets are sexually active, for the next sphere is that of the Moon, the traditional dividing line of the upper and lower worlds, of ether and air, stability and mutability. Just above the Moon are the Elysian Fields, inhabited by happy spirits; just below it is the turbulent and changeable sphere of Earth.

Weary from their long journey, the two goddesses stop at the Moon to rest, and Urania avails herself of this brief respite to lecture Natura on the heavens. In this prose section, Urania points out that this place is the middle of the golden chain, the navel of the upper and lower worlds. She then explains that heaven is full of life, since it is full of God ("Caelum ipsum Deo plenum est"). The fiery stars are themselves animals ("Sua caelo animalia, ignes siderei"). Below the stars and above man, in whom both worlds meet, are the angels, sharing with the stars the divine attribute of immortality and with man the propensity to be excited by the passions. Between the Sun and the Moon are benevolent angels who provide a medium between God and man. Below the Moon dwell a variety of spirits; some have an affinity for the neighboring ether and live quiet, serene lives, while others oversee the lives of individual men, having been assigned to them at birth (identified as genii, these are tutelary spirits and should not be confused with the "oyarses/ genius" situated in the aplanes). Urania explains that nearer the earth's atmosphere are other spirits assigned by God to torment the evil. These have the power to assume corporeal or ghostly shapes and are identified as fallen angels ("angelos desertores"). Still lower are the "Silvani, Panes et Nerei" who inhabit the earth's mountains, forests, and streams. They are quite harmless, and though long-lived because of being composed of the elements in a pure state, they too in time will pass away.

At last, Natura and Urania arrive at the home of Physis and her two daughters. Named Granusion, the home is a secret garden that basks in the rays of the youthful sun. It is a kind of paradise, having a lovely forest, a murmuring river, a variety of grasses and herbs, and a perpetually pleasant climate, which are the most salient features of the *locus amoenus*. It is the only place of its kind on earth. Though she has not yet seen Natura, Physis senses her approach ("Quippe matrem generationis Naturam praesenserat adventare"). Sharing Physis' presentiment, the living things of the garden respond to the approach of Natura, but Physis remains in a state of deep contemplation, studying the origins, potencies, and properties of all natural things. As she meditates on the divine principles of genera and species, on the various characteristics of animals and the medicinal qualities of herbs, she anticipates, as if in a dream, the imminence of the creation of man. Awakened from her reverie by the reflection of Urania's face in the garden well, Physis and her daughters, Theory and Practice, joyfully greet the two goddesses. Then Noys suddenly appears among them.[6]

Noys' purpose in appearing at this point is twofold. First, she explains the nature of the man that is to be fashioned, and second, she gives the goddesses their final instructions. Man will be a world himself, an image of the greater world. His soul is from heaven, his body from the earth; and though his body lives on earth, his soul will be capable of reaching heaven. This union of the heavenly and earthly in man is necessary because he is to live for a double purpose, to serve the world with his prudence and the gods with his religion or piety. As for his concerns on earth, Noys will make him knowledgeable in the ways of the things of the earth. Natura will hide nothing from his understanding. He will understand the causes of all things, the breadth of the land, the depth of the sea, the seasons, earthquakes, storms at sea, and why the days are longer in summer. What is more, Noys will make him primate and pontifex over all things of the earth. The land will provide him with fruit, the sea with fish, his flocks will graze on the mountains, the forests will supply him with wild animals. He shall rule the earth, Noys concludes in this eloquent meter.

Ready to begin their work, the three goddesses receive final instructions from Noys. The composition of the soul out of Endelechia and the building up of its virtues is the responsibility of Urania. The preparation of the body out of matter is Physis' task. And the joining of soul to body in emulation of the celestial order is Natura's duty. Noys then gives the *speculum providentiae* to Urania, the *tabula fati* to Natura, and the *liber recordationis* to Physis.

These three textbooks are to guide the goddesses in their labors. The description of each book supplies an account of each goddess' responsibility in the act that is about to take place. The speculum providentiae reflects the divine mind, the eternal ideas in it, the copies of those ideas, and the heavens. In the world of ideas Urania finds the outlines for the divine image of man ("imaginarium hominis imaginem certis indiciis inveniret"). Natura's tabula fati represents the ways in which the movements of the celestial bodies dispense the will of providence in the material world. Bernard carefully distinguishes between the functions of these two texts, for both share the image of the heavens. The cause of change in the world of time is relegated to the care of the three sister fates—Atropos, Clotho, and Lachesis—who are the fatal administrators of providence in the created world. The tabula fati is the succession of fatal decrees that manage the destiny of all things existing in space and time, in the world of becoming and change. Since the world's comings and goings—its destiny—are ruled by the heavenly motions, Natura, the mater generationis, carefully seeks out in the tabula fati its concealed humanity, for the entire history and condition of mankind are written there, from the Golden Age to the Iron. The liber recordationis, which Noys gives to Physis, is a book of memory in which are recorded observations on natural history, as on the behavior of the animal and plant kingdoms, or on whatever comes into being through generation or loses its being, destroyed by corruption ("Illic quicquid vel ingressus ad substantiam generatio prohevit, vel egressus a substantia destruit corruptela"). Out of this great record of natural things, Physis seizes the glimmering form of mankind, which is subtly inscribed on its final page.

Having prepared the goddesses for their work, Noys encourages them to begin. The actual shaping of man's body out of what was left of the four elements after the ordering of the macrocosm then takes place. He is supplied with the four complexions out of the four elements, and his body is arranged in three major parts: head, breast, and loins. Finally, after he is given his five senses, man is complete. The *De mundi universitate* concludes with a series of verse sections in which each of the five senses is celebrated. The sexual organs, especially, are frankly praised for their function in perpetuating the race. When the time, place, and manner are suitable, their use will be both delightful and proper. They fight against death and restore nature. That which is subject to death will not die, the transitory will not disappear, and man will not wither away.

BIBLIOGRAPHY, NOTES,
AND INDEX

ABBREVIATIONS

AHDLMA	Archives d'histoire doctrinale et littéraire du moyen âge
AnM	Annuale Mediaevale
CE	College English
ChauR	The Chaucer Review
CL	Comparative Literature
ClPh	Classical Philology
EHR	English Historical Review
ELH	Journal of English Literary History
GCFI	Giornale critico della filosofia italiana
JEGP	Journal of English and Germanic Philology
JHI	Journal of the History of Ideas
JTS	Journal of Theological Studies
MAE	Medium Aevum
MKNAL	Mededelingen der Koninklijke Nederlandse Akademie, Afdeling Letterkunde
MLN	Modern Language Notes
MP	Modern Philology
MRS	Mediaeval and Renaissance Studies
MS	Mediaeval Studies
PhR	Philosophical Review
PMLA	Publications of the Modern Language Association of America
PQ	Philological Quarterly
RCSF	Rivista critica di storia della filosofia
RDM	Revue des deux mondes
RES	Review of English Studies
RPh	Romance Philology
RR	Romanic Review
RS	Research Studies
SATF	Société des anciens textes français
SMed	Studi medievali
UCPES	University of California Publications in English Studies
ZRP	Zeitschrift für romanische Philologie

BIBLIOGRAPHY

PRIMARY SOURCES

Alan of Lille. *Anticlaudianus.* Ed. Robert Bossuat. Paris: Librairie Philosophique J. Vrin, 1955.
————. *De planctu naturae.* Ed. Thomas Wright. *The Anglo-Latin Satirical Poets and Epigrammatists,* vol. II. Rerum Britannicarum Medii Aevi, Rolls Series, 59. Wiesbaden: Kraus Reprint, 1964.
————. *Liber poenitentialis.* Ed. Jean Longère. 2 vols. Analecta mediaevalia Namurcensia, vols. 17 and 18. Louvain and Lille: Nauwelaerts, 1965.
————. *Textes inédits.* Ed. Marie-Thérèse d'Alverny. Paris: Librairie Philosophique J. Vrin, 1965.
Ambrose, Saint. *Hexaemeron.* Ed. J. P. Migne. *Patrologia Latina,* XIV, 131–288. Paris, 1866.
Apuleius. *The Golden Ass.* Trans. William Aldington, rev. Stephen Gaselee. Loeb Classical Library. Cambridge, Mass.: Harvard University Press, 1935.
Aristotle. *De caelo.* Trans. W. K. C. Guthrie. Loeb Classical Library. Cambridge, Mass.: Harvard University Press, 1939.
————. *The Complete Works of Aristotle.* Ed. W. D. Ross. 11 vols. Oxford: The Clarendon Press, 1926–1952.

———— (pseud.). *De mundo.* Trans. D. J. Furley. Loeb Classical Library. Cambridge, Mass.: Harvard University Press, 1955.

————. *Physics.* Trans. Philip H. Wicksteed and Frances M. Cornford. 2 vols. Loeb Classical Library. Cambridge, Mass.: Harvard University Press, 1929.

Bernardus Silvestris. *Commentum super sex libros Eneidos Virgilii.* Ed. Wilhelm Riedel. Greifswald: J. Abel, 1923.

————. *De mundi universitate.* Ed. Carl Sigmund Barach and Johann Wrobel. Frankfurt: Minerva, 1964 (first published 1876).

Boethius. *Tractates and The Consolation of Philosophy.* Trans. H. F. Stewart and E. K. Rand. Loeb Classical Library. Cambridge, Mass.: Harvard University Press, 1962.

Chalcidius. *Timaeus: A Calcidio translatus commentarioque instructus.* Ed. J. H. Waszink. *Plato Latinus: Corpus Platonicum Medii Aevi,* ed. Raymond Klibansky, vol. IV. London and Leiden: The Warburg Institute and E. J. Brill, 1962.

Chaucer, Geoffrey. *The Works of Geoffrey Chaucer.* Ed. F. N. Robinson. 2nd ed. Boston: Houghton Mifflin, 1957.

Cicero. *De finibus.* Trans. Harris Rackham. Loeb Classical Library. Cambridge, Mass.: Harvard University Press, 1951.

————. *De inventione.* Trans. H. M. Hubbell. Loeb Classical Library. Cambridge, Mass.: Harvard University Press, 1949.

————. *De natura deorum.* Trans. Harris Rackham. Loeb Classical Library. Cambridge, Mass.: Harvard University Press, 1951.

Clarembald of Arras. *The Life and Works of Clarembald of Arras.* Ed. Nikolaus M. Häring. Toronto: Pontifical Institute of Mediaeval Studies, 1965.

Claudian. *Claudian.* Trans. Maurice Platnauer. 2 vols. Loeb Classical Library. Cambridge, Mass.: Harvard University Press, 1922.

Corpus Hermeticum. Trans. and ed. A. D. Nock and A. J. Festugière. 4 vols. Paris: Société d'édition "Les belles lettres," 1945.

Ellebaut. *Anticlaudien.* Ed. Andrew Creighton. Washington, D.C.: Catholic University of America Press, 1944.

Gilbert of Poitiers. *The Commentaries on Boethius by Gilbert of Poitiers.* Ed. Nikolaus M. Häring. Toronto: Pontifical Institute of Mediaeval Studies, 1966.

Hermetica. Trans. and ed. Walter Scott. 4 vols. Oxford: The Clarendon Press, 1924.

Hugh of Saint Victor. *The Didascalicon of Hugh of St. Victor.* Trans. Jerome Taylor. New York: Columbia University Press, 1961.

John of Salisbury. *The Metalogicon of John of Salisbury*. Trans. Daniel McGarry. Berkeley and Los Angeles: University of California Press, 1962.

John Scotus Erigena. *Annotationes in Marcianum*. Ed. Cora E. Lutz. Cambridge, Mass.: The Mediaeval Academy of America, 1939.

————. *De divisione naturae*. Ed. J. P. Migne. *Patrologia Latina*, vol. CXXII. Paris, 1866.

Lactantius. *Divinarum institutionum*. Ed. J. P. Migne. *Patrologia Latina*, VI, 111–818. Paris, 1844.

Liber Hermetis Mercurii Triplicis de vi rerum principiis, ed. Theodore Silverstein, *AHDLMA* XXII (1955), 217–302.

Lorris, Guillaume de, and Jean de Meun. *Le Roman de la Rose*. Ed. Ernest Langlois. 5 vols. *SATF*, 71. Paris: Firmin-Didot, 1920–1924.

————. *The Romance of the Rose*. Trans. Charles Dahlberg. Princeton: Princeton University Press, 1971.

Lucretius. *De rerum natura*. Trans. W. H. D. Rouse. Loeb Classical Library. Cambridge, Mass.: Harvard University Press, 1947.

Macrobius. *Commentarius in somnium Scipionis*. Ed. Franz Eyssenhardt. Leipzig: B. G. Teubner, 1868.

————. *Macrobius' Commentary on the Dream of Scipio*. Trans. William Harris Stahl. New York: Columbia University Press, 1952.

Orphei Hymni. Ed. Wilhelm Quandt. Berlin: Weidmann, 1955.

Orpheus. *The Mystical Hymns of Orpheus*. Trans. Thomas Taylor. London, 1896.

Ovid. *Fasti*. Trans. James George Frazer. Loeb Classical Library. Cambridge, Mass.: Harvard University Press, 1951.

————. *Metamorphoses*. Trans. Frank Justus Miller. Loeb Classical Library. Cambridge, Mass.: Harvard University Press, 1951.

Plato. *The Collected Dialogues of Plato*. Ed. Edith Hamilton and Huntington Cairns. Bollingen Series LXXI. New York: Pantheon, 1961.

Plotinus. *The Enneads*. Trans. Stephen MacKenna. London: Faber and Faber, 1930.

Proclus. *The Commentaries of Proclus on the Timaeus of Plato*. Trans. Thomas Taylor. 2 vols. London, 1820.

Prudentius. *Prudentius*. Trans. H. J. Thomson. 2 vols. Loeb Classical Library. Cambridge, Mass.: Harvard University Press, 1949.

Scriptores rerum mythicarum latini tres Romae nuper reperti. Ed. Georg Heinrich Bode. Hildesheim: Georg Olms, 1968.

Statius. *Statius.* Trans. J. H. Mozley. 2 vols. Loeb Classical Library. Cambridge, Mass.: Harvard University Press, 1945.

Thierry of Chartres. "De sex dierum operibus," ed. Nikolaus Häring, *AHDLMA,* XXII (1955), 137–216.

SECONDARY SOURCES

Alton, E. H. "The Mediaeval Commentators on Ovid's *Fasti," Herma-thena,* XX (1930), 119–151.

Auerbach, Erich. *Literary Language and Its Public in Late Latin Antiquity and in the Middle Ages.* Trans. Ralph Manheim. Bollingen Series LXXIV. New York: Pantheon, 1965.

Baldwin, Charles Sears. *Medieval Rhetoric and Poetic.* New York: Macmillan, 1928.

Bennett, J. A. W. *The Parlement of Foules: An Interpretation.* Oxford: The Clarendon Press, 1957.

Bethurum, Dorothy. "Chaucer's Point of View as Narrator in the Love Poems," *PMLA,* LXXIV (1959), 511–520.

Bett, Henry. *Johannes Scotus Erigena.* Cambridge: Cambridge University Press, 1925.

Bloomfield, Morton W. "A Grammatical Approach to Personification Allegory," *MP,* LX (1963), 161–171.

Boas, George. *Essays on Primitivism and Related Ideas in the Middle Ages.* Baltimore: The Johns Hopkins Press, 1948.

Bréhier, Emile. *The Philosophy of Plotinus.* Trans. Joseph Thomas. Chicago: University of Chicago Press, 1958.

Brewer, D. S., ed. *The Parlement of Foulys.* New York: Nelson, 1960.

Bronson, Bertrand H. "In Appreciation of Chaucer's *Parlement of Foules," UCPES,* III (1935), 193–224.

———. " *The Parlement of Foules* Revisited," *ELH,* XV (1948), 247–260.

Brown, Emerson, Jr. "*Hortus Inconclusus*: The Significance of Priapus and Pyramus and Thisbe in the *Merchant's Tale," ChauR,* IV (1970), 31–40.

Chenu, Marie–Dominique. *Nature, Man, and Society in the Twelfth Century.* Trans. Jerome Taylor and Lester K. Little. Chicago: University of Chicago Press, 1968.

———. *La théologie au douzième siècle.* Paris: Librairie Philosophique J. Vrin, 1957.

Clemen, Wolfgang. *Chaucer's Early Poetry.* Trans. C. A. M. Sym. 2nd ed. New York: Barnes and Noble, 1964.

Clerval, L'Abbé. *Les écoles de Chartres.* Frankfurt: Minerva, 1965 (first published Paris, 1895).

Close, A. J. "Commonplace Theories of Art and Nature in Classical Antiquity and in the Renaissance," *JHI*, XXX (1969), 467–486.

Collingwood, R. G. *The Idea of Nature*. New York: Oxford University Press, 1960.

Cornford, Francis M. *Plato's Cosmology*. London: Routledge & Kegan Paul, 1948.

Courcelle, Pierre. *La consolation de philosophie dans la tradition littéraire*. Paris: Etudes Augustiniennes, 1967.

Curtius, Ernst Robert. *European Literature and the Latin Middle Ages*. Trans. Willard R. Trask. Bollingen Series XXXVI. New York: Pantheon, 1953.

————. "Zur Literarästhetik des Mittelalters," *ZRP*, LVIII (1938), 129–232.

Dahlberg, Charles. "Love and the *Roman de la Rose*," *Speculum*, XLIV (1969), 568–584.

Deane, Herbert A. *The Political and Social Ideas of St. Augustine*. New York: Columbia University Press, 1963.

De Lage, G. Raynaud. *Alain de Lille*. Paris: Librairie Philosophique J. Vrin, 1951.

Denomy, A. J. "The *De amore* of Andreas Capellanus and the Condemnation of 1277," *MS*, VIII (1946), 107–149.

Dronke, Peter. *Medieval Latin and the Rise of European Love-Lyric*. 2 vols. Oxford: The Clarendon Press, 1965.

Düring, Ingemar, and G. E. L. Owen, eds. *Aristotle and Plato in the Mid-Fourth Century*. Papers of the Symposium Aristotelicum held at Oxford in August 1957. Göteborg: Studia Graeca et Latina Gothoburgensia, 11, 1960.

Economou, George D. "Januarie's Sin Against Nature: The *Merchant's Tale* and the *Roman de la Rose*," *CL*, XVII (1965), 251–257.

Emerson, O. F. "Some Notes on Chaucer and Some Conjectures," *PQ*, II (1923), 81–96.

Everett, Dorothy. *Essays on Middle English Literature*. Oxford: The Clarendon Press, 1955.

Faral, Edmond. *Les arts poétiques du XIIe et du XIIIe siècles*. Paris: E. Champion, 1958.

————. "Le manuscrit 511 de 'Hunterian Museum' de Glasgow," *SMed*, IX (1936), 69–88.

————. "*Le Roman de la Rose* et la pensée française au XIIIe siècle," *RDM*, XXXV (1926), 430–457.

Fisher, John H. *John Gower: Moral Philosopher and Friend of Chaucer*. New York: New York University Press, 1964.

Fleming, John V. "The Moral Reputation of the *Roman de la Rose* before 1400," *RPh*, XVIII (1965), 430–435.
———. *The Roman de la Rose: A Study in Allegory and Iconography*. Princeton: Princeton University Press, 1969.
Frank, Robert Worth, Jr. "Structure and Meaning in the *Parlement of Foules*," *PMLA*, LXXI (1956), 530–539.
Fredén, Gustaf. *Orpheus and the Goddess of Nature*. Göteborgs Universitets Arsskrift, LXIV, no. 6. Stockholm: Almqvist and Wiksell, 1958.
Friedman, Lionel J. "'Jean de Meung,' Antifeminism, and 'Bourgeois Realism,'" *MP*, LVII (1959), 13–23.
Garin, Eugenio. *Studi sul platonismo medievale*. Florence: Felice Le Monnier, 1958.
Gilson, Etienne. "La cosmogonie de Bernardus Silvestris," *AHDLMA*, III (1928), 5–24.
———. *History of Christian Philosophy in the Middle Ages*. New York: Random House, 1955.
Green, Richard Hamilton. "Alan of Lille's *Anticlaudianus*: Ascensus Mentis in Deum," *AnM*, VIII (1967), 3–16.
———. "Alan of Lille's *De planctu naturae*," *Speculum*, XXXI (1956), 649–674.
———. "Dante's 'Allegory of Poets,'" *CL*, IX (1957), 118–128.
Gregory, Tullio. *Anima mundi. La filosofia di Guglielmo di Conches e la scuola di Chartres*. Florence: G. C. Sansoni, 1955.
———. *Giovanni Scoto Eriugena*. Florence: Felice Le Monnier, 1963.
———. *Platonismo medievale*. Rome: Istituto Storico Italiano per il Medio Evo, 1958.
Gunn, Alan M. F. *The Mirror of Love*. Lubbock: Texas Tech Press, 1952.
Guthrie, W. K. C. *The Greeks and Their Gods*. Boston: Beacon Press, 1951.
———. *A History of Greek Philosophy*. 3 vols. Cambridge: Cambridge University Press, 1962.
Hoffman, Richard L. *Ovid and the Canterbury Tales*. Philadelphia: University of Pennsylvania Press, 1966.
Huizinga, Johan. "Über die Verknüpfung des Poetischen mit dem Theologischen bei Alanus de Insulis," *MKNAL*, LXXXIV, Series B, No. 6 (1932), 89–198.
Huppé, Bernard F., and D. W. Robertson, Jr. *Fruyt and Chaf*. Princeton: Princeton University Press, 1963.
Inge, William Ralph. *The Philosophy of Plotinus*. 2 vols. 3rd ed. London: Longmans, Green, 1929.

Jackson, W. T. H. "Allegory and Allegorization," *RS*, XXXII (1964), 161–175.

———. "The *De amore* of Andreas Capellanus and the Practice of Love at Court," *RR*, XLIX (1958), 243–251.

———. *The Literature of the Middle Ages*. New York: Columbia University Press, 1960.

Jeauneau, Edouard. "Macrobe, source du Platonism Chartrain," *SMed*, I (1960), 3–24.

———. "Note sur l'école de Chartres," *SMed*, V (1964), 821–865.

———. "L'usage de la notion d'*integumentum* à travers les gloses de Guillaume de Conches," *AHDLMA*, XXIV (1957), 35–100.

Jourdain, Charles, ed. "Des commentaires inédits de Guillaume de Conches et de Nicolas Triveth sur *La consolation de la philosophie* de Boèce," *Notices et extraits des manuscrits de la Bibliothèque Impériale*, XX (1862), 40–82.

Jung, Marc-René. *Etudes sur le poème allégorique en France au moyen âge*. Romanica Helvetica, vol. 82. Bern: Editions Francke, 1971.

Kerényi, Karl. "Die Göttin Natur," *Eranos-Jahrbuch*, XIV (1946), 39–86.

Klibansky, Raymond. *The Continuity of Platonic Tradition during the Middle Ages*. London: The Warburg Institute, 1950.

Knowlton, Edgar C. "The Allegorical Figure Genius," *ClPh*, XV (1920), 380–384.

———. "Genius as an Allegorical Figure," *MLN*, XXXIX (1924), 89–95.

———. "The Goddess Natura in Early Periods," *JEGP*, XIX (1920), 224–253.

———. "Nature in Middle English," *JEGP*, XX (1921), 186–207.

———. "Nature in Old French," *MP*, XX (1922), 309–329.

Labriolle, Pierre de. *History and Literature of Christianity from Tertullian to Boethius*. Trans. Herbert Wilson. London: Knopf, 1924.

Langlois, Ernest. *Origines et sources du Roman de la Rose*. Paris: E. Thorin, 1891.

Lewis, C. S. *The Allegory of Love*. London: Oxford University Press, 1953.

———. "Dante's Statius," *MAE*, XXV (1956), 133–139.

———. *The Discarded Image*. Cambridge: Cambridge University Press, 1964.

Liebeschütz, Hans. *Fulgentius Metaforalis: Ein Beitrag zur Geschichte der antiken Mythologie im Mittelalter*. Leipzig: B. G. Teubner, 1926.

Lovejoy, Arthur O. *Essays in the History of Ideas*. New York: Putnam's, 1960.

———. *The Great Chain of Being*. New York: Harper & Brothers, 1960.

————. "The Meaning of *Physis* in the Greek Physiologers," *PhR*, XVIII (1909), 369–383.

————, and George Boas. *Primitivism and Related Ideas in Antiquity.* Baltimore: The Johns Hopkins Press, 1935.

Lumiansky, R. M. "Chaucer's *Parlement of Foules*: A Philosophical Interpretation," *RES*, XXIV (1948), 81–89.

McDonald, Charles O. "An Interpretation of Chaucer's *Parlement of Foules*," *Speculum*, XXX (1955), 444–457.

McKeon, Richard. "Poetry and Philosophy in the Twelfth Century: The Renaissance of Rhetoric," *MP*, XLIII (1946), 217–234.

Manitius, Max. *Geschichte der lateinischen Literatur des Mittelalters.* 3 vols. Munich: Beck, 1911–1931.

More, Paul Elmer. *The Religion of Plato.* Princeton: Princeton University Press, 1921.

Müller, Franz Walter. *Der Rosenroman und der lateinische Averroismus des 13. Jahrhunderts.* Frankfurt: V. Klostermann, 1947.

Muscatine, Charles. *Chaucer and the French Tradition.* Berkeley and Los Angeles: University of California Press, 1957.

Mysteries, The. Ed. Joseph Campbell. Papers from the *Eranos Yearbooks*, Bollingen Series XXX, vol. II. New York: Pantheon, 1955.

Nasr, Seyyed Hossein. *An Introduction to Islamic Cosmological Doctrines.* Cambridge, Mass.: Harvard University Press, 1964.

Nelson, William. *The Poetry of Edmund Spenser.* New York: Columbia University Press, 1963.

Neumann, Erich. *The Great Mother.* Trans. Ralph Manheim. Bollingen Series XLVII. New York: Pantheon, 1955.

Owen, Charles A., Jr. "The Role of the Narrator in the *Parlement of Foules*," *CE*, XIV (1953), 264–269.

Panofsky, Erwin. *Studies in Iconology.* New York: Harper & Row, 1962.

Paré, Gérard. *Les idées et les lettres au XIIIᵉ siècle: Le Roman de la Rose.* Montreal: Bibliothèque de Philosophie, 1947.

————. *Le Roman de la Rose et la scolastique courtoise.* Paris: Librairie Philosophique J. Vrin, 1941.

Parent, J. M. *La doctrine de la création dans l'école de Chartres.* Publications de l'Institut d'Etudes Mediévales d'Ottawa, VII. Ottawa: Librairie Philosophique J. Vrin, 1938.

Patch, Howard Rollin. *The Goddess Fortuna in Mediaeval Literature.* Cambridge, Mass.: Harvard University Press, 1927.

————. *The Other World.* Cambridge, Mass.: Harvard University Press, 1950.

————. *The Tradition of Boethius.* New York: Oxford University Press, 1935.

Pauly-Wissowa. *Real-Encyclopädie der Classischen Altertumswissenschaft.* Vol. XX. Stuttgart: J. B. Metzler, 1941.

Pépin, Jean. *Mythe et allégorie.* Paris: Aubier, 1958.

Poole, Reginald Lane. *Illustrations of the History of Medieval Thought and Learning.* 2nd ed., rev. New York: Dover, 1960.

————. "The Masters of the Schools of Paris and Chartres in John of Salisbury's Time," *EHR*, XXXV (1920), 326–331.

Pratt, Robert A. "Chaucer's Use of the *Teseida*," *PMLA*, LXII (1947), 598–621.

Raby, F. J. E. *A History of Christian Latin Poetry.* 2nd ed. Oxford: The Clarendon Press, 1953.

————. *A History of Secular Latin Poetry in the Middle Ages.* 2 vols. Oxford: The Clarendon Press, 1934.

————. "*Nuda Natura* and Twelfth-Century Cosmology," *Speculum*, XLIII (1968), 72–77.

Rand, E. K. *Founders of the Middle Ages.* New York: Dover, 1957.

Robertson, D. W., Jr. *A Preface to Chaucer.* Princeton: Princeton University Press, 1962.

Rosán, Laurence Jay. *The Philosophy of Proclus.* New York: Cosmos, 1949.

Ross, W. D. *Aristotle.* 5th ed. London: Methuen, 1949.

————. *Plato's Theory of Ideas.* Oxford: The Clarendon Press, 1951.

Rowland, Beryl, ed. *Companion to Chaucer Studies.* Toronto: Oxford University Press, 1968.

Sandys, Sir John Edwin. *A History of Classical Scholarship*, vol. I, *From the Sixth Century B.C. to the End of the Middle Ages.* 3rd ed. New York: Hafner, 1964.

Santillana, Giorgio de. *The Origins of Scientific Thought.* Chicago: University of Chicago Press, 1961.

Schless, Howard. "Chaucer and Dante," *Critical Approaches to Medieval Literature.* Selected Papers from the English Institute, 1958–1959, ed. Dorothy Bethurum, pp. 134–154. New York: Columbia University Press, 1960.

Seznec, Jean. *The Survival of the Pagan Gods.* Trans. Barbara F. Sessions. New York: Harper & Brothers, 1961.

Silk, Edmund Taite. "Pseudo-Johannes Scottus, Adalbold of Utrecht, and the Early Commentaries on Boethius," *MRS*, III (1954), 1–40.

————. ed. "Saeculi noni auctoris in Boetii Consolationem philosophiae commentarius," *Papers and Monographs of the American Academy in Rome*, IX. 1935.

Silverstein, Theodore. "Chaucer's Modest and Homely Poem: *The Parlement*," *MP*, LVI (1959), 270–276.

———. "The Fabulous Cosmogony of Bernardus Silvestris," *MP*, XLVI (1948–1949), 92–110.

Stewart, Hugh Fraser. *Boethius*. London: W. Blackwood & Sons, 1891.

———, ed. "A Commentary by Remigius Autissiodorensis on the *De consolatione philosophiae* of Boethius," *JTS*, XVII (1915–1916), 22–42.

Stillwell, Gardiner. "Chaucer's Eagles and Their Choice on February 14," *JEGP*, LIII (1954), 546–561.

———. "Unity and Comedy in the *Parlement of Foules*," *JEGP*, XLIX (1950), 470–495.

Tayler, Edward William. *Nature and Art in Renaissance Literature*. New York: Columbia University Press, 1964.

Thorndike, Lynn. *A History of Magic and Experimental Science*. 8 vols. New York: Macmillan, 1923–1958.

Tuve, Rosemund. *Allegorical Imagery*. Princeton: Princeton University Press, 1966.

Van Winden, J. C. M. *Calcidius on Matter: His Doctrine and Sources*. Leiden: E. J. Brill, 1959.

Vasoli, Cesare. "Le idee filosofiche di Alano di Lilla nel *De planctu* e nell'*Anticlaudianus*," *GCFI*, XL (1961), 462–498.

———. "La 'theologia apothetica' di Alano di Lilla," *RCSF*, XVI (1961), 153–187.

Waddell, Helen. *The Wandering Scholars*. New York: Doubleday, 1955 (first published London, 1927).

Ward, C. F. *The Epistles on the "Romance of the Rose" and Other Documents in the Debate*. Chicago: n.p., 1911.

Wetherbee, Winthrop. "The Literal and the Allegorical: Jean de Meun and the 'de Planctu Naturae,'" *MS*, XXXIII (1971), 264–291.

———. "The Function of Poetry in the *De planctu naturae* of Alain de Lille, *Traditio*, XXV (1969), 87–125.

Whittaker, Thomas. *The Neo-Platonists*. 2nd ed. Cambridge: Cambridge, University Press, 1928.

Williams, George. *A New View of Chaucer*. Durham: Duke University Press, 1965.

Wood, Chauncey. *Chaucer and the Country of the Stars*. Princeton: Princeton University Press, 1970.

Woolsey, Robert B. "Bernard Silvester and the Hermetic *Asclepius*," *Traditio*, VI (1948), 340–344.

NOTES

I. THE PHILOSOPHICAL BACKGROUND

1. Marie-Dominique Chenu, *Nature, Man, and Society in the Twelfth Century*, trans. Jerome Taylor and Lester K. Little (Chicago, 1968), p. 3; Giorgio de Santillana, *The Origins of Scientific Thought* (Chicago, 1961), p. 28. See also Edgar C. Knowlton, "The Goddess Natura in Early Periods," *JEGP*, XIX (1920), 224–253; "Nature in Middle English," *JEGP*, XX (1921), 186–207; "Nature in Old French," *MP*, XX (1922), 309–329; Ernst Robert Curtius, "Zur Literarästhetik des Mittelalters," *ZRP*, LVIII (1938), 129–232; *European Literature and the Latin Middle Ages*, Bollingen Series XXXVI (New York, 1953), pp. 106–127; J. A. W. Bennett, *The Parlement of Foules: An Interpretation* (Oxford, 1957), pp. 194–212.

2. See J. M. Parent, *La doctrine de la création dans l'école de Chartres*, Publications de l'Institut d'Etudes Mediévales d'Ottawa, VII (Ottawa, 1938), pp. 92, 93, 110; Theodore Silverstein, "The Fabulous Cosmogony of Bernardus Silvestris," *MP*, XLVI (1948–1949), 105–107; Arthur O. Lovejoy and George Boas, *Primitivism and Related Ideas in Antiquity* (Baltimore, 1935), pp. 28, 64; Chenu, *Nature, Man, and Society*, pp. 1–48; Tullio Gregory, *Anima mundi: La filosofia di Guglielmo di Conches e la scuola di Chartres* (Florence, 1955), pp. 175–246.

3. C. S. Lewis, *The Discarded Image* (Cambridge, 1964), pp. 34–40.

4. Cicero, *De inventione* I.xxiv.34; *Metaphysics* 1014b–1015a, in *The Complete Works of Aristotle*, trans W. D. Ross, vol. VIII, (Oxford, 1928); *The Commentaries of Proclus on the Timeaus of Plato*, trans. Thomas Taylor, vol. I (London, 1820), I.8–9; *Contra Evtychen* I.i, in Boethius, *Tractates and The Consolation of Philosophy*, trans. H. F. Stewart and E. K. Rand, Loeb Classical Library (Cambridge, 1962), pp. 76–80, *The Didascalicon of Hugh of St. Victor*, trans. Jerome Taylor (New York, 1961), I.10.56–57; *The Metalogicon of John of Salisbury*, trans. Daniel McGarry (Berkeley and Los Angeles, 1962), I.8.28–29.

5. Pauly-Wissowa, *Real-Encyclopädie der Classischen Altertumswissenschaft*, XX, 1129–1164; Lovejoy and Boas, *Primitivism*, pp. 447–456; Curtius, "Zur Literarästhetik des Mittelalters," pp. 182–185; R. G. Collingwood, *The Idea of Nature* (New York, 1960). This chapter is greatly indebted to this work.

6. See Tullio Gregory, *Platonismo medievale* (Rome, 1958), p. 176, where he states that Natura is also the personification of reason and morality.

7. Morton W. Bloomfield, "A Grammatical Approach to Personification Allegory," *MP*, LX (1963), 161–171; W. T. H. Jackson, *The Literature of the Middle Ages* (New York, 1960), pp. 354–355.

8. *Metaphysics* 1014b–1015a. All quotations from this work are from the *Complete Works*, cited above. If not otherwise noted, all translations are my own.

9. See Collingwood, *The Idea of Nature*, pp. 80–82. See also Aristotle, *Physics*, vol. I, trans. Cornford and Wicksteed, Loeb Classical Library (Cambridge, 1929) p. 114, note *b*. All translations of *Physics* are from this edition.

10. See W. K. C. Guthrie, *A History of Greek Philosophy*, vol. I, *The Earlier Presocratics and the Pythagoreans* (Cambridge, 1962), pp. 82–83, where he explains that the sense of "constitution or developed form . . . is likely to have predominated in the sixth century," as evidenced by the description of *moly* in the *Odyssey* X.303. See also Lovejoy, "The Meaning of *Physis* in the Greek Physiologers," *PhR*, XVIII (1909), 376; Lovejoy and Boas, *Primitivism* p. 104, where *physis* is defined as "the intrinsic and permanent qualitative constitution of things"; Collingwood, *The Idea of Nature*, pp. 43–44, where "nature," understood as a principle "in the proper sense of that word, a *principium*, *arche*, or source . . . refers to something which makes its possessor behave as it does; this source of its behavior being something within itself."

11. Throughout the *Physics* Aristotle emphasizes this meaning: I.ii.185a; II.i.192b–193a; III.i.200b; VIII.iii.253b; as does *De caelo*, trans. W. K. C. Guthrie, Loeb Classical Library (Cambridge, 1939), III.ii.301b. See also C. S. Lewis, *The Discarded Image*, pp. 3–5. *Metaphysics* 1072b: "On such a principle, then, depend the heavens and the world of nature." Cf. Dante, *Paradiso* xxviii.42: "From that point hang the heavens and all nature." For an exception, see *De caelo* II.viii.290b, where Physis is said to have provided the heavenly bodies with their spherical shapes.

12. My discussion of Plato and Aristotle is indebted to the essay by Friedrich Solmsen, "Platonic Influences in the Formation of Aristotle's Physical System," in Ingemar Düring and G. E. L. Owen, eds., *Aristotle and Plato in the Mid-Fourth Century*, Papers of the Symposium Aristotelicum held at Oxford in August 1957 (Göteborg, 1960), pp. 213–235.

13. *De planctu naturae*, ed. Thomas Wright, in *Anglo-Latin Satirical Poets*, vol. II, Rerum Britannicarum Medii Aevi, Rolls Series, 59 (Wiesbaden, 1964), p. 516; See also Lovejoy and Boas, *Primitivism*, pp. 447–456, nn. 37, 38, 64.

14. In the *Phaedrus* 245c.–246a, from *The Collected Dialogues of Plato*, ed. Edith Hamilton and Huntington Cairns, Bollingen Series LXXI (New York, 1961), Plato places locomotion above all modes of movement and puts it in the soul: "And now that we have seen that that which is moved by itself is immortal, we shall feel no scruple in affirming that precisely that is the essence and definition of soul, to wit, self-motion" (245e). The entire passage was translated by Chalcidius in his commentary, LVII. See also Plato's *Laws* 896a–b. All quotations of Plato are from the above edition. Like Plato, Aristotle puts locomotion first among the kinds of movement: "Now of the three kinds of motion (in the larger sense of change in general), to wit change of quantity, change of quality, and change of place, which we call 'locomotion,' this last named must come first." *Physics* VIII.260a. As in Plato, where the priority of self-movement in the soul places soul at the head of all movement and of all that is, Aristotle's "local motion" stands prior to all that exists: "Yet again it can be proved that local motion takes precedence of others by the following considerations. In regard to motion, as in regard to everything else, 'priority' has several meanings: (1) that has priority without which the things to which it is said to be prior cannot exist, whereas it can exist without them; (2) the priority may be in time; and (3) in respect of perfection and nature." *Physics* VIII.260b.

15. Solmsen, "Platonic Influences" p. 230. "We have shown that motion must be eternal and can never cease: so there must be some prime mover, whether singular or plural, that is eternal and not itself movable." *Physics* VIII.vi.258b. On the *primum mobile*, what is directly moved by the prime mover, its eternity and constant motion, see *Physics* VIII.vi.259b; *Metaphysics* 1072a; Collingwood, *The Idea of Nature*, pp. 89–91; W. D. Ross, *Aristotle*, 5th ed. (London, 1949), pp. 179–186.

16. *Physics* VIII.vi.259b. "The final cause, then, produces motion as being loved, but all other things by being moved." *Metaphysics* 1072b. The hierarchy of moving agents is explained: "But if there really is such an existence (A), causing motion but itself unmoved and eternal, (B) which is immediately moved by it must likewise be eternal. This is evident from the very fact that genesis and evanishment and change occur to all else for no other reason than that they are moved by something that is itself in motion; for the motion caused by the unmoved (A) will be a single motion caused always in the same way, since it in no way changes in relation to the mobile: whereas that (C) which is moved by an agent (B) that is in motion, though that motion be immediately caused by the unmoving, inasmuch as it (C) changes in relation to things (D) it moves, will not cause a uniform movement, but because of its contrasted positions or characteristics will produce contrary movements in each of the things it affects, and any such movements will be intermittent . . . The reason is now obvious, namely, that some things derive their motion from an eternal and immovable cause, and therefore their motion is constant, whereas others derive their motion from a cause which is in itself in motion and changing, and therefore they also must necessarily be changing." *Physics* VIII.vi.260a.

17. Collingwood, *The Idea of Nature*, p. 87.

18. Collingwood, *The Idea of Nature*, p. 88. This longing and its classification are discussed in Lovejoy, *The Great Chain of Being* (New York, 1960), pp. 55–58.

19. Solmsen, "Platonic Influences," pp. 226–227. See *De mundo*, trans. D. J. Furley, Loeb Classical Library (Cambridge, 1955), 392a: "The substance of the heaven and the stars we call *aether*, not, as some think, because it is fiery in nature and so burns (they fall into error about its function, which is quite different from that of fire), but because it always moves in its circular orbit: it is an element different from the four elements, pure and divine." As Lewis suggests (*The Discarded Image*, p. 4, n. 3) it does not matter in this case that the *De mundo* is pseudo-

Aristotelian. (Actually, it was attributed to Apuleius.). The same distinction can be found in *De caelo* I.ii.269a–b.

20. This is to a great degree a result of the new astronomy of Eudoxus and others wherein the planets move in a direction opposite that of the fixed stars and are no longer considered errant bodies because they repeat eternally and at unvarying speed the same movements. See *Laws* 822; *Timaeus* 38d; *De caelo* 291b, 292a; *Metaphysics* 1073b. For the four classes of change see *Physics* I.i.

21. Ingemar Düring, "Aristotle on Ultimate Principles from 'Nature and Reality,'" in Düring and Owen, eds., *Aristotle and Plato*, p. 47. For the concept of the inseparability of form and matter, see *Physics* II.i.193b. For the idea that nature is a "goal-directed cause," see *Physics* II.viii. 199b.

22. Ross, *Aristotle*, pp. 78–79. The quotations are from *De generatione animalium* 744.b16.a36; *De caelo* 291.b13.a24; *De partibus animalium* 686.a22—all cited by Ross.

23. *De mundo* 397b.

27. For the fundamental differences between the two, see Lovejoy, *The Great Chain of Being*, pp. 24–66.

25. Düring, "Aristotle," pp. 54–55. Compare the definition of *physis/natura* given in *Physics* II.i.193b with Plato's repudiation of the pre-Socratic notion in *Laws* 852c: "Why, by *nature* they mean what was there to begin with, but if we can show that soul came first—that it was not fire, nor air, but soul which was there to begin with—it will be perfectly true to say that it is the existence of soul which is most eminently *natural*." See also Collingwood, *The Idea of Nature*, pp. 70–79; W. D. Ross, *Plato's Theory of Ideas* (Oxford, 1951), pp. 120–121.

26. Lewis, *The Discarded Image*, p. 36.

27. For William's own commentary, see Edouard Jeauneau, *Guillaume de Conches, Glosae super Platonem* (Paris, 1965).

28. See also *Laws*, 896c.

29. "Soul, then, by her own motions stirs all things in sky, earth, or sea—and the names of these motions are wish, reflection, forsight, counsel, judgment, true or false, pleasure, pain, hope, fear, hate, love—stirs them, I say, by these and whatever other kindred or primary motions there may be. They, in turn, bring in their train secondary and corporeal movements, and so guide all things to increase and decrease, disintegration and integration, with their attendant characters of heat and cold, weight and lightness, hardness and softness, white and black, dry and sweet." *Laws* 897a,b.

30. *Timaeus* 43a. Nature in this sense of the corporeal world is in Plato "a rambling series of phenomena, a mechanism ruled by necessity and the 'errant cause.'" Düring "Aristotle," p. 39. On the doctrine of necessity, see *Timaeus* 48a; Francis M. Cornford, *Plato's Cosmology* (London, 1948), pp. 160–177. See also Paul Elmer More, *The Religion of Plato* (Princeton, 1921), p. 231.

31. See Lovejoy, *The Great Chain of Being*, pp. 24–66, esp. 61–66; Paul Henry, S. J., "Plotinus' Place in the History of Thought," in *The Enneads*, trans. Stephen MacKenna (London, 1930), pp. xxxvii–xliv.

32. Chenu, *Nature, Man, and Society*, pp. 49–50. See also Raymond Klibansky, *The Continuity of Platonic Tradition during the Middle Ages* (London, 1950); Thomas Whittaker, *The Neoplatonists*, 2nd ed. (Cambridge, 1928); Etienne Gilson, *History of Christian Philosophy in the Middle Ages* (New York, 1955), pp. 67–153; Laurence Jay Rosán, *The Philosophy of Proclus* (New York, 1949), pp. 223–224.

33. Klibansky, p. 22. See also *Macrobius' Commentary on the Dream of Scipio*, trans. William Harris Stahl (New York, 1952), pp. 22, 37; William Ralph Inge, *The Philosophy of Plotinus*, vol. I, 3rd ed. (New York, 1929), p. 111; Lovejoy, *The Great Chain of Being*, pp. 61–66; Whittaker, *The Neo-Platonists*, pp. 40–97.

34. *Contra Evtychen* I.41–42. See also Howard Rollin Patch, *The Tradition of Boethius* (New York, 1935); Hugh Fraser Stewart, *Boethius* (London, 1891); E. K. Rand, *Founders of the Middle Ages* (New York, 1957), pp. 135–180.

35. "The One is all things and no one of them; the source of all things is not all things; and yet it is all things in a transcendental sense— all things, so to speak, having run back to it: or, more correctly, not all as yet are within it, they will be." *Enneads* V.2.1. All quotations are from the MacKenna translation, cited above. Plotinus explains nous in this way: "Its knowing is not by search but by possession, its blessedness inherent, not acquired; for all belongs to it eternally and it holds the authentic Eternity imitated by Time which, circling round the Soul, makes towards the new thing and passes by the old. Soul deals with thing after thing—now Socrates; now a horse: always some one entity from among beings—but the Intellectual-Principle is all and therefore its entire content is simultaneously present in that identity," *Enneads* V.1.4. Of the world-soul he writes: "But the Soul has the distinction of possessing at once an action of conscious attention within itself, and an action towards the outer. It has the function of giving life to all that does not live by prior right, and the life it gives is commensurate with its

own; that is to say, living in reason, it communicates reason to the body—an image of the reason within itself, just as the life given to the body is an image of Real-Being—and it bestows, also, upon that material the appropriate shapes of which it contains the Reason-Forms," *Enneads* IV.3.10. See also II.3.17; V.9.3.

36. Proclus also calls this lower, or second, word-soul "nature". See Rosán, pp. 115–116. Proclus explains Plato's meaning of nature thus: "Plato, however, does not think fit to give the appellation of nature primarily, either to matter, or material form, or body, or physical powers, but is averse to call it immediately soul. Placing, however, the essence of it in the middle of both, I mean between soul and corporeal powers, the latter being inferior to it, in consequence of being divided about bodies, and incapable of being converted to themselves, but nature surpassing things posterior to it, through containing the reasons or productive principles of all of them, and generating and vivifying all things, he has delivered to us the most accurate theory concerning it. For, according to common conceptions, nature is one thing, and that which subsists according to, and by nature, another ... For nature, indeed, verges to bodies, is inseparable from them." *The Commentaries of Proclus* I.i.8–9.

37. Inge, *Philosophy of Plotinus*, I, 155. Plotinus does not admit ether, the Aristotelian fifth element. See Emile Bréhier, *The Philosophy of Plotinus*, trans. Joseph Thomas (Chicago, 1958), p. 178. The heavens in Plotinus are made of fire, which soul bends into a circle. *Enneads* II.1.6.

38. *Macrobius' Commentary on the Dream of Scipio* I.xiv.5.145. In the Latin edition of *Commentarius in somnium Scipionis*, ed. Franciscus Eyssenhardt (Leipzig, 1868) p. 530, this passage reads: "secundum haec ergo cum ex summo deo mens, ex mente anima fit, anima uero et condat et uita conpleat omnia quae secuntur, cunctaque hic unus fulgor illuminet et uniuersis appareat, ut in multis speculis per ordinem positis uultus unus, cumque omnia continuis successionibus se sequantur degenerantia per ordinem ad imum meandi: inuenientur pressius intuenti a summo deo usque ad ultimum rerum faecem una mutuis se uinculis religans et nusquam interrupta conexio. et haec est Homeri catena aurea, quam pendere de caelo in terras deum iussisse commemorat." Cf. *Enneads* I.1.8; Chalcidius, *Timaeus: A Calcidio translatus commentarioque instructus*, ed. J. H. Waszink, vol. IV of *Plato Latinus*, ed. Raymond Klibansky (London and Leiden, 1962) CLXXXVIII. 212–213, cited hereafter as Chalcidius.

39. For an essay that complements Lovejoy on this subject, see Ludwig Edelstein, "The Golden Chain of Homer," in *Studies in Intellectual History* (New York, 1968), pp. 48–66.

40. *Macrobius' Commentary* I.xiv.8.143–144. Cf. *Commentarius*, p. 529.

41. *Macrobius' Commentary* I.xiv.9.143–144. Macrobius records the Aristotelian classification of life into reasoning (man), sensitive (animals), and vegetative (plant life), from *De anima* II.ii–iii. Man is endowed with all three attributes, the beasts with the lower two, and plants with the last only. Cf. *Commentarius*, p. 529: "in inferiora uero ac terrena degenerans fragilitatem corporum caducorum deprehendit meram diuinitatem mentis sustinere non posse . . . soli ergo homini rationem id est uim mentis infudit cui sedes in capite est." The spherical shape of man's head permits him to participate in the divine mind because, being similar to the heavenly spheres, that shape is the only one capable of containing mind. Cf. *Timaeus* 44d and Chalcidius, CCXXXI.245: "Rationibili uelut arx corporis et regia, utpote uirtuti quae regali quadam eminentia praestet, id est domicilium capitis, in quo habitet animae principale."

42. *Macrobius' Commentary* I.xvii.8–11.156–157. Cf. *Commentarius*, pp. 541–542. The entire Neoplatonic cosmological scheme would then proceed like this: the One, mind, the world-soul, the celestial sphere, the spheres of Saturn, Jupiter, Mars, Venus, Mercury, Sun, Moon, and the stationary earth.

43. *Macrobius' Commentary* I.vi.20.104. Cf. *Commentarius*, p. 488.

44. *Macrobius' Commentary* I.xxi.33.180–181. Cf. *Commentarius*, p. 566: "sed omnia haec, quae de summo ad lunam usque peruenient, sacra incorrupta diuina sunt, quia in ipsis est aether semper idem nec umquam recipiens inaequalem uarietatis aestum. infra lunam et aer et natura permutationis pariter incipiunt, et sicut aetheris et aeris ita diuinorum et caducorum luna confinium est." See also, *Macrobius' Commentary* I.xi.4–7. 131–132. Chalcidius marks the sublunary world as the realm of mutability and death: "Namque generatio et item mors in isto loco sub luna, incrementa quoque et imminutiones et omnifarium commutatio transitioque ex locis as loca." LXXVI.123. Cf. *Enneads* II.1.5.

45. *Macrobius' Commentary* II.xxi.13–15.224–225. Cf. *Commentarius*, p. 615: "nihil intra uiuum mundum perire sed eorum quae interire uidentur solam mutari speciem, et illud in originem suam atque ipsa elementa remeare, quod tale quale fuit esse desierit . . . a ceteris enim corporibus quod effluit recedit, elementorum fluxus numquam ab ipsis

recedit elementis, ergo in hoc mundo pars nulla mortalis secundum uerae rationis adserta."

46. This is also one of the key points made by Chalcidius in the section headed "De silua," CCLXVIII–CCCLV.

47. *Macrobius' Commentary* II.xii.10–11.224. Cf. *Commentarius*, p. 614.

48. *Macrobius' Commentary* I.vi.63.112. Cf. *Commentarius*, p. 498: "uerum semine semel intra formandi hominis monetam locato hoc primum artifex natura molitur ut die septimo folliculum genuinum circumdet humori ex membrana tam tenui qualis in ouo ab exteriore, teste clauditur et intra se claudit liquorem." See also I.vi.14.102, where it is stated that *natura* establishes the term of nine months for human births.

49. *De planctu naturae*, ed. Wright, p. 469.

50. *Macrobius' Commentary* I.ii.17.86. Cf. *Commentarius*, pp. 471–472: "de dis autem ut dixi ceteris et de anima non frustra se nec ut oblectent ad fabulosa conuertunt sed quia sciunt inimicam esse naturae apertam nudamque expositionem sui, quae sicut uulgaribus hominum sensibus intellectum sui uarro rerum tegmine operimentoque subtraxit, ita a prudentibus arcana sua uoluit per fabulosa tractari."

51. Lewis, *The Discarded Image*, p. 36, n. 1. It is doubtful that Chalcidius was one of Macrobius' sources. Yet this should not eliminate the possibility of common sources or their basic similarities, for the works of both display "the widespread borrowing that characterizes the compilations of ancient encyclopedists." Stahl, *Macrobius' Commentary*, p. 16.

52. J. C. M. Van Winden, *Chalcidius on Matter: His Doctrine and Sources* (Leiden, 1959), pp. 191–192; Chalcidius, CCCXXX.324–325: "ac distinguit intellectum imperata animi conceptione tali, ut *tria genera* nobis occurrant, genera nunc improprie appelans—neque enim silua nec uero exemplum genera sunt—sed ut appellatio generum significet primas substantias. *Illud quidem*, inquit, *quod fit et quod gignitur* —generata uidelicet species, quae in silua subsistit et ibidem dissoluitur —, *item aliud in quo gignitur*—*in quo* est ipsa silua, in hac quippe species dissolubiles substantiam sortiuntur—, *tertium praeterea, ex quo similitudinem trahit mutuaturque quod gignitur*, idea scilicet, quae exemplum est rerum omnium quas natura progenuit, hoc est eorum, quae siluae quasi quodam gremio continentur exemplorumque imagines esse dicuntur. Deinde euidenti quadam comparatione atque exemplo quaestionem reuelat. Comparat enim *quod percipit* in se species *matri*, uidelicet siluae—haec enim recipit a natura proditas species—, *illud uero ex quo* similitudo commeat *patri*, hoc est ideae—huius enim similitudinem

memoratae species mutuantur—, quod uero ex his duobus est *proli*, generatae scilicet speciei—est enim haec posita inter naturam uere existentem constantem eandemque semper, nimirum idean, quae intellectus dei aeterni est aeternus, et inter eam naturam quae est quidem, sed non eadem semper, id est siluam; quippe haec natura sua nihil est eorum quae sunt, cum sit aeterna. Ergo quod inter has duas naturas positum est uere non est. Cum enim sit imago uere existentis rei, uidentur esse aliquatenus, quia uero non perseuerat patiturque immutationem sui, non est existens uere, et sunt exempla; illa quippe exempla rata et immutabili constantia uigent. Erunt igitur tria haec: quod semper est, item quod semper non est, deinde quod non semper est." In the second part of this passage—beginning "est enim haec posita"—*natura* seems to be synonymous with *substantia* in the first half. Note also the idea of the negative eternity of matter.

53. Van Winden, *Chalcidius on Matter*, p. 33. Cf. Chalcidius CCLXIX.274: "non enim ex his mixtus est mundus, sed consultis prouidae mentis ex necessitatis rationibus constitit operante quidem prouidentia et agente, silua uero perpetiente exornationique se facilem praebente, penetram siquidem eam usque quaque diuina mens format plene, non ut artes formam tribuentes in sola superficie, sed perinde ut natura atque anima solida corpora permeantes uniuersa uiuificant."

54. Chalcidius XCVIII–CXVIII.150–164, a section headed "De caelo."

55. Chalcidius LVII.104–106; *Phaedrus* 245c–246a. Despite the great influence of Numenius on him, Chalcidius rejects his view that matter has a soul of its own. See Van Winden, *Chalcidius on Matter*, p. 123.

56. Chalcidius CCXXVI.242: "cum Plato tan dignitate quam uirtutem praestantia uenerabilem dicit esse animam et plane corporis dominam"; *Timaeus* 34c.

57. Chalcidius offers two explanations of the *indiuidua substantia* and the *diuidua substantia*. In the first, the indivisible stands for the *species intelligibilis mundi* and the divisible for *silua* (XX.80). In the second, the indivisible stands for *anima incorporalis* and the divisible for *anima stirpea*, which is purely rational and material (XXXI.80–81). He expresses no personal preference, though he may favor the second since he places it last.

58. Chalcidius XXIX.79. On Chalcidius' doctrine of *silua*, see Van Winden, *Chalcidius on Matter*, *passim*, esp. pp. 243–245. Throughout his commentary on the *commentarius*, Van Winden stresses that the Chalcidian doctrine on matter insists that matter is eternal, without motion

or quality, and that it is the sole source of evil in the universe since it is wholly negative.

59. Chalcidius XXIII.73–74: "Omnia enim quae sunt uel dei opera uel naturae uel naturam imitantis hominis artificis." *De mundo* 396b; *Physics* II.viii.199a.

60. Curtius, *European Literature*, p. 108. See also *The Didascalicon of Hugh of St. Victor*, p. 189; Theodore Silverstein, "De vi rerum principiis," *AHDLMA*, XXII (1955), 217–302. There are numerous extant manuscripts of the Latin *Ascelepius*, the earliest dating from the eleventh century. The Greek original was probably last known to Lactantius. See *Hermetica*, trans. and ed. Walter Scott (Oxford, 1924) I, 49, 53, 55. All translations of the *Asclepius* are from this edition.

61. *Hermetica* I.289–291. Cf. *Corpus Hermeticum*, trans. and ed. A. D. Nock and A. J. Festugière (Paris, 1975), vol. II, *Asclepius* 2.12–17.298: "Anima et mundus a natura conprehensa agitantur, ita omnium multiformi imaginum qualitate uariata, ut infinitae qualitatum ex interuallo species esse nascantur, adunatae tamen ad hoc, ut totum unum et ex uno omnia esse uideantur." See also *Hermetica*, p. 291 (*Mundus-hyle*, n. 14). Cf. *Asclepius* 3.11–15.299: "Mundus autem praeparatus est a deo receptaculum omniformium specierum, natura autem, per species imaginans mundum per quattuor elementa, ad caelum usque producit cuncta dei uisibus placitura."

62. *Hermetica*, p. 293. Cf. *Asclepius* 4.13–18. 300: "Divinitatis enim genus et ipsum et species immortales sunt. Reliquorum genera quorum aeternitas est generis, quamvis per species occidat, nascendi fecunditate servantur: ideoque species mortales sunt [genera non sunt]; ut homo mortalis sit, inmortalis humanitas."

63. *Hermetica*, p. 333. Cf. *Asclepius* 20.3–17.321.

64. *The Works of Geoffrey Chaucer*, ed. F. N. Robinson, 2nd ed. (Cambridge, Mass., 1957), p. 145.

65. See Edward William Tayler, *Nature and Art in Renaissance Literature* (New York, 1964); A. J. Close, "Commonplace Theories of Art and Nature in Classical Antiquity and the Renaissance," *JHI*, XXX (1969), 467–486.

II. BOETHIUS AND THE POETIC BACKGROUND

1. Erich Auerbach, *Literary Language and Its Public in Late Latin Antiquity and in The Middle Ages*, trans. Ralph Manheim (New York, 1965), p. 85. For studies of Boethius, see E. K. Rand, *Founders of the*

Middle Ages (New York, 1957), pp. 135–180; Max Manitius, *Geschichte der Lateinischen Literatur des Mittelalters* I, 22–36; Howard Rollin Patch, *The Tradition of Boethius* (New York, 1935); Hugh Fraser Stewart, *Boethius* (London, 1891); Pierre Courcelle, *La consolation de philosophie dans la tradition littéraire* (Paris, 1967). All quotations are from the Loeb Classical Library edition, *Tractates and the Consolation of Philosophy*, with the English translation of "I.T." (1609), revised by H. F. Stewart (Cambridge, 1962).

2. For the gifts of the goddesses Fortuna and Natura in medieval literature, see Howard Rollin Patch, *The Goddess Fortuna in Medieval Literature* (Cambridge, Mass., 1927), pp. 65–66, 75–77; Courcelle, *La consolation*, pp. 101–158.

3. The argument that man must base the correct and good life on an understanding of the whole plan of nature appears explicitly in Cicero, *De finibus*, trans. Harris Rackham, Loeb Classical Library (Cambridge, 1951), III.xxii.73: "Nor again can anyone judge truly of things good and evil, save by a knowledge of the whole plan of nature and also the life of the gods, and of the answer to the question whether the nature of man is or is not in harmony with that of the universe." On the goddess Fortuna's wheel, see Patch, *The Goddess Fortuna*, pp. 146–177. See also Courcelle, *La consolation*, pp. 141–151.

4. On this sense of "nature," which was variously defined by ancient philosophers, see Arthur O. Lovejoy and George Boas, *Primitivism and Related Ideas* (Baltimore, 1935), Appendix 49 and pp. 187–188.

5. Etienne Gilson, *History of Christian Philosophy* (New York, 1955) p. 105.

6. Chalcidius CLXXXVIII. 212–213.

7. On William, see Courcelle, *La consolation*, pp. 302–303, 306–313. Edmund Taite Silk abandoned his original attribution of the earlier commentary to John Scotus in his "Pseudo-Johannes Scottus, Adalbold of Utrecht, and the Early Commentaries on Boethius," *MRS*, III (1954), 2. Courcelle reviews the controversy over the authorship of the Carolingian commentary, *La consolation*, pp. 248–254. On John Scotus, see Tullio Gregory, *Giovanni Scoto Eriugena* (Florence, 1963); Henry Bett, *Johannes Scotus Erigena* (Cambridge, 1925).

8. *Saeculi noni auctoris in Boetii consolationem philosophiae commentarius*, ed. Edmund Taite Silk, Papers and Monographs of the American Academy in Rome, IX (1935), 157: "Omne enim opus aut Dei aut opus naturae aut artificis imitantis naturam. Opus Dei est sicuti nous, id est mens diuina scilicet uerbum Patris et mundus et anima mundi et

illud chaos quod olim erat, scilicet elementorum confusio quae hyle, appellatur. Opus naturae est duplex: uel quando aliquid surgit ex iactis seminibus, sicut homo ex homine et arbores ex arboribus, uel per se surgit, sicut quaedam arbores per se surgunt absque iacto semine. Opus uero artificis imitantis naturam est sicut statua alicuius."

9. *Saeculi noni auctoris*, pp. 155–156: "Quicumque de mundi constitutione dixerunt, siue catholici uel ethnici, id est gentiles, fuerunt, duos mundos esse asseruerunt: unum quidem dictum archetypum alium uocatum sensilem, id est exemplarem mundum. Archetypum uero mundum uocauerunt conceptionem et imaginationem huius sensilis mundi quae fuit in mente diuina antequam est sensilis mundus fieret . . . Et totius huius mundi imago in mente Dei erat, ad cuius imaginis exemplum mundus iste sensilis factus est."

10. J. M. Parent, *La doctrine de la création dans l'école de Chartres* (Ottawa, 1938), p. 131: "Probat hoc idem scilicet Deum mundum gubernare per ordinem nature, et est ordo nature quod similia nascantur ex similibus ut homines ex hominibus, asini ex asinis." William repeats this statement in his commentary on *Timaeus*: "Opus nature est quod similia nascantur ex similibus ex semine vel ex germine, quia est natura vis rebus insita similia de similibus operans." Parent, *La doctrine de la création*, p. 147.

11. Parent, *La doctrine de la création*, p. 131: "Sed quicquid est conjunctum ex diversis, vel ab homine conjunctum est vel operante natura vel creatore; ab homine, ut partes imaginis; a natura, ut membra hominis."

12. Parent, *La doctrine de la création*, p. 128: "Opus nature est quod similia nascantur ex similibus, homines ex hominibus, asini ex asinis. At dicet aliquis: nonne hoc est opus creatoris quod homo ex homine nascatur? Ad quod respondeo: nichil detraho Deo; omnia que in mundo sunt Deus fecit preter malum sed alia facit operante natura rerum que est instrumentum divine operationis et ea dicuntur opera nature que a Deo fiunt natura subserviente."

13. Silk, *Saeculi noni auctoris*, p. 213: "Quod si aliquis Deo uelit contraire nil proficit. Bene dicit NATVRAM SERVANS, quia in quantum naturam seruat bene agit et a Deo regitur; in quantum autem a Deo discedit male agit et contra naturam. Diabolus enim in sui natura bonus est et potestas quidem eius iusta: uoluntas autem eius mala. Sed Deus malo illius bene utitur; ideoque dum aliquid conatur malum uoluntate Deo tantum resistit." See also Parent, *La doctrine de la création*, p. 158; H. F. Stewart, "A Commentary by Remigius Autissiodarensis

on the *De consolatione philosophiae* of Boethius," *JTS*, XVII (1915–1916), 29.

14. Charles Jourdain, ed., "Des commentaires inédits de Guillaume de Conches et de Nicolas Triveth sur *La consolation de la philosophie* de Boèce," *Notices et extraits des manuscrits de la Bibliothèque Impériale*, XX (1862), 81.

15. See Erich Neumann, *The Great Mother*, trans. Ralph Manheim, Bollingen Series XLVII (New York, 1955).

16. Chaucer's trans., in *The Works of Geoffrey Chaucer*, ed. Robinson, (Boston, 1957) p. 342. In his vast work Courcelle does not once discuss or even mention III.m.2.

17. Ernst Robert Curtius, *European Literature and the Latin Middle Ages* (New York, 1953), pp. 106–107.

18. *The Mystical Hymns of Orpheus*, trans. Thomas Taylor (London, 1896), pp. 29–33. The Greek text may be read in *Orphei Hymni*, ed. Wilhelm Quandt (Berlin, 1955), pp. 10–12. Gustaf Fredén, who in "Orpheus and the Goddess of Nature," *Göteborgs Universitets Arsskrift*, LXIV, no. 6 (1958), 15, also translates the hymn, sees a remarkable resemblance between Physis and the medieval goddess but, other than citing Curtius, adduces no evidence in support of the statement (p. 27).

19. See Karl Kerényi, "Die Göttin Natur," *Eranos-Jahrbuch*, XIV (1946), 39–86. Kerényi indicates the numerous associations that can be made, not only with other divinities in the Orphic hymns, but also with later figures and philosophical concepts of nature. For example, on p. 84, n. 3, he points out the similarity between the predicate "fire-breathing" in verse 26 and Zeno's definition of nature as "a craftsman-like fire," reported by Cicero in *De natura deorum* II.xxii. Kerényi's conclusions, however, have a tendency to tie the many senses of nature from the Orphic hymns to Cicero into a whole that is deceptively coherent and unified. Although philosophy made use of Orphic material, the aims and discipline of philosophy are not necessarily synonymous with those of popular religion. See W. K. C. Guthrie. *The Greeks and Their Gods* (Boston, 1951), pp. 308–312; Walter Wili, "The Orphic Mysteries and the Greek Spirit," in *The Mysteries*, ed. Joseph Campbell, trans. Ralph Manheim, Bollingen Series XXX, vol. 2 (New York, 1955), pp. 64–92.

20. Apuleius, *The Golden Ass*, trans. William Aldington, rev. Stephen Gaselee, Loeb Classical Library (London, 1935), XI.5.

21. C. S. Lewis, *The Discarded Image*, (Cambridge, 1964) p. 36.

22. Ovid, *Metamorphoses*, trans. Frank Justus Miller, Loeb Classical

Library (Cambridge, 1951), I.506. See also Curtius, *European Literature*, p. 106.

23. Lucretius, *De rerum natura*, trans. W. H. D. Rouse, Loeb Classical Library (Cambridge, Mass., 1947), I.21. See also II.1117; V.1362.

24. Pauly-Wissowa, *Real-Encyclopädie*, XX.1129. Of interest is *De rerum natura* III.931–1101, where Natura speaks a reproach to the foolish man who fears death. Though this passage is of doubtful significance to the development of the medieval Natura in a strictly historical sense, it shows that the allegorical technique was at work in Latin poetry before Statius and Claudian.

25. Ernst Robert Curtius, "Zur Literarästhetik des Mittelalters," *ZRP*, LVIII (1938), 182, has arranged a list of fourteen classes of functions, the first seven of which represent Latin literature up to Claudian: (1) Natura artifex mundi, (2) Natura parens omnium rerum, (3) Natura domina omnium rerum, (4) Natura plasmatrix terrae et locorum, (5) Natura dotatrix hominum, (6) Natura formatrix hominum, and (7) Natura domitrix feritatis et mater pietatis. It would not be difficult to relate any of these functions of nature, either explicitly or implicitly, to the broadly based figure of Physis of the Orphic hymn. But more important, numbers 3–6 appear frequently in medieval Latin poetry. According to Curtius, Claudian adds five more functions and Prudentius two.

26. C. S. Lewis in *The Allegory of Love* (London, 1953), after asserting that "the twilight of the gods is the mid-morning of the personifications" (p. 52), demonstrates that in the *Thebaid* the gods become "more and more like mere personifications" and the personifications become figures of gravity, representing more than do the gods the religious feelings and intellectual concerns of the poet (pp. 50–55).

27. *Statius*, trans, J. H. Mozley, Loeb Classical Library (Cambridge, 1975), vol. I, *Silvae* I.iii.15–17. All references and quotations are from this edition. The second passage is in II.ii.15–16. In the quoted passage, although Statius gives the upper hand to nature in the division between nature and art, a few lines later he praises the landscaping efforts of man (52–53). Statius then describes the improvements made by the master who tamed the place. On this conflict between the creativities of nature and art, see Edward William Tayler, *Nature and Art in Renaissance Literature* (New York, 1964).

28. *Statius*, vol. II, *Thebaid* XI. 466; XII.561.

29. Lewis, *The Allegory of Love*, p. 55. For references to Natura in the *Thebaid* not cited here, see VIII.330; X.88; XI.607.

30. *Statius* I.xv–xvi. See also Lewis, *The Allegory of Love*, p. 58.

31. Cicero, *De natura deorum*, trans. Harris Rackham (London, 1951) II.xi.152. For the Stoic tendency to personify the gods, see Lewis, *The Allegory of Love*, pp. 57–58. However, this practice was not limited to the gods alone, as demonstrated by Balbus' lengthy discussion of personified powers in *De natura deorum* II.xxiii–xxviii. In addition to the gods, divine gifts, virtues, passions, departed human benefactors, natural phenomena, and mythological personalities were also commonly personified. See Jean Pépin, *Mythe et allégorie* (Paris, 1958), pp. 125–127, where he summarizes the Stoic method of allegorization: "Essentiellement par l'observation étymologique de son nom, qui est le plus souvent en rapport étroit avec la réalité psychologique ou cosmique qu'il désigne. Cette rationalisation des mythes sauve d'ailleurs leur valuer religieuse; on renonce bien au culte des dieux populaires, mais c'est pour retrouver dans les forces physiques qu'ils incarnent autant de spécifications de la véritable divinité, la seule qui appelle la vénération" (p. 127).

32. Lewis believes that Dante's interest in Statius stemmed in part from finding in his poem something "modern," the figure of Natura. C. S. Lewis, "Dante's Statius," *MAE*, XXV (1956), 135.

33. *Claudian*, trans. Maurice Platnauer, Loeb Classical Library (London, 1922), I.vii. All quotations are from this edition.

34. Curtius, "Zur Literarästhetik des Mittelalters," p. 185.

35. Curtius, *European Literature*, p. 106.

36. *Claudian* II.XXIX.

37. *Claudian* II.XXVII.62–64.

38. *Claudian* II; *De consulatu Stilichonis*, II.424–436.

39. The snake represents eternity. See Platnauer's note, p. 32; Hans Leisegang, "The Mystery of the Serpent," in *The Mysteries*, ed. Campbell, pp. 194–260. Lewis' identification of the *Senex* as a Genius figure in *The Allegory of Love*, p. 361, is not definitive, for the old man's presence and activity in the cave suggests that he is figure related to Time the revealer. See Erwin Panofsky, *Studies in Iconology* (New York, 1962), pp. 73, 83.

40. In "Zur Literarästhetik des Mittelalters," p. 184, Curtius describes Claudian's Natura as a full personification; she is a mighty, divine being who orders chaos and stands near the supreme God.

41. See Lewis, *The Discarded Image*, pp. 38–39.

42. Silk, *Saeculi noni auctoris*, p. 15: "Hic accipit uiolentiam uim inferentium haereticorum praue intelligentium, qui scindunt sanam doctrinam suis haeresibus, qui non habent perfectam sapientiam."

III. THE LATIN MIDDLE AGES

1. George Boas, *Essays on Primitivism and Related Ideas in the Middle Ages* (Baltimore, 1948), p. 97.

2. Two of these aspects, *Natura Dei serva* and *altrix hominum*, constitute numbers 13 and 14 in Curtius' list, "Zur Literarästhetik des Mittelalters," *ZRP*, LVII (1938), 185.

3. *Prudentius*, trans. H. J. Thomson, Loeb Classical Library (Cambridge, Mass., 1949), vol. I. All quotations and references are to this edition.

4. Lactantius, *Divinarum institutionum*, ed. J. P. Migne, *Patrologia Latina*, VI, 436–437: "Illi enim, cum aut ignorarent, a quo esset effectus mundus, aut persuadere vellent, nihil esse divina mente perfectum, naturam esse dixerunt rerum omnium matrem, quasi dicerent, omnia sua sponte esse nata: quo verbo plane imprudentiam suam confitentur. Natura enim, remota providentia et potestate divina, prorsus nihil est. Quos si Deum naturam vocent, quae perversitas est, naturam potius quam Deum nominare? Si autem natura ratio est, vel necessitas, vel conditio nascendi, non est per seipsam sensibilis: sed necesse est mentem esse divinam, quae sua providentia nascendi principium rebus omnibus praebeat. Aut si natura est coelum atque terra, et omne, quod natum est, non est Deus natura, sed Dei opus."

5. See Pierre de Labriolle, *History and Literature of Christianity from Tertullian to Boethius*, trans. Herbert Wilson (London, 1924), pp. 281–283.

6. Migne, ed., *Patrologia Latina*, XIV, 153, 158, 220, 265: "Melior enim magistra veritatis natura est. Haec sine ullius magisterio suavitatem sanitatis nostris infundit sensibus, eadem doloris acerbitatem docet esse fugiendam. Hinc vita dulcior, hinc mors amarior." See also Boas, *Essays on Primitivism*, pp. 88–92. Natura as teacher and guide to men can be found in Lactantius, Tertullian, and Saint Augustine, to name three Christian writers.

7. *Patrologia Latina*, XIV, 260.

8. *Patrologia Latina*, XIV, 202: "Bonus quidem sol, sed ministerio, non imperio; bonus meae fecunditatis adjutor, sed non creator; bonus meorum altor fructum, sed non auctor ... Mecum assistens laudat auctorem, mecum hymnum dicit Domino Deo nostro."

9. For instances of personified nature in medieval Latin poetry prior to the works of Bernard and Alan, albeit brief and for the most part echoing functions 1–7, see Curtius, "Zur Literarästhetik des Mittelalters," pp. 182–183.

10. Chenu, *Nature, Man, and Society in the Twelfth Century* (Chicago, 1968), p. 25.

11. Manitius, *Geschichte der lateinischen Literatur des Mittelalters* (Munich, 1931), III, 205. Reginald Poole, in "The Masters of the Schools of Paris and Chartres in John of Salisbury's Time," *EHR*, XXXV (1920), 331, dates this work 1145 or 1147–1148. Edmond Faral, in "Le manuscript 511 du 'Hunterian Museum' de Glasgow," *SMed*, IX (1936), 71, set 1156 as the date. As for the identity of the author, Bernard Silvestris should not be confused with Bernard of Chartres, as he was by Carl Barach and Johann Wrobel in their edition of *De mundi universitate* (Frankfurt, 1964), and by Poole in the first edition of his *Illustrations of the History of Medieval Thought and Learning*, an error corrected in the second revised edition (New York, 1960), p. 101. The mistaken identity was cleared up by the Abbé Clerval, *Les écoles de Chartres* (Frankfurt, 1965), pp. 158–163, and is discussed by Lynn Thorndike, *A History of Magic and Experimental Science*, II (New York, 1923), 99–100.

12. See Ernst Robert Curtius, *European Literature and the Latin Middle Ages* (New York, 1953), pp. 108–112; F. J. E. Raby, *A History of Secular Latin Poetry in the Middle Ages*, II (Oxford, 1934), 11–13; Theodore Silverstein, "The Fabulous Cosmogony of Bernardus Silvestris," *MP*, XLVI (1948), 95–98. See also Thorndike, *A History of Magic*, pp. 100–106. Thorndike gives a thorough account of Bernard's unfinished poem *Mathematicus*, whose plot hinges on astrological prediction, pp. 106–109. He also discusses the geomantic book *Experimentarius*, supposedly translated from the Arabic into Latin by Bernard, pp. 110–115.

13. Bernardus Silvestris, *Commentum super sex libros Eneidos Virgilii*, ed. Wilhelm Riedel (Greifswald, 1923); Edouard Jeauneau, "Note sur l'école de Chartres," *SMed*, V (1964), 855–864; from his books on poetics and rhetoric stem "the most important Latin arts-of-poetry of the twelfth and thirteenth centuries," Curtius, *European Literature*, p. 108.

14. *De mundi universitate*, p. 5. All quotations and references are to book, chapter, and page of this edition. For summaries of its action, see Curtius, *European Literature*, pp. 109–111; Etienne Gilson, "La cosmogonie de Bernardus Silvestris," *AHDLMA*, III (1928), 9–10; C. S. Lewis, *The Allegory of Love*, (London, 1953) pp. 90–97; Manitius, III, 205–206; Raby, *History of Secular Latin Poetry*, II, 8–11; Helen Waddell, *The Wandering Scholars* (New York, 1955), pp. 128–132.

15. See Gilson, "La cosmogonie de Bernardus Silvestris," pp. 5, 7–9, 19–20, 23; Curtius, *European Literature*, pp. 112–113, n. 21; Curtius, "Zur Literarästhetik des Mittelalters," pp. 185–190; Silverstein, "The

Fabulous Cosmogony," pp. 93, 109–110, 112–116. Silverstein argues strongly against Gilson's dualism theory, pointing out that whatever Bernard's "view of creation, this is conceived as anterior to the conditions described in the *De mundi*, hence beyond the scope of the work" (pp. 100–101). He shows that nowhere does Bernard indicate that he believes in the eternity of matter (pp. 100–102) and corrects Gilson's view that the figure of Noys is the second person of the Trinity by pointing out that the Trinity appears as the triple-shafted light in the mansion of Tugaton, whereas Noys is a completely separate figure, "a separate fabulous construction, characterized by certain qualities recognizably analogous to those of *Filius Dei*, since she is, as it were, His figurative representative in the physical world of the *De mundi*" (pp. 107–110). On the treatment of a Christian theme in mostly pagan terms in a philosophical poem, see Richard McKeon, "Poetry and Philosophy in the Twelfth Century: The Renaissance of Rhetoric," *MP*, XLIII (1946), 223–224.

16. For twelfth-century poetics, see Winthrop Wetherbee, "The Function of Poetry in the *De planctu naturae* of Alain de Lille," *Traditio*, XXV (1969), 87–125, esp. 87–99. Bernard distinguishes between and defines *allegoria* and *integumentum* in this way: "Est autem allegoria oratio sub historica narratione verum et ab exteriori diversum involvens intellectum, ut de luctu Iacob. Integumentum vero est oratio sub fabulosa narratione verum claudens intellectum, ut de Orpheo. Nam et ibi historia et hic fabula ministerium habent occultum, quod alias discutiendum erit. Allegoria quidem divine pagine, integumentum vero philosophice competit." Jeauneau, "Note sur l'école de Chartres," pp. 856–857. See also Edouard Jeauneau, "L'usage de la notion d'*integumentum* à travers les gloses de Guillaume de Conches," *AHDLMA*, XXIV (1957), 35–100, esp. the analysis of Abelard's *Introductio ad theologiam*, pp. 47–48; Richard Hamilton Green, "Dante's 'Allegory of Poets,'" *CL*, IX (1957), 118–128.

17. Wetherbee, "The Function of Poetry," p. 100. For the philosophical difficulties in Bernard, particularly that of matter, see Eugenio Garin, *Studi sul platonismo medievale* (Florence, 1958), pp. 54–62.

18. *The Life and Works of Clarembald of Arras*, ed. Nikolaus M. Häring (Toronto, 1965), p. 50; *Tractatulus* 9–10.229–230. On the creation *ex nihilo*, see *Tractatulus* 25.237: "Mutabilitas enim ab immutabilitate ex necessitate descendit. Immutabilitas vero est aeternitas quae Deus est. Quare necesse est mutabilitatem ab aeternitate descendere. Et sic primordialis materia a Deo descendit. Et ita non est coaeterna

Deo." Häring notes that this is based on Thierry (*Lectio* 2.25) n. 91.237.

19. See Silverstein, "The Fabulous Cosmogony," pp. 104–116.

20. *De mundi* II.v.40: "Ibi summi et superessentialis Dei sacrarium est, si theologis fidem praebas argumentis." It is possible that Bernard means Macrobius here, for a few lines later he speaks of Tugaton as residing in that supreme place. Tugaton, the Platonic idea of the Good, is discussed in *Macrobius, Commentary*, I.ii.14. See Curtius, *European Literature*, p. 111. Cf. *Saeculi noni auctoris*, ed. Silk, Papers and Monographs of the American Academy in Rome, IX (1935), 181.

21. *Tractatulus* 9.229–230: "Mundus iste ex contrariis elementis coniunctus est: calidis, frigidis, humidis, siccis. Natura ergo vel casus vel artifex haec tam adversantia sibi coniunxit. Sed natura similia similibus applicat, refugit vero contraria. Non ergo natura mundum fecit."

22. See Gilson, "La cosmogonie de Bernardus Silvestris," pp. 17–18. Robert B. Woolsey, "Bernard Silvester and the Hermetic *Asclepius*," *Traditio*, VI (1948), 341–342, declares that Bernard took the term *imarmene* from the *Asclepius* III.19b.14–15. On Bernard's use of the term *endelechia* for the world-soul, see Gilson, "La cosmogonie de Bernardus Silvestris," pp. 15–16, n. 4, where it is explained that Bernard carries over the Aristotelian definition of the human soul to the Platonic definition of world-soul.

23. William of Conches, like Abelard, had identified the world-soul with the Holy Spirit, "In Boetium," III.m.9, and then abandoned the idea, in Parent, *La doctrine de la création dans l'école de Chartres* (Ottawa, 1938), pp. 74–75. Thierry of Chartres also makes the identification in "De sex dierum operibus," ed. Nikolaus Häring, *AHDLMA*, XXII (1955), p. 193, par. 27. On the merging of *anima mundi* and the idea of Natura, see Tullio Gregory, *Platonismo medievale* (Rome, 1958), pp. 122–150.

24. See Silverstein, "The Fabulous Cosmogony of Bernardus Silvestris," pp. 104–107. In this article Silverstein seems much more certain that the *De vi rerum principiis* was a definite source than he does in his introduction to his edition of the work, "*Liber Hermetis Mercurii Triplicis de vi rerum principiis*," *AHDLMA*, XXII (1955), 217–302. See also *Didascalicon* I.vii.54 and 189.

25. II.xiii.61: "Unitas deus. diversum non aliud quam hyle eaque indigens forma."

26. Chenu, *Nature, Man, and Society*, p. 23.

27. John Scotus Erigena, *De divisione naturae*, ed. J. P. Migne, *Patro-*

logia Latina, CXXII, 893 B–C. For more on the microcosm, see 760 A and 912 C.

28. *Didascalicon*, p. 3. It is quite likely that the *De vi rerum principiis* is indebted to the *Didascalicon*. The date is difficult to set, though 1135–1147 is possible, especially if Bernard used it as a source. See Silverstein, *De vi rerum principiis*, pp. 224–225, 236–237.

29. For Hugh's three definitions of nature, see *Didascalicon*, p. 57: (1) "Nature is that which gives to each thing its being" (this is nature as "illud archetypum exemplar rerum omnium, quod in mente divina est"); (2) "The peculiar difference giving form to each thing is called its nature" ("proprium esse uniuscuiusque rei . . . Natura unamquam-que rem informens propria differentia dicitur"); (3) "Nature is an artificer fire coming forth from a certain power to beget sensible objects" ("Natura est ignis artifex, ex quadam vi procedens in res sensibles procreandas"). The Latin definitions are from Silverstein, "The Fabulous Cosmogony," p. 104, and Taylor's notes, *Didascalicon*, p. 193. The second definition derives from Boethius, and the third has its ultimate source in Cicero, *De natura deorum* II.xxii, cited by Taylor, *Didascalicon*, p. 193. Silverstein believes that assimilating either definition of nature as a cosmic power to the second definition reveals similarities to the description of nature in he *De vi rerum principiis*, though he admits that there are still significant differences (p. 104).

30. See *De vi rerum principiis*, pp. 249 and 289. On the subject of man, see Woolsey, "Bernard Silvester," pp. 343–344, who finds notions in the *Asclepius* that parallel those in Bernard's description.

31. Parent, *"La doctrine de la création*, p. 17.

32. See W. T. H. Jackson, "Allegory and Allegorization," *RS*, XXXII (1964), 164.

33. Geoffroi de Vinsauf, *Documentum de modo et arte dictandi et versificandi* II.22–23: "*Prosopopeia* est conformatio novae personae, quando scilicet res non loquens introducitur tanquam loquens," in Edmond Faral, *Les arts poétiques du XIIe et du XIIe siècles* (Paris, 1958), p. 275.

34. Faral, *Les arts poétiques*, p. 73.

35. *Commentum super sex libros Eneidos*, p. 3. For the literary background of integument and other figures of thought and expression, see Chenu, *Nature, Man, and Society*, pp. 99–145.

36. See F. J. E. Raby, "*Nuda Natura* and Twelfth-Century Cosmology," *Speculum*, XLIII (1968), 72–77.

37. Though the exact dating of these two works is uncertain, the three most recent critics and editors of Alan's works all date the *De*

planctu naturae prior to the *Anticlaudianus*. See G. Raynaud De Lage, *Alain de Lille* (Montreal and Paris, 1951), p. 42; Alan of Lille, *Anti-claudianus*, ed. Robert Bossuat (Paris, 1955), p. 13; Alan of Lille, *Textes inédits*, ed. Marie-Thérèse d'Alverny (Paris, 1965), p. 34. All three agree that the *Anticlaudianus* was composed during 1181–1184, and that because of its influence on the *Architrenius*, finished in 1184, 1182–1183 is an even more likely date. De Lage and d'Alverny date the *De planctu* during 1160–1170, while Bossuat prefers 1179–1182.

38. See Johan Huizinga, "Über die Verknüpfung des Poetischen mit dem Theologischen bei Alanus De Insulis," *MKNAL*, LXXXIV, Series B, No. 6 (1932), 128; Cesare Vasoli, "Le idee filosofiche di Alano di Lilla nel *De planctu* e nell' *Anticlaudianus*," *GCFL*, XL (1961), 465–466; Wetherbee, "The Function of Poetry"; R. H. Green, "Alan of Lille's *De planctu naturae*," *Speculum*, XXXI (1956), 649–674; Green, "Alan of Lille's *Anticlaudianus*: Ascensus Mentis in Deum," *AnM*, VIII (1967), 3–16.

39. See Curtius, *European Literature*, pp. 118–121; Lewis, *The Allegory of Love*, pp. 98–109; Manitius, III, 797–799; F. J. E. Raby, *A History of Christian Latin Poetry*, 2nd ed. (Oxford, 1953), pp. 298–302.

40. See Charles Sears Baldwin, *Medieval Rhetoric and Poetic* (New York, 1928), p. 174. See also De Lage, *Alain de Lille*, pp. 109–111.

41. The edition of *De planctu naturae* cited throughout is Thomas Wright's, *The Anglo-Latin Satirical Poets and Epigrammatists*, Rerum Britannicarum Medii Aevi Scriptores (Rolls Series 59), II, 429–522. For the portrait of Natura, see pp. 431–443. In the very last lines of the work Alan identifies the events that have taken place as a vision: "Hujus igitur imaginariae visionis subtracto speculo, me ab extasi excitatum in somno prior mysticae apparitionis dereliquit aspectus" (p. 522).

42. "In qua, prout oculis pictura imaginabatur, animalium cele-bratur concilium." *De planctu naturae*, ed. Wright, p. 427. According to Robinson, this line possibly suggested to Chaucer the idea for his *Parlement of Foules*. *The Works of Geoffrey Chaucer*, ed. F. N. Robinson, 2nd. edition (Cambridge, Mass., 1957), p. 794.

43. See Vasoli, "Le idee filosofiche," pp. 472–473.

44. In one of its senses the word *natura* means genitals. See *Harper's Latin Dictionary* (New York, 1879), def. D, p. 1190; *Lexicon Totius Latinitatis*, III, 336–337; Arthur O. Lovejoy, *Essays in the History of Ideas* (New York, 1960), p. 332, n. 43. Though there is little reason to believe that Alan intended his readers to take the word in this sense, to the modern reader, who is ever ready to detect the slightest shade of

meaning, it is a distinct if slightly grotesque possibility for the genitals, abused by sodomites and adulterers, to cry out their own complaint.

45. See Wetherbee, "The Function of Poetry," pp. 103–104. The symbolic charioteer goes back to Plato's *Phaedrus* 253d–254e.

46. Barach and Wrobel, *De mundi universitate* II.ix.53; *De planctu naturae*, pp. 445–447. For an interesting parallel see the hymn to Venus, opening of Book I in Lucretius' *De rerum natura*.

47. Curtius, *European Literature*, p. 119. That Alan could not completely escape the Neoplatonic hierarchy is evident in such a passage as the fourth stanza of the narrator's hymn to Natura. Contemplating the pure ideas of Noys, Natura coins the species of all things ("Quae noys puras recolens ideas, / Singulas rerum species monetas"). *De planctu naturae*, p. 458.

48. See d'Alverny, *Textes inédits*, p. 82. "Hec autem generantur nature ministerio, que nichil aliud est quam potentia inferioribus causis indita ex similibus procreandi similia. Natura ergo non creatrix, sed procreatrix dicitur, quasi ex alio creatrix. Eius operatio, procreatio, eius vero opus, procreatum dicitur." From the *Expositio prosae de Angelis*, in d'Alverny, *Textes inédits*, pp. 199–200. In his *Contra haereticos*, Alan explains that God gives procreation to things through his intermediary, Natura, and that the law of Natura was not altered by Adam's sin: "Cum ergo Deus mediante Natura, res procreaturus esset, propter peccatum Adae noluit mutare legem naturae. Haec enim fuit lex naturae ab origine, ut ex similibus similia procrearentur, ut de homine homo, de rationali rationalis." Cited by De Lage, *Alain de Lille*, p. 63. See also *Summa quot modis seu distinctiones*, eleventh definition of natura, cited by De Lage, *Alain de Lille*, p. 65; *Anticlaudianus* II.71–73.75.

49. De Lage believes Alan's hymn was inspired by III.m.ix, which is addressed to God, the Father of all things. *Alain de Lille*, p. 106. Though this is a reasonable assumption, it is more likely that Alan was primarily inspired by this poem to Natura, to which he seems to allude quite deliberately.

50. See Green, "Alan of Lille's *De planctu naturae*," p. 655. esp. n. 14.

51. See Wetherbee, "The Function of Poetry," for the implications in Natura's speeches of the failings of poetic fable and the use of mythology. As products of the imagination of fallen man, they are themselves examples of his corruption. Natura, who uses this technique herself, is unable to supply satisfactory interpretations of the mythological figures "which veil her principles from the unenlightened mind. Alain's allegory amounts to a powerful criticism of the assumptions of Chartrian

'natural philosophy' and the pursuit of wisdom in secular literature"
(p. 109).

52. *De planctu naturae*, p. 270. Natura's preference for the stable
ethereal world indicátes that Alan does not identify her with the sublunary world. She is its queen and ruler, as indicated by the words of
Generosity (Largitas) to her, "O mundanae regionis regina!" (p. 516).

53. See Lovejoy, *Essays in the History of Ideas*, p. 336; Boas, *Essays on
Primitivism*, p. 103. On Macrobius as a source of Platonism to the
Chartrians, see Edouard Jeauneau, "Macrobe, source du Platonism
Chartrain," *SMed*, I (1960), 3–24.

54. See Hans Liebeschütz, *Fulgentius Metaforalis: ein Beitrag zur
Geschichte der antiken Mythologie im Mittelalter* (Leipzig, 1926), p. 45; E.
H. Alton, "The Mediaeval Commentators on Ovid's *Fasti*," *Herma-
thena*, XX (1930), 136; John Scotus Erigena, *Annotationes in Marcianum*,
ed. Cora E. Lutz (Cambridge, Mass., 1939), p. 67; *Scriptores rerum
mythicarum Latini tres Romae nuper reperti*, ed. G. H. Bode (Hildesheim,
1968), p. 239; Saint Augustine, *Contra Faustum, Opera Omnia*, VIII
(Paris, 1841), XX.ix.374.

55. *Commentum super sex libros Eneidos*, p. 9: "Veneres vero legimus
duas esse, legitimam et petulantiae deam. Legitimam Venerm dicimus
esse mundanam musicam, i.e., aequalem mundanorum proportionem,
quam alii Astream, alii naturalem iustitiam vocant. Haec enim est in
elementis, in sideribus, in temporibus, in animantibus. Impudicam
autem venerem, petulantiae deam, dicimus esse carnis concupiscentiam
quia omnium fornicationem mater est." For the double Venus background, see Green, "Alan of Lille's *De planctu naturae*," pp. 667–669.
Although Green's identification of Alan's *Venus scelestis* with John
Scotus' "generalis et specialis libido" (*Annotationes in Marcianum*, pp.
13, 91–92), the source of all vice, is well-supported by Alan's text, his
identification of *Venus caelestis* as a figure of "providential love" does
not enjoy equally strong textual support. The assumption that Alan
made unqualified use of this tradition raises unnecessary difficulties.
Bernard associated Astrea with *Venus legitima*, probably based on Ovid's
Metamorphoses I.146–150, and the implications of the departure of the
last divinity to live among men after the advent of the degenerate
bronze age is paralleled by Alan's treatment of Venus: after man's
upsetting of the natural order, the legitimate aspect of Venus recedes,
and the evil aspect dominates earthly love.

56. On homosexuality, see Alan's *Liber Poenitentialis*, ed. Jean Longère
(Louvain, 1965), II.110–111; Herbert A. Deane, *The Political and*

Social Ideas of St. Augustine (New York, 1963), p. 88; Curtius, *European Literature*, pp. 113–117; De Lage, *Alain de Lille*, p. 82.

57. On grammar, see M.-D. Chenu, *La théologie au douzième siècle* (Paris, 1957), pp. 90–107; *The Metalogicon of John of Salisbury*, trans. Daniel McGarry (Berkeley and Los Angeles, 1962), I.14.38–41; III.2.150–155.

58. See the passage beginning, "Sed cum ipsa genialis concubitas regula," *De planctu naturae*, pp. 475–476. Natura's instructions to Venus on lawful propagation consist largely of grammatical metaphors. Venus is enjoined, for example, to take care that the noun, the feminine sex, and the adjective, the male sex, always keep their proper relationship. There is a remarkable resemblance between Alan's doctrine of love and that given by Plotinus, *The Enneads*, trans. Stephen McKenna (London, 1930), III.5. Though it is impractical here to demonstrate a direct line of influence from Plotinus to Alan, it is important to recognize the possibility of an indirect filtering of Plotinian concepts through intermediate writers.

59. Wetherbee, "The Function of Poetry," pp. 111–112.

60. On the Genius figure, see Wetherbee, "The Function of Poetry," pp. 112–118; De Lage, *Alain de Lille*, pp. 89–93; Edgar C. Knowlton, "The Allegorical Figure Genius," *CP*, XV (1920), 380–84; Knowlton, "Genius as an Allegorical Figure," *MLN*, XXXIX (1924), 89–95; Lewis, *The Allegory of Love*, pp. 361–363.

61. De Lage, *Alain de Lille*, p. 92.

62. See Chalcidius, CCXXX, 324–325; *De mundi universitate* I.ii.11; II.xiii.62; d'Alverny, *Textes inédits*, pp. 167–180; De Lage, *Alain de Lille*, pp. 92–93. The same concept can be found in the *Anticlaudianus* I.450–510.70–71, in Reason's contemplation of her triple mirror.

63. Wetherbee, "The Function of Poetry," p. 114. See also Vasoli, "Le idee filosofiche," pp. 477–478. On the union of form and matter, cf. Alan's *Sermo de sphaera intelligibili* in d'Alverny, *Textes inédits*, pp. 299–301.

64. Wetherbee, "The Function of Poetry," pp. 112–114. For other works in which Genius appears as god of generation, see De Lage, *Alain de Lille*, pp. 89–90; Lewis, *The Allegory of Love*, pp. 360–361. For the etymological relation of *genius* to *genialis* and *gignere*, see De Lage, *Alain de Lille*, p. 89. Following Knowlton, Lewis identifies the *senex* who sits inside the cave of Aevum in Claudian's *De consulatu Stilichonis* II.424.32 as a vague Genius figure (*The Allegory of Love*, p. 361). This identification is by no means conclusive, because the duties of the

senex include activities not associated with Genius and the name Genius is not connected with the figure anywhere in the text, as it is in other references. De Lage does not list Claudian in this connection at all.

65. See Wetherbee, "The Function of Poetry," pp. 117–118; p. 116, n. 119, on the kiss "as symbol of the Incarnation, of the Holy Spirit, and of the imparting of Christian doctrine," and on the implied analogy between matter and the Virgin. Wetherbee argues that the description of the genial kiss is indebted to Noys' greeting of Natura as "uteri mei beata fecunditas" (I.ii.9) in the *De mundi*, which echoes the *Ave Maria* and provides the basis for Alan's suggesting "a natural analogue to the Annunciation." See also J. A. W. Bennett, *The Parlement of Foules* (Oxford, 1957), p. 108.

66. Wetherbee, "The Function of Poetry," pp. 118–119.

67. Charles Jourdain, ed., "De commentaires inédit de Guillaume de Conches et de Nicolas Triveth sur *La consolation de la philosophie* de Boèce," *Notices et extraits des manuscrits de la Bibliothèque Imperiale*, XX (1862), 81. The text is also supplied and discussed by Jeauneau, "L'usage de la notion d'*integumentum*," pp. 44–47. The source in Horace is *Epistles* II.2.188–189.

68. Wetherbee, "The Function of Poetry," pp. 121–122. The quotations are from Chenu, *La théologie au douzième siècle*, p. 295. Vasoli has also discussed Alan's place in this movement, particularly as reflected by his *Regulae de sacra theologia* and the later *De planctu naturae* and *Anticlaudianus*. Cesare Vasoli, "La 'theologia apothetica' di Alano di Lilla," *RCSF*, XVI (1961), 153–163.

69. *Anticlaudianus*, ed. Bossuat, p. 199. All references are to this edition, by page for the *summarium* and by book, line, and page for the poem.

70. Curtius, *European Literature*, p. 120; Vasoli, "Le idee filosofiche," pp. 483–484; De Lage, *Alain de Lille*, pp. 117–129.

71. "Alan of Lille's *Anticlaudianus*," p. 4.

72. On the question of whether the work also refers to Claudianus Mamertus, whom Alan had confused with Claudian the poet in his *Contra haereticos*, see *Anticlaudianus*, p. 34; De Lage, *Alain de Lille*, p. 51. Bossuat does not believe that the poem is necessarily a refutation of Saint Hilary of Poitiers' theory of the creation of the soul, reported by Claudianus Mamertus in his *De statu animae*. Hilary had said the soul comes from something, *ex aliquo*, while Alan states in his poem that the soul was created out of nothing by the immediate act of God. See Raby, *A History of Christian Latin Poetry*, p. 298. On the literary sources of the poem, see *Anticlaudianus* pp. 34–42.

73. Green, "Alan of Lille's *Anticlaudianus*," pp. 12-16, provides an analysis of this complex figure, who is variously called Fronesis, Sophia, Minerva, but who is identified by the poem's action as *sapientia*, "the soul's purest cognitive power by which, through the mediation of theology and the light of faith, the vision of God can be achieved" (p. 14). See also Vasoli, "Le idee filosofiche," pp. 487-488.

74. *Metalogicon* IV.17.230.

75. See Alan's *Hierarchia* in d'Alverny, *Textes inédits*, pp. 227-228.

76. In *Anticlaudianus*, p. 35, n. 6, Bossuat suggests that the idea for the perfect man might have come to Alan from Boethius' *Contra Evtychen* II, where the humanity of Christ is described. He also points out that some of the commentaries on the *Anticlaudianus* consider the perfect man a symbol of Christ, as does Ellebaut, who wrote an adaptation of the poem in the thirteenth century. See Ellebaut, *Anticlaudien*, ed. Andrew Creighton (Washington, D.C., 1944), p. 6.

77. See, e.g., Peter Dronke, *Medieval Latin and the Rise of the European Love-Lyric*, 2 vols. (Oxford, 1965).

78. Jean and Chaucer certainly knew Alan's and Bernard's works. Jean adapted many passages from the *Anticlaudianus* and translated Alan's description of Fortuna's home almost verbatim. See Howard Rollin Patch, *The Goddess Fortuna in Medieval Literature* (Cambridge, Mass, 1927), pp. 126-167. See also Patch, *The Other World* (Cambridge, Mass., 1950), pp. 150-151. On Chaucer's use of the *De mundi*, see Chauncey Wood, *Chaucer and the Country of the Stars* (Princeton, 1970), pp. 208-219.

79. Text in Wright, *Anglo-Latin Satirical Poets*, I, 240-392. See also Lewis, *The Allegory of Love*, pp. 109-110; Manitius, III.805-809; Raby, *A History of Secular Latin Poetry*, II, 100-102.

IV. JEAN DE MEUN

1. The most important studies of the poem are Gérard Paré, *Les idées et les lettres au XIIIᵉ siècle: Le Roman de la Rose* (Montreal, 1947), which supersedes his earlier work, *Le Roman de la Rose et la scolastique courtoisie* (Paris and Ottawa, 1941); Alan M. F. Gunn, *The Mirror of Love* (Lubbock, 1952); John V. Fleming, *The Roman de la Rose: A Study in Allegory and Iconography* (Princeton, 1969). Fleming's interpretation is not considered in this study. Winthrop Wetherbee, "The Literal and the Allegorical: Jean de Meun and the 'de Planctu Naturae'," *MS*, XXXIII (1971), 264-291; and Marc-René Jung, *Etudes sur le poème allégorique en France au Moyen Âge*, Romanica Helvetica, 82 (Bern, 1971) both appeared

after this work was completed. On sources, see Charles Dahlberg, "Love and the *Roman de la Rose*," *Speculum*, XLIV (1969), 568–584; Ernest Langlois, *Origines et sources du Roman de la Rose* (Paris, 1891).

2. *Le Roman de la Rose*, ed. Ernest Langlois, 5 vols. *SATF*, 71 (Paris, 1921–1924), IV and V.15891–20683. All references are to this edition, by volume and line number. Translations are from *The Romance of the Rose*, trans. Charles Dahlberg (Princeton, 1971), which is based on Langlois' edition.

3. See Langlois, *Origines et sources*, pp. 148–150.

4. See Paré, *Les idées*, pp. 203–278, which points out the affinities between many passages of Jean's poem and the works of Albert the Great.

5. *Roman* IV.15891–16016, and note, p. 296.

6. A few lines earlier Jean tells the story of the phoenix, 15975–16004. In *Origines et sources*, p. 165, Langlois lists Ovid, Lactantius, and Claudian as Jean's sources of the well-known story, but does not mention that Claudian's poem on the phoenix directly involves Natura in the bird's regeneration.

7. Gunn, *Mirror of Love*, pp. 128–129, analyzes the speech in terms of the rhetorical figure *expeditio*, logical exclusion.

8. Paré, *Les idées*, pp. 207, 227–230, 252–271. For a discussion of the sublunary world in Islamic cosmology, which Jean may have known indirectly, see Seyyed Hossein Nasr, *An Introduction to Islamic Cosmological Doctrines* (Cambridge, Mass., 1964), pp. 139–150.

9. Jean's description of Art's attempt to rival Natura (*Roman* IV.16005–16148) does not come from Alan. The superiority of Natura's creations over those of Art lies in their ability to reproduce themselves, a distinction made by Aristotle in the *Physics* II.i.193b.10. See Gunn, *Mirror of Love*, pp. 260–265. For Jean's interest in alchemy, see Paré, *Les idées*, pp. 68–71. For Jean's place in the history of the concept of nature versus art, see Edward Tayler, *Nature and Art in Renaissance Literature* (New York, 1964), pp. 74–77.

10. See Gunn, *Mirror of Love*, pp. 276–297.

11. Gunn, *Mirror of Love*, pp. 267, 269–270.

12. Edmond Faral, "*Le Roman de la Rose* et la pensée française au XIIIᵉ siècle," *RDM*, XXXV (1926), 443.

13. Ernst Robert Curtius, *European Literature and the Latin Middle Ages* (New York, 1953), p. 126.

14. See Paré, *Les idées*, pp. 283–285.

15. Paré, *Les idées*, pp. 322–325. See also Curtius, *European Literature*, p. 126; Etienne Gilson, *History of Christian Philosophy in the Middle Ages*

(New York, 1955), pp. 412–420. For the possible relationship between the *Roman* and Latin Averroism, see Franz Walter Müller, *Der Rosen-roman und der lateinische Averroismus des 13. Jahrhunderts* (Frankfurt, 1947).

16. In his article "The Moral Reputation of the *Roman de la Rose* before 1400," *RPh*, XVIII (1965), 430–435, John V. Fleming attacks the view that Natura and Genius necessarily represent Jean's personal attitude. He argues against the position that Jean's poem caused a "furore" and that it was one of the targets of the 1277 condemnation, particularly in light of the fact that neither poet nor poem is mentioned in the condemnation. See also A. J. Denomy, "The *De amore* of Andreas Capellanus and the Condemnation of 1277," *MS*, VIII (1946), 107–149. Denomy's assumption that Andreas' work, which is included *nominatim* in the condemnation, anticipates the Averroistic doctrine of the double truth (pp. 148–149) illustrates the danger in relating literary works to a philosophical movement simply on the basis of chronology. See W. T. H. Jackson, "The *De amore* of Andreas Capallanus and the Practice of Love at Court," *RR*, XLIX (1958), 249. Fleming also establishes that the attacks on the *Roman* by Christine de Pisan and Jean Gerson around 1400 were a novelty, just as Jean's defender in the quarrel, Pierre Col, originally pointed out. See C. F. Ward, *The Epistles on the "Romance of the Rose" and Other Documents in the Debate* (Chicago, 1911).

17. Gunn, *Mirror of Love*, pp. 141–198, 396–405, 435–436, 478, 498–505.

18. D. W. Robertson, Jr., *A Preface to Chaucer* (Princeton, 1962), p. 202. See also p. 199: "He who seeks Jean de Meun's opinions will find them here, not in the discourses of the other characters, who, with Ciceronian decorum, speak as their natures demand. Raison explains the function of delight in love and the folly of pursuing it for its own sake rather than using it as a stimulus to the perpetuation of the species." Robertson's argument implies that Raison does not speak according to her own nature but rather to the editorial needs of Jean.

19. Rosemund Tuve, *Allegorical Imagery* (Princeton, 1966), pp. 273–276, agrees that taken alone, Natura's position expresses an inadequate view of love, and that Love and his barons make Genius their servant.

20. See Faral, "*Le Roman de la Rose*," p. 437; Lionel J. Friedman, "'Jean De Meung,' Antifeminism, and 'Bourgeois Realism,'" *MP*, LVII (1959), 16. Friedman points out that Jean transformed the figure of Raison from "the conventional moment in the love process" in the work of Guillaume, into "the proponent of several doctrines of rational love."

21. Cf. Alan's "Prosequitur, si tu sequeris; fugiendo fugatur; / Si cedis, cedit; si fugis illa fugit," *De planctu naturae*, p. 474.

22. Raison's recognition that Natura presides over procreation as God's representative is clear in her explanation to the Lover of God's purpose in creating man with sexual organs, so as to ensure the continuity of His creation (III.6956–6976). The Lover, on whom Raison's words have been wasted, attacks her for the frankness with which she refers to the sexual organs, an illustration of how tenaciously he clings to the code of "good manners" demanded of him by the God of Love, although he understands little of what he is about.

23. See Friedman, "'Jean de Meung,'" pp. 19–20: "Genius, in concluding, excepts Natura from the general ranks of women in lines considered ironic. If irony there is, it stems not from Genius' saying what he does not believe but from the exploitation of the dual aspect of Natura, who here appears, on the one hand, as a macrocosmic force transcending human foibles and, on the other, as a microcosmic woman, subject to the characteristics of that animal . . . Only when an abstraction has been completely humanized may the irony between *res* and *signum* be exploited humorously."

24. On Gunn's point (*Mirror of Love*, p. 405) that Genius' exhortation is announced as "la diffinitive sentence" (*Roman* V.19504.4), it is likely that the *sententia* referred to is Natura's judgment rather than the poet's.

V. CHAUCER'S *THE PARLEMENT OF FOULES*

1. The most thorough study of Chaucer's poem and its background to date is J. A. W. Bennett, *The Parlement of Foules: An Interpretation* (Oxford, 1957). For accounts of *Parlement* criticism, see Donald C. Baker, "The Parliament of Fowls," in *Companion to Chaucer Studies*, ed. Beryl Rowland (Toronto, 1968), pp. 355–369; R. M. Lumiansky, "Chaucer's *Parlement of Foules*: A Philosophical Interpretation," *RES*, XXIV (1948), 81–83; George Williams, *A New View of Chaucer* (Durham, N.C., 1965), pp. 82–83; F. N. Robinson, *The Works of Geoffrey Chaucer*, 2nd. ed., pp. 791–792. All quotations of Chaucer are from this edition.

2. For Chaucer's use of the rhetorical figures *sententia*, *contentio*, and *comparatio* in this stanza and his use of *repetitio* in his summary (technically, a *digressio*) of the *Dream of Scipio*, see Dorothy Everett, *Essays on Middle English Literature* (Oxford, 1955), pp. 103–106.

3. For Chaucer's use of the rhetorical conventions of the love vision in the *Parlement*, see Dorothy Bethurum, "Chaucer's Point of View as Narrator in the Love Poems," *PMLA*, LXXIV (1959), 511–520.

4. Africanus and Scipio's view of the universe from "a sterry place" implies a cosmic journey, a motif noted in the *De mundi universitate* and the *Anticlaudianus*.

5. On the possible significances of "north-north-west," see Robinson's note on *Parlement of Foules, Works of Chaucer*, p. 793.

6. For the planetary denotation of Cytherea elsewhere in Chaucer and in medieval poetry, see Bennett, *The Parlement of Foules*, pp. 57–58.

7. See Jean Seznec, *The Survival of the Pagan Gods*, trans. Barbara F. Sessions (New York, 1961, first published 1940), p. 44; Robinson's note on *The Merchant's Tale* IV.1777, *Works of Chaucer*, p. 517; Bertrand Bronson, "In Appreciation of Chaucer's *Parlement of Foules*," *UCPES*, III (1935), 204–205; Bronson, "*The Parlement of Foules* Revisited," *ELH*, XV, (1948), 252.

8. On the echo in these stanzas of the inscription over the entrance to Dante's *Inferno*, see Everett, *Essays*, p. 143.

9. The word "were," which means "weir" as used in the passage, can also mean "a state of anxiety or uncertainty." Perhaps Chaucer intended the double meaning, for anxiety and uncertainty are indeed characteristic of the kind of love described in the passage. The two words, however, are not exact homonyms.

10. It is possible that the inscriptions over the entrance to Chaucer's park may have been suggested by Jean's opposition of the Garden of Deduit and the Good Shepherd's Park. On Chaucer's use of this opposition elsewhere, see George D. Economou, "Januarie's Sin Against Nature: *The Merchant's Tale* and the *Roman de la Rose*," *CL*, XVII (1965), 251–257.

11. On the convention of the catalogue of trees, see Robinson's note on *Parlement of Foules, Works of Chaucer* pp. 793–794. On *silva*, see the discussion of Servius' commentary on the term in the *Aeneid* I.314, in William Nelson, *The Poetry of Edmund Spenser* (New York, 1963), pp. 158–159.

12. Verses 199–203 are original with Chaucer. See O. F. Emerson, "Some Notes on Chaucer and Some Conjectures," *PQ*, II (1923), 81–96.

13. On "Wille," see Robinson's note on *Parlement of Foules*, p. 794. It is possible Chaucer meant "Wille" in the sense of the Italian *voluttá* (*voluptas*).

14. *Metamorphoses* I.468–473. See Erwin Panofsky, *Studies in Iconology* (New York, 1962), pp. 101–104. This characterization is followed

in the *Roman*. See also Chaucer's description of the God of Love in the Prologue to *The Legend of Good Women* F.226–240; G.158–172.

15. Bennett, *The Parlement of Foules*, p. 84.

16. For Chaucer's modifications, see Bennett, *The Parlement of Foules*, pp. 78–98; Bronson, "In Appreciation of Chaucer's *Parlement*," pp. 209–211; Charles O. McDonald, "An Interpretation of Chaucer's *Parlement of Foules*," *Speculum*, XXX (1955), 449–450; Robert A. Pratt, "Chaucer's Use of the *Teseida*," *PMLA*, LXII (1947), 605–608. Of these critics, Pratt alone does not see Chaucer's adaptation of Boccaccio as thematically relevant.

17. Chaucer never identifies this temple as the temple of Venus, as he does in his other adaptation of the scene in *The Knight's Tale* I.1918–1966.

18. The story of Priapus and Lotis appears in Ovid, *Fasti*, trans. James George Frazer, Loeb Classical Library (Cambridge, Mass., 1951), I.415–440. Priapus is the "god of gardyns" in the *Merchant's Tale* IV.2034–2035, which is probably based on the same Ovidian passage, vs. 415, where Priapus is called "hortorum decus et tutela." The interpretation of Priapus as a representation of frustrated lust is supported by Emerson Brown, Jr., "*Hortus Inconclusus*: The Significance of Priapus and Pyramus and Thisbe in the *Merchant's Tale*," *ChauR*, IV (1970), 33–34. See also Richard L. Hoffman, *Ovid and the Canterbury Tales* (Philadelphia, 1966), 154–156. McDonald's suggestion in "An Interpretation," p. 449, that "Priapus represents love and fertility at its most natural" is surely wrong. See Bernard F. Huppé and D. W. Robertson, Jr., *Fruyt and Chaf* (Princeton, 1963), p. 120. Despite these critics' provocative view of the poem, I cannot agree with their position that the *Parlement* is essentially against earthly love.

19. For Chaucer's subduing of Boccaccio's rich description of Venus, see Bronson, "In Appreciation of Chaucer's *Parlement*," pp. 209–211; McDonald, "An Interpretation," p. 449.

20. See Robinson's note on *Parlement of Foules*, p. 794, and *The Faerie Queene* III.i.39–45, where Baccante is named as one of Malecasta's knights. Bacchilatria, one of the daughters of Idolatry, was also loosed upon the world after Venus' adulterous affair with Antigamus in the *De planctu naturae*, pp. 485–486.

21. See Robinson's note on *Parlement of Foules*, p. 794, which suggests the list is a combination of Boccaccio and Dante (*Inferno* V.58–69). See also Howard Schless, "Chaucer and Dante" *Critical Approaches to Medieval Literature*, Selected Papers from the English Institute, 1958–1959, ed. Dorothy Bethurum (New York, 1960), pp. 134–154, who

shows that "it is more likely that Chaucer's 'stock list' [of lovers] developed from Boccaccio's stanza on the basis of common knowledge and reading in the standard classical authors" (p. 141).

22. The only other reference to Cytherea in Chaucer comes in *The Knight's Tale* I.2215–2216, where she is identified as beneficent. See also the invocation to Venus at the beginning of the third book of *Troilus and Criseyde*.

23. *Paradiso* XXXIII.14–39. This speech anticipates Troilus' song, III.1744–1771, which is based on Boethius, II.m.viii. See also *The Knight's Tale*. I.2987–3016.

24. The relation of charity to "Thi moder ek, Citherea the swete," seems to have reference to the early Christian assimilation of the Neoplatonic *Venus Ourania* to heavenly love, *caritas*. See Panofsky, *Studies in Iconology*, pp. 142–144. Chaucer nevertheless closely associates Cytherea with heavenly love.

25. The *De mundi universitate* places Cupid (even though as an infant) with the planet Venus: "Sinistro super ab ubere Cupido parvulus dependebat" (II.45).

26. On the use of the four classes of birds to represent the four classes of human society, see Robinson's note on *Parlement of Foules*, p. 795. The birds of prey stand for the nobles, the worm-fowl for the bourgeoisie, the seed-fowl for the agricultural class, and the water-fowl for the merchant class.

27. Theodore Silverstein, "Chaucer's Modest and Homely Poem: The *Parlement*," *MP*, LVI (1959), 274, suggests that Chaucer's source for the first three lines of this stanza was the pseudo-Aristotelian *De mundo*, trans. D. F. Furley, Loeb Classical Library (Cambridge, 1955) although he does not supply a specific reference. Investigation of the *De mundo* bears out the fact that "nature" is said to knit together the elements (396b). Moreover, sexuality is related to this activity, just as it is in the quoted stanza from the *Parlement*: "But perhaps nature actually has a liking for opposites; perhaps it is from them that she creates harmony, and not from similar things, in just the same way as she joined the male to the female, and not each of them to another of the same sex, thus making the first harmonious community not of similar but of opposite things" (396b).

28. Fisher maintains erroneously that "Chaucer himself did some perverting of the Chartrian tradition ... For his Nature ... is the priestess of marriage, the instrument of human law by which the unruly life force is regulated." John H. Fisher, *John Gower: Moral Philosopher and Friend of Chaucer* (New York, 1964), p. 219.

29. See McDonald, "An Interpretation," p. 453.

30. For the opposite view, see Gardiner Stillwell, "Chaucer's Eagles and Their Choice on February 14," *JEGP*, LIII (1954), 546–561; Stillwell, "Unity and Comedy in the *Parlement of Foules*," *JEGP*, XLIX (1950), 470–495.

31. See Robert Worth Frank, Jr., "Structure and Meaning in the *Parlement of Foules*," *PMLA*, LXXI (1956), 538. Frank identifies Nature with Love, and the fact that Love is irrational leads him to interpret "If I were Resoun" as meaning that Nature (Love?) is not reasonable. McDonald's undocumented statement that Reason is "Nature's opposite number in allegorical tradition" ("An Interpretation," p. 454) ignores both Boethius and Alan and seems to be based on Jean de Meun. See Bennett, *The Parlement of Foules*, p. 132.

32. Robinson, *Parlement of Foules*, *Works of Chaucer*, p. 796.

33. See Everett, *Essays*, p. 112; Charles Muscatine, *Chaucer and the French Tradition* (Berkeley and Los Angeles, 1957), p. 115; Charles A. Owen, Jr., "The Role of the Narrator in the *Parlement of Foules*," *CE*, XIV (1953), 267–268; *The Parlement of Foulys*, ed. D. S. Brewer (New York, 1960), p. 43; McDonald, "An Interpretation," p. 456; Wolfgang Clemen, *Chaucer's Early Poetry*, trans. C. A. M. Sym (New York, 1964), pp. 148–151.

34. This view opposes that of Lumiansky, "Chaucer's *Parlement of Foules*," p. 88, which states that the end of the poem leaves the poet with the problem of reconciling true and false felicity. The final stanza of the poem, which to Lumiansky expresses the poet's desire to find a solution in future reading, actually means that the narrator intends to continue reading so that he might, as he has after reading the *Dream of Scipio*, "mete som thyng for to fare / The bet."

APPENDIX. A SUMMARY OF BERNARD SILVESTRIS' *DE MUNDI UNIVERSITATE*

1. Because of matter's imperfection, Noys does not impress it with the eternal ideas, for they are immovable and cannot mix with matter. Instead, she invests matter with copies of the divine ideas (I.ii.11). This distinction between ideas and their copies is reiterated in II.xiii.62. On the currency of this concept at Chartres, see J. M. Parent, *La doctrine de la création dans l'école de Chartres* (Ottawa, 1938), pp. 90–94; Theodore Silverstein, "The Fabulous Cosmogony of Bernardus Silvestris," *MP*, XLVI (1948), *The Commentaries on Boethius of Gilbert of Poiters*, ed. Nikolaus M. Häring (Toronto, 1966), *De trinitate* I.2.98.100.

2. Cf. John Scotus Erigena, *Annotationes in Marcianum*, ed. Cora E. Lutz (Cambridge, Mass., 1939), p. 10.

3. *Annotationes*, p. 40.

4. A combination of two Hermetic figures, Pantomorphos, the cosmic form-giver, and *ousiarch*, of which "oyarses" is a Latinized corruption, ruler of a heavenly sphere. Robert B. Woolsey, "Bernard Silvester and the Hermetic *Asclepius*," *Traditio*, VI (1948), 342–343. Bernard also identifies Saturn and Jupiter as having "oyarses" of their own (II.v.41 and 42). Woolsey argues that Bernard meant his readers to understand each of the seven planets as possessing an "oyarses," a term which in the *Asclepius* "is a designation for each ruler of each stratum of the material world," although Bernard "discarded the sense of rule; in *Oyarses* he employs only the notion of essence or true quality" (p. 343). See also C. S. Lewis, *The Allegory of Love* (London, 1953), p. 361.

5. II.iv.31–34.39. The distinction between the three fates, the *parcae*—Atropos, Clotho, and Lachesis—and the general, more comprehensive fate is not unusual. Later in the work, Bernard explains that the three fates dispense the laws of providence in the created world. Atropos presides over the fixed stars, Clotho over the planets, and Lachesis the earth or sublunary world (II.xi.58). Bernard's source was probably Chalcidius, CXLVI.182–183: "At uero in substantia positum fatum mundi anima est, tripertita in aplanem sphaeram inque eam quae putatur erratica et in sublunarem tertiam; quarum elatam quidem ad superna dici Atropon, mediam Clotho, imam Lachesin."

6. Though no source for Physis has been discovered, her meaning for Bernard is fairly clear. Theodore Silverstein, in "Chaucer's Modest and Homely Poem: The *Parlement*," *MP*, LVI (1959), 276, sees Physis as a separate figuration of the sublunary sphere of nature, while the figure of Natura represents the divine, or superlunary sphere, of nature. A slightly different view is expressed by Edgar C. Knowlton, "The Goddess Natura in Early Periods," *JEGP*, XIX (1920), p. 237. On the name *Granusion*, see Etienne Gilson, "La cosmogonie de Bernardus Silvestris," *AHDLMA*, III (1928), 19, n. 1; C. S. Lewis, *The Discarded Image* (Cambridge, 1964), pp. 59–60. The name is based on a misunderstanding of Chalcidius, CXXIX.172, where the lower and upper air in the atmosphere are distinguished. Because this lower air, called *hygran usian* by the Greeks, is moist, men are able to breathe it ("post humectae substantiae, quam Graeci hygran usian appellant, quae humecta substantia aer est crassior, ut sit aer iste quem homines spirant"). Whatever the reason, Bernard took *hygran usian* as a proper name.

INDEX

Abelard, 189n*16*

Abraham, 99

Academics, 3

Adam, 82, 193n*48*

Aevum, cave of, 49, 195n*64*

Africanus, 126, 127, 128, 131, 149

Alan of Lille, 1, 3, 6, 22, 27, 37, 51, 57, 58, 59, 69, 107, 125; *Anticlaudianus*, 2, 35, 48, 53, 72, 79, 97, 98–102, 111, 112; *De planctu naturae*, 2, 19, 36, 48, 53, 72–97, 101, 102, 103, 106, 109, 111, 112, 118, 121, 130, 138, 140

Albert the Great, 198n*4*

Alecto, 100

allegoria, defined by Bernard Silvestris, 189n*16*. *See also* Allegory

Allegory, 20, 102–103, 124, 147

Ambrose, Saint, 78; *Hexaemeron*, 56–58

amplificatio, 68

Anaximander, 4

Anaximenes, 4

Andreas Capellanus, 144, 199n*16*

anima, 23. *See also* Endelechia; World-soul

animae (unborn souls), 50, 70–71

Antigamus, 73, 86, 88, 138

Antirufinus, 98

apeiron, 4–5

Aphrodite, 91. *See also* Venus

aplanes, 17

Apologetics, 56

Apuleius, 24; *The Golden Ass*, 42

Aray, 134

Aristotle, 1, 2, 4–10, 13, 14; *De caelo*, 10; *Metaphysics*, 2, 4–5, 7; *Physics*, 7, 10

Aristotelianism, 109

Arithmetic, 99

Art *vs.* Nature, 26–27, 185n*27*, 198n*9*

artifex natura, 19–20, 26, 153. *See also* Natura

Asclepius, 25

Asclepius (pseudo-Apuleius), 24–25, 59, 65

Astrea, 194n*55*

Astronomy, 99
Atropos, 88, 113, 157, 205n5. *See
also* Fates; Parcae
Augustine, Saint, 14, 84, 88
Avarice (Nummulatria) 85
Averroism, 116, 199n*16*

Bacchus, 137
Beauty, 98
Bellona, 45
Bennett, J. A. W., 134
Bernard Silvestris, 75, 92, 94, 103,
107; *Commentum super sex libros
Eneidos Virgilii*, 85; *De mundi
universitate*, 2, 35, 47, 48, 53, 58–72,
77, 78, 92, 102, 151–158; *Liber
de metrificatura*, 59; *Summa
dictaminis*, 59
Beute, 134
Boas, George, 3
Boccaccio, Giovanni: *Teseida*,
132–137 *passim*
Boethius, 11, 14, 33, 35, 36, 59, 64,
69, 110, 120; *The Consolation of
Philosophy*, 28–33, 37–40, 49, 50,
72, 75, 79, 81–82, 84, 109;
Contra Evtychen, 3; *De trinitate*, 92

Ceres, 48, 137
Chain of Being, Great, 17, 114,
149
Chalcidius, 11, 14, 15, 18, 22, 25,
31, 33, 34, 59, 65, 79, 92;
*Timaeus: a Calcidio translatus
commentarioque instructus*, 16, 20–24
Chartres, school of, 1, 2, 24, 34, 53,
58, 92, 96
Chastity (Castitas), 74, 85
Chaucer, Geoffrey, 1, 27, 37, 57,
59, 102, 103; *Knight's Tale*, 49;
Parlement of Foules, 2, 48, 72, 88,
89, 119, 125–150; *Physician's
Tale*, 26–27; *Troilus and Criseyde*,
138

Chenu, M.-D., 1, 67, 95
Christine de Pisan, 199n*16*
Church, figural relation to Natura, 93
Cicero, 2, 18, 45, 84; *De natura
deorum*, 3; *Somnium Scipionis
(Dream of Scipio)*, 64, 114, 126,
127–128, 130, 143, 148–149
Clarembald of Arras, 64; *Tractatulus
super librum Genesis*, 62
Claudian, 2, 40, 48–49, 63; *De
consolatu Stilichonis*, 49–50; *De
raptu Proserpinae*, 46–48; *In
Rufinum*, 98; "Magnes," 49;
"Phoenix," 49
Claudianus Mamertus, *De statu
animae*, 196n72
Clementia, 45
Clotho, 157, 205n5. *See also* Fates;
Parcae
Col, Pierre, 199n*16*
Collingwood, R. G., 3, 7–8
comparatio, 133
Concord, 98, 99, 101–102
contentio, 128
Craft, 134
Creation, the: in Saint Ambrose,
57; in Genesis and *Timaeus*,
69–70; *ex nihilo*, 79, 189–190n*18*
Creativity, threefold division of: in
Chalcidius, 23–24; mentioned, 26,
79; in pseudo-John Scotus
Erigena, 34–35; in William of
Conches, 35–36
Criseyde, 138
Cupid, 71, 73, 84, 86, 87, 88, 91,
121, 122, 154. See also *descriptio
Cupidinis*; Love; Mirth
Curteysie, 134
Curtius, E. R., 3, 40, 43, 60, 97,
115, 116
Cyllenius, 154
Cytherea: as *Venus legitima* in
Parlement of Foules, 127, 128–129,
143. *See also* Aphrodite; Venus